ANALYSIS OF
AMBULANCE COMPLAINTS:
DATABASING, STATISTICAL REPORTING, AND MORE

STEVEN GILBERT

ANALYSIS OF AMBULANCE COMPLAINTS: DATABASING, STATISTICAL REPORTING, AND MORE

iUniverse books may be ordered through booksellers or by contacting:

iUniverse
1663 Liberty Drive
Bloomington, IN 47403
www.iuniverse.com
1-800-Authors (1-800-288-4677)

Because of the dynamic nature of the Internet, any web addresses or links contained in this book may have changed since publication and may no longer be valid. The views expressed in this work are solely those of the author and do not necessarily reflect the views of the publisher, and the publisher hereby disclaims any responsibility for them.

Any people depicted in stock imagery provided by Getty Images are models, and such images are being used for illustrative purposes only.
Certain stock imagery © Getty Images.

ISBN: 978-1-5320-9598-6 (sc)
ISBN: 978-1-5320-9597-9 (e)

Library of Congress Control Number: 2020903603

Print information available on the last page.

iUniverse rev. date: 03/19/2020

DEDICATION

This book is dedicated to a special group of investigators, six of whom I hired, trained, and closely worked with for many years, and one I often worked with on selective sensitive and confidential cases, many involved varying degrees of corruption. These seven investigators, no matter what the challenge in front of them was, always maintained a special combination of high-level investigational skills, experience, knowledge and attitude, and they completely grasped the concept of what the word "integrity" means in the context of EMS investigations. I know that without them I would not have been able to do my job as effectively as I did, or certainly for as long as I did.

INTRODUCTION

This new book does not replace my original book, "*Conducting Emergency Ambulance Investigations*", which was published in 2011 and contains a wealth of relevant information for any ambulance investigator, EMS investigative unit director, or anyone who is interested in EMS investigations for any reason. It supplements it. Many different topics were examined in my original book with the major emphasis being on complaints, the investigative process, receiving and processing the complaint, conducting interviews, investigative reports and much more.

This second book is different. While its first section covers a potpourri of topics that for the most part were not addressed in my original book, the focus of the remaining sections pertain to the importance and utilization of the investigative unit's database. This includes what type of investigative information needs to be databased, various database reports, and the vast benefits that a "well-kept" database provides both for the investigative unit and the organization. These benefits include the ability to develop stats, informative reports, graphs, charts and official investigative unit presentations relating to ambulance complaints and investigative activities.

Why did I write this second book? Primarily because I feel that it is important to share the information, ideas, and concepts. I have always believed in this profession and wanted to give something back to the EMS investigators of today and tomorrow. The job of ambulance investigator provided me with much enjoyment, intrigue and fulfillment. It enabled me to meet and interact with some great people along the way, people who sat on "both sides of the interview table". Today I am still in contact with many of these people

Secondly, I have attempted to sublimity portray a very important premise throughout this book, A premise that was taught by our Medical Director early on in my career, that first and foremost, proper patient care is what any EMS organization is all about. In other words, it's the top priority issue. Besides refreshers and quality assurance (QA) reviews, another way to ensure the best patient care possible is being provided, is to professionally investigate and document each individual complaint as well as to track and monitor the various complaint types and trends that are associated with the complaints. I eventually learned that although they seem to serve similar purposes, QA reviews and investigative unit (IU) investigations are two very different animals. Simply put, a QA review is educational, while IU investigations often lead to discipline. From my perspective, employees were much less reluctant to attend a QA review than they were to appear at an IU investigation. But both are both important tools that should be available in the "organizational" patient care toolbox.

The contents of this book will assist EMS investigators, EMS administrators and attorneys with much information concerning this highly specialized field. Whether an ambulance organization is government run, hospital based, or a commercial service, complaints will be received, and investigations will be required. This book will be of assistance regardless of whether your organization has an existing investigations unit or is considering establishing one.

I also wrote this book is to educate EMS system managers. There were times over the span of my career where people were hired into the managerial ranks of my organization, who had little or no EMS experience, and certainly no direct EMS investigative experience. But for whatever reason, their responsibilities always seemed to include interacting with, or overseeing the investigative unit. While most were professional and personable, and while many seemed to have had the best of intentions, when it came to EMS investigations, most seemed "not to have a clue" (not my term). Most wanted to, or were directed to "reinvent the wheel", although usually it was not broken. They also had no understanding about the variables that can come into play during an EMS investigation, or how important understanding the term "semantics" is in the EMS investigative field. And finally, they had no understanding about potential investigative involvement and interaction with the local Department of Health (DOH), the involvement of the Municipal Investigative Unit, as well as Federal or local law enforcement agencies. And they certainly had no idea what havoc the media could cause if media related matters weren't handled properly.

I quickly learned that if you continuously resisted their managerial idea's, you wouldn't be around very long. Unfortunately, that's what happened to my predecessor. So rather than outright resist, my modus-operandi was always to work with them and to embrace their ideas if they were legal, and if I saw a benefit, incorporate some into our investigative repertoire. If something negative occurred because of some direction they provided or some action that they took, even though I had previously warned them about it, I never said "I told you so", but I did continuously try to educate them about EMS investigations and their potential ramifications, both short and long term. It frequently took time to make them understand. Most finally did realize that EMS investigations are different than they originally thought, and most came to the realization that I was not the enemy. So, I wanted to have easily obtainable proven information available for administrators so that it might be easier for them to understand the world of EMS investigations, and just as importantly, to help them realize that the "wheel" does not always require reinvention. That is what this book, in tandem with my first one tries to accomplish.

This book is sub-divided into the following sections:

SECTION 1 - A POTPOURRI OF TOPICS

- Complaints-Investigations-Cases
- Slicing, dicing and peeling away the outer skin and inner layers of complaints
- Who benefits from complaint investigations?
- Formal investigative process
- Four important words
- The importance of an investigator contacting a complainant as soon as possible after being assigned the case
- A cover-up is always worse than the original incident
- How long should it take for an investigation to be completed?
- Negative EMS perception
- The Media
- The Zebra Principle
- The use of drones in EMS investigations
- Investigative vital signs
- Internal organizational investigative notifications
- History of the Investigative Unit
- Video, video, video
- Humorous surveillance story
- It's all a matter of semantics
- Untested investigative techniques used for priority investigations
- Site visit addendum
- Missing property addendum
- A word about audits

SECTION 2 - DATABASE RELATED INFORMATION

- What should the Investigative Unit's director do when a serious statistical spike or other potentially negative information is discovered?
- Why input so much information into the investigative unit's database?
- What investigative information should be databased?

- The need to database investigative related information and the subsequent benefits that this will reap for both the investigative unit and the respective EMS organization
- Database reports
- Four important sources for statistical information
- Tracking complaints/investigations involving a patient death
- Final investigative dispositions

SECTION 3 - COMPLAINT TYPES

- General complaint types
- Presenting a concept that I call the "family of complaints"
- 494 "family of complaints" related database reports

SECTION 4 - INVESTGATIVE REPORTS

- 543 Investigative Unit database reports pertaining to one or more of 46 different investigative categories

SECTION 5 - PRESENTATION OF STATS

- Development of stats and graphical presentations of statistical reports and related simple but powerful charts pertaining to complaints and investigations, and related subjects

SECTION 6 - ANNUAL INVESTIGATIVE UNIT RECAP REPORT

Probably the most important historical investigative document for the Investigative Unit (IU) to prepare would be a year-in-review (recap type report) report strictly concerning IU activities

SECTION 7- FINAL THOUGHTS

For the above topics to work properly, I present them making the following organizational and/or investigative unit assumptions:

- Your EMS organization has a well-thought-out, tested and working "formal investigative process" in place which is what I am usually referring to when I use the term "Investigative Unit", (IU). This process must have the unwavering support from the top echelon of your organization, as well as from administrative and supervisory ranks.
- The Organization must have a foolproof "notification system" in place which is operational during business hours and non-business hours. This notification system ensures that a designated Investigative Unit (IU) investigator is made aware of complaints or incidents that are either serious or unusual, and likely will require immediate investigative action, whether the notification is done telephonically, or in-person, it must be done in a timely fashion. A properly set up notification system, although bothersome at times, will prove to be beneficial to both the IU as well as the organization itself, and on occasion, can save an investigator's job.
- Your organization is not afraid of complaints and will not try to hide, downplay, cleanse, or refuse to accept them. Instead, all complaints, no matter what the severity of the allegations are, and no matter who might be involved, will be officially documented, properly managed, fairly investigated and after the investigation is completed, the complainant needs to receive an official organizational dispositional response. (I addressed organizational dispositional responses in my first book).
- Your organization's philosophy accepts the reality that in the emergency ambulance business there will always be complaints, and the more 9-1-1 calls an organization responds to, the more complaints will be received, and the more complaints that are received, means additional experienced investigators will be required.
- Your organization wants the investigative unit to be proactive and thereby encourages appropriate self-generated investigations.

- At the conclusion of any investigation, a final internal investigative report needs be prepared which individually addresses each original allegation as well as any subsequent additional issues which were identified during course of the investigation. The final report should completely document the investigation, including a final determination identifying which employees were subjects of the investigation, and which employees were witnesses (there is a very important difference between these two classifications).
- Once the final investigative report has been endorsed (approved), all information which was developed during the investigation must be entered into the Investigative Unit's (IU's) database.
- In a perfect world there should be no access to the Investigative Unit's (IU) database by outsiders (people outside of the IU). Unfortunately, the world is not perfect, and some level of access may have to be provided to select organizational outsiders. This is something that you never want, but if you have no choice about it, you should set it up this way. Full access should only be provided to active IU members. If you are forced to provide database access to anyone outside of the IU, it must be "read-only" access. In other words, the outsiders must not be able to enter, delete or alter any information. If the IU is set up in such a way that it is part of a larger organizational department, any such department staff should also only get "read only" access. Additionally, and most importantly, the IU database should be set up so that there are electronic security "footprint" records of whomever logs into it, and documentation of what specific records were accessed (including "read only access") and this information should be permanently documented, which should prevent "tampering-of-information".
- All the investigative unit's investigators must be properly vetted and must possess the highest level of integrity possible. They should all want to be conducting investigations for the investigative unit, and continually demonstrate that they are maintaining the confidentiality of their assigned investigations.
- The organization provides the investigative unit with all the necessary equipment that is required to operate efficiently, which includes an appropriate array of vehicles to conduct day-to-day investigational business, and which also includes specialized vehicles to conduct covert surveillances. Surveillance vehicles

when not in use, should be parked at safe, hidden away non-descript locations.

- Individual records must be maintained for each vehicle that is assigned to the Investigative Unit (IU), be it day-to-day vehicles or covert surveillance vehicles. Such records should include daily mileage figures, gasoline usage, preventive maintenance and the daily identity of driver(s). Such records should be maintained in a safe place within the IU. If toll records come into play in your area, they too should be maintained. All of these records need to be reviewed periodically just to make sure that there isn't any "monkey-business" going on, which is the last thing the IU would want. I have seen some investigators from other investigative unit's balk at preparing such records which was always a red flag to me suggesting that trouble was brewing. I have always believed that if you do nothing wrong, there is nothing to hide. These records must be prepared, reviewed, and securely maintained.

- All investigative activities which are conducted by the investigative unit must be legal, and after examination been determined to fall within the scope of your organization's medical, administrative and investigative guidelines.

- If your investigative unit is only authorized to conduct "administrative investigations", a mechanism must be in place which details how to properly handle the receipt of a complaint which involves a potentially "criminal allegation", such as a theft of patient property, assault of a patient, assault of a member of the service, sexual abuse of a patient by a crew member, or the diversion of controlled substances. This mechanism should include both assisting the complainant in getting his/her complaint to the proper investigative authority in a timely fashion, as well as confidentially documenting some of the information into the investigative unit's database. (The investigative unit may not be allowed to investigate these matters, but the basic information absolutely needs to be entered into the database for reference purposes).

- In many areas of the country, EMS is part of, is managed by, or responds along with the local Fire Department to "medical calls" (their term). In some areas, this has been going on for a long time, while in other areas this relationship is relatively new. If the Fire Department is medically involved in your area, I personally hope that the primary reason for their involvement is to reduce medical response times, and to provide the best patient care possible. Whatever the actual reason is, and this concept is very important, if the Fire Department does respond to medical calls, and if a complaint is received, or if a self-generated investigation is initiated, the Fire Department personnel who were involved, must be investigated to the same degree that the EMS personnel would be investigated. The only caveat is the Fire Department personnel are likely to have a lower level of medical training than the EMTs and Paramedics do, so in some instances, such as patient care, their level of education might play a part in "investigative equality". But other than that, there can't be two separate sets of rules, standards, or level of investigation, (one for EMS and one for the Fire Department). If there are, that opens the door to all sorts of negative issues, including the loss of credibility of the Fire Department, as well as the organization.

- All investigative actions taken by the investigators must be strictly business related and should never be based upon any type of a personal agenda or vendetta.

- Politics cannot be allowed to infiltrate the investigative unit at any level. Unfortunately, this is one of those topics that could be a book all by itself. Everyone is entitled to his/her own idea as to who they will vote for. That is fine, but it is my opinion that politics as well as all ancillary political activities must remain outside of the investigative unit's door.

- If a subject employee of a new complaint has had several past complaints of a similar nature, with respect to a new complaint you cannot just say the employee is guilty, solely based upon the employee's complaint history. You must conduct a new investigation into the new complaint. You can however, put additional investigative efforts into investigating the new complaint.

- No favoritism can be shown to any employee during an investigation, no matter what connections, title, relations or relationships they might currently have, or have had in the past. Favoritism should not be confused with "investigative politeness" or "investigative professionalism".

- A separate unit must handle any discipline that results from any investigative unit investigation.

Since all of my EMS investigational experience was with a major municipal ambulance service which responded to over a million EMS runs a year, and whose investigative unit handled over a thousand investigations during most years, I came to understand and appreciate the concept that many of the confidential investigations that were conducted, when completed, might have had some degree of operational impact on my EMS organization, sometimes a major operational impact. By this I mean that as a result of a particular investigation, or a series of investigations, a guideline, operational directive, or a medical directive might have had to be created, revised, partially revoked or completely revoked.

Over time, I also became aware that throughout this country, EMS related investigations are not exclusively conducted by the respective EMS organization's Investigative Unit. Some investigations are handled by outside entities, such as the local State Department of Health (DOH) or other State agency. In some cases which involve drug related issues, Federal agencies can also become involved. It took me a long time to become comfortable with this, but I eventually did.

SECTION 1

COMPLAINTS-INVESTIGATIONS-CASES

My personal perspective on complaints

Every EMS organization is going to receive complaints. It's going to happen, period. Similarly, the more responses an organization does, the more complaints they are going to receive. It's as simple as that. Complaints can be minor, major, or somewhere in between. Once you accept this premise about complaints, the issues become:

- How are complaints going to be received?
- How are complaints going to be documented?
- How are complaints going to be managed?
- How are complaints going to be investigated?
- How are complaints going to be responded to?
- How is an organization going to learn from complaints?

The answer to these questions is to have a "formal investigative process" in place.

Once we agree that complaints are part of doing business in the EMS world, we must determine what an organization's "normal" complaint receipt rate is. To do this, you need to determine how many complaints an organization has received in the past reviewing specific time increments, and then comparing those numbers to how many they are currently receiving. These figures should be broken down into specific time frames, be it daily, weekly, monthly, semi-annually, yearly or by decade. This is where your database comes in. You should go back years and years to obtain related historical information. Looking at these complaint numbers will provide you with a complaint volume figure. This figure will constantly be changing so it must be continuously monitored for trends and spikes.

The next thing that you want to monitor is specific complaint types, especially the ones your organization considers to be major. However, I would recommend monitoring them all. They should be monitored the same way I just suggested that complaints be monitored.

One of the most asked about issues that an EMS Investigative Unit (IU) or organization must be able to answer with specificity concerns "complaints". In almost all cases, a complaint will involve an actual person contacting the IU or EMS organization, either in person, by phone, e-mail, letter, or through a municipal complaint intake system to register their complaint

The three most common complaint related questions that will likely be asked are:

- How many complaints were received,
- What kinds of complaints were received, and
- How many of the complaints were substantiated.

While "complaints" are certainly the major investigative barometer of how an organization is doing, and it is the term that is always asked about, it should not be the only type of inquiry that is conducted by the investigative unit (IU). The IU should also be conducting "self-generated investigations", which includes investigations involving select internal EMS organizational reports and related documents. So now we have two different, but related important terms; "complaints" and "investigations". Both are important, but have different meanings, and both must be individually and collectively counted, measured, examined and documented. And if you lump these two terms (complaints and investigations), together, you can collectively refer to them as "cases". Now we have three terms, "complaints", "investigations" and "cases", which are related-by-definition, but differ from each other. You may think what I am saying is just a matter of semantics. It is, but it's much more than just that. Throughout this book, I have made a purposeful distinction between these three related-but-different terms, purposely putting a greater emphasis on the most important one; "complaints".

SLICING, DICING AND PEELING AWAY THE OUTER SKIN AND INNER LAYERS OF COMPLAINTS

Individual complaints or investigations with few exceptions provide minimal insight into EMS organizational problems. However, as more information becomes available, and when all cases are entered into a database, the pool of information grows and becomes fruitful.

Another important focus of this book is to suggest ways to slice, dice, and peel away the various layers of complaints, (much like peeling an onion), where each layer that an investigator removes brings you closer to the truth. Each layer can then be analyzed turning the layers into a group of useful informational investigative nuggets. This process should allow you to compare each new nugget to previously obtained nuggets, and then transpose all of them into graphical reports and charts. Here is a quick topical listing of how complaints can be sliced, diced and grouped into useful nugget related query fields:

- ambulance stations
- average number
- call, tour, shift
- call volume
- complainants
- complaint sources
- complaint types
- complaint volume
- day
- day of the week
- employee
- final disposition
- geographic area
- hospital times
- investigations
- investigative activity
- investigative classifications
- investigators
- number
- observers
- on assignment versus off assignment

- on-scene times
- patients
- patient death
- patient injury
- percentages
- re-availability time
- relationship to payday
- response time
- sensitive locations
- straight time versus overtime
- time
- total number
- total percentage
- total types
- turn-around-time
- weather

WHO BENEFITS FROM COMPLAINT INVESTIGATIONS?

The answer in a nutshell is that many people can (or should) learn a lot from complaints. There are two ways that the learning process works. The first way is from individual cases, but with very few exceptions what we will learn from one individual case will be minimal. Having said that, information that comes from one case can open the investigative floodgates by involving other cases, both past and present.

The second is from all of the cases collectively.

Who specifically can learn from complaints? The answer is the following:

- **Individual Complainants**
  Within established organizational guidelines, complainants will be able to find out what happened during the call he/she/they complained about, and what administrative action(s), if any, is the organization is going to take against the subject employees.

- **Investigators**

  Investigators will get to assist the complainant by conducting an appropriate investigation using various approved investigative techniques and will be able to find out what occurred and determine if the crew acted inappropriately. They will also be able to determine if there are any issues that require immediate attention, or subsequent disciplinary action.

- **Investigative Unit Director**

  Will supervise how all of the complaints that were received were managed and handled. He/she will also determine if new investigative techniques are needed in the future. By reviewing database information, the director will determine if there are specific issues that need to be immediately brought to the organization's attention. By utilizing historical complaint information will also help the director determine if the staffing level in the investigative unit is at the proper level.

- **The Organization's top echelon**

  EMS organizational administrators on a regular basis need to be presented with data that documents how many complaints were received, what types of complaints were received, and what their final dispositions were. This information might suggest that additional EMS resources (vehicles and equipment) are required to properly manage the volume of calls.

- **The subject employees**

  They should learn which of their actions during the call were incorrect (if any), and which of their actions were appropriate.

- **The Organization's media liaison**

  When I refer to the "media liaison", I am referring to the Organization's "public information officer". He/she will learn about the results of individual complaints that the media has inquired about and should also learn that any information which the investigative unit provides to him/her is "solid information".

- **The Organization's legal staff**
  It is not unusual for some complaints to later develop into civil or criminal cases. Over time, the legal staff should understand that information which is provided by the investigative unit is always solid information. There may be related areas that will be of interest to the legal staff that wasn't part of the investigation, so there likely will be some information finding interactions between the legal staff and the investigative unit, which is usually a good thing.

- **The Media**
  The media will receive information via the media liaison, which was developed by the investigative unit, and over time will learn that such information was developed by the investigative unit. Over time they should consider the Investigative Unit to be a trustworthy resource of information. Once this occurs, more times than not, when the media is told that the matter is under investigation by the investigative unit, that will be acceptable, and the media pressure should decline, at least until the investigation has been completed.

- **Local politicians**
  Complainants frequently reach out to local politicians prior to contacting the EMS organization directly to register their complaint. In these cases, the politicians may become co-complainants, and will be seeking the final disposition to the complaint. Over time they should come to the conclusion that the investigative unit is trustworthy.

- **Authorized outside investigative agencies**
  Investigators from outside agencies, including law enforcement agencies, will learn that the Investigative Unit (IU) is trustworthy and competent. This may allow complaints that fall into a grey area, to be investigated by the IU rather than the respective outside agency. This may also allow subsequent joint investigations where the IU and outside agency work together.

- **Local State Department of Health**
  Most EMS organizations are subject to the rules and regulations promulgated by the by the state's Department of Health (DOH). It is a huge benefit to EMS administrators if the State DOH has confidence that the EMS organization can investigate and adjudicate its own complaints. This will only happen over time when the DOH determines that the organizational investigative unit is trustworthy.

- **Area citizens**
  Based upon the above, citizens who reside, work or travel through the organization's response area should come to the conclusion that they have confidence in the investigative unit.

So, as you can see, many people can benefit from complaint investigations.

FORMAL INVESTIGATIVE PROCESS

Even though I addressed this topic in my original book, I will be re-presenting it again here, because in the EMS investigative field it is of the upmost importance. It is the cornerstone in which all facets of EMS organizationally related investigations, usually but not exclusively administrative investigations, are processed. My experience has taught me that there must be a "formal investigative process" in place to properly investigate ambulance complaints. If constructed carefully, this process will provide your Investigative Unit (IU), and your EMS organization with the necessary credibility and public trust required to effectively deal with complainants, patients, politicians and the media.

The IU for the most part is a "post incident investigatory unit". It should also be set up to conduct self-generated investigations, and to have unfettered access to all internal organizational reports, whether or not they directly pertain to complaints or investigations. Internal organizational reports that don't rise to the level of an investigation, can be filed and entered into the IU's database for "information and intelligence purposes" (a term I learned of in 1996, and which I immediately became enamored with, because it made good investigative sense).

For the "formal investigative process" to work properly, you must have trained investigators assigned to the IU whose sole purpose is to receive, process, review and investigate EMS related complaints, self-generated investigations and internal organizational reports. It is imperative that these investigators be a combination of seasoned and certified EMTs, Paramedics and EMS Supervisors. The investigators must be trustworthy and possess the highest level of integrity and understand the concept that "investigations-come-first".

The "formal investigative process" starts when the complaint is received, and continues through the following five phases:

- Case management
- Investigative report writing
- Final dispositions
- Databasing of information
- Testifying at administrative hearings

All investigative findings need to be accurate, comprehensive, and above all, fair to both the complainant and the subject crew members. Being fair is of paramount importance. Not only must findings be fair, employees, whether they are classified as subjects or witnesses in an investigation, need to be treated professionally and compassionately, no matter what the allegation(s) are that they are accused of.

For investigative managerial purposes, you need to divide your investigations up into a small number of investigative categories, or classifications, which range from the most serious to the least serious. Doing this will allow you to devote the proper amount of time to your most serious cases while at the same time still being able to manage the less serious ones. I recommend utilizing the following four categories:

- A complete "internal" investigation. This is reserved for the most serious allegations.
- A preliminary investigation. After a review this type of case can either upgraded to an internal investigation or is downgraded to a referral (either internal or external).
- An immediate referral to an organizational field unit or authorized outside investigatory agency. Each complaint must be carefully scrutinized for hidden indicators of potentially serious infractions

prior to using this category. Just because the matter is being managed as a referral, the case shouldn't be taken lightly.
- A case filed for "information and intelligence" (I&I) purposes.

FOUR IMPORTANT WORDS

These words are tied into the formal investigative process. They are important for any type or classification of investigation. Their definitions do overlap and are somewhat interchangeable at times. You could think of them as four "magic-linking-rings". Once they are "magically-linked" and they remain that way and should never come apart, or more importantly, be allowed to come apart. If they do become unlinked, there is a major problem. I am talking about the following four words which are listed in alphabetical order, not in order of importance:

- Accountability
- Behavior
- Consistency
- Integrity

Accountability

The Merriam-Webster dictionary partially defines accountability as the quality or state of being accountable, especially an obligation or willingness to accept responsibility, or to account for one's actions. From an investigative point of view, the Investigative Unit (IU) is accountable in the following three ways:

- It's accountable to the respective EMS organization, specifically not to slant investigations, or to cover things up, but to conduct truthful, proper and fair investigations into all complaints.
- It is accountable to all organizational employees (EMTs, Paramedics, Supervisors, Firefighters and civilian employees) in that they all must be treated fairly.
- Just as important if not more so, the IU is also accountable to complainants. I always thought the symbol for the IU as being

the "scales of justice", where the scales are at an equal height, not one higher than the other. The IU must obtain all relevant information, conduct a complete investigation, which includes giving all involved a "fair shake". The investigation must come to an objective conclusion based solely on the evidence obtained.

Behavior

The Merriam-Webster-Learner's dictionary partially defines "behavior" as the manner of conducting oneself.

It has been said that the best way to predict a person's future behavior is to examine their past behavior. I have read that this theory is taught to investigators although in practice it's not as reliable as it sounds. I believe that from an investigative perspective, employee organizational and investigative unit complaint histories must be reviewed during an investigation (whether it's a complaint or a self-generated investigation).

Behavior is important to the organization and to the investigative unit in varying degrees, in the following ways:

- Prior to employment by the organization (pure organizational issue). Behavior prior to being hired is not an issue for the IU, nor should it be.
- During their probation period once hired by the organization (organization and IU equally). The IU's interest would only be if a complaint was received or if a situation developed during the probation period where the organization asked that the IU begin an investigation into a particular matter.
- After the probation period has concluded (IU issue). For the most part this would involve complaints and self-generated investigations.
- Discipline at field level (organization issue). This would generally be of little interest to the IU with the exception of being able to fully examine an employee's work background.
- Complaints (pure IU issue)
- Discipline as a result of an IU investigation (organization issue and IU issue).
- Integrity testing (IU issue and/or outside investigative unit issue).

Consistency

Investigations must be consistent no matter what the allegation is. A lack of consistency will work against what the investigative unit is trying to accomplish.

Integrity

The Merriam-Webster-Learner's dictionary partially defines integrity as the quality of being honest and fair. He has a reputation for integrity (honesty) in his business dealing. A second dictionary partially defines it as a firm adherence to a code of especially moral values. Incorruptibility.

It is of the upmost importance that:

- Integrity must be intertwined with the IU's reputation
- The IU director has integrity
- Individual investigators have integrity

If the IU has an integrity laced reputation, that one element alone will generally make investigations easier to conduct (when it comes to internal and external interactions). It is important to have integrity when dealing with organizational employees as well as outside investigators. Because of this reputation, significantly more subject and witness employees will more freely cooperate with investigators. This only occurs because of the "perception of integrity", and not because they are required to cooperate. They believe that they will receive a fair-shake, and they should.

In the case of my investigative unit the "perception" was "actual reality". I often saw employees cooperate and surprisingly confess to behavior under investigation because by doing so, they felt that they would be treated fairly. There were also instances of employees coming forward and volunteering unsolicited information about matters and behavior which was previously unknown to the IU. Again, this was solely the result of the "perception of integrity" that took us many years to develop and put into place. When employees did come forward, I was always gratified, because I knew the investigative process was working as it was designed to work.

As I prepared this section of this book, I gave a lot of thought to the word "integrity". A word that I often thought about over the years. I always preached this word to my investigators, and most grasped the importance of this subject, and it ultimately did become part of their "investigative DNA".

One last word on this topic. Long ago I had this brick made, and it was a fixture in my office for many years. The inscription says it all.

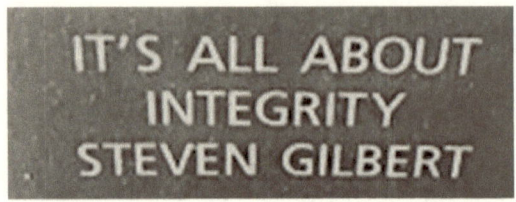

THE IMPORTANCE OF AN INVESTIGATOR CONTACTING THE COMPLAINANT AS SOON AS POSSIBLE AFTER BEING ASSIGNED THE CASE

This is probably the easiest investigative technique there is. My personal goal was to make initial contact with the complainant on the same day that I received a new case. It didn't matter if another investigator had received the complaint and had already interviewed the complainant. Since I was the "assigned investigator", I needed to establish a working relationship with the complainant, so I contacted them. To me, this was not being redundant, it was being a prudent investigator. I always believed that it was important for a complainant to know that their complaint did not fall on "deaf ears". I learned a long time ago that if a complainant felt that someone was actually listening to their concerns, something that unfortunately doesn't happen often enough in government, they would almost always be cooperative and reasonable. In addition, developing an early dialogue with the complainant provides the investigator with a better chance of obtaining accurate information.

If I was unable to make immediate verbal contact that same day, I would document all of my unsuccessful attempt(s) in the respective case folder, and then prepare and mail out an "if-we-don't-hear-from-you letter" to the complainant. This was a specific form letter which I created back in the early 1980's, which had three primary purposes:

- To prompt the complainant to call me
- For documentation purposes in the respective case file

- For statistical purposes

After realizing how quickly my investigative unit (IU) routinely made their initial complainant contacts, I created a stat for initial complainant contact. It was such an easy and positively reflective stat to qualify this time frame. It was an easy stat to obtain and without fail, was a consistent positive reflection on the IU. It always confirmed the initiative which was routinely demonstrated by the IU investigators. I have found that not all investigative units consider this a priority, some even wait weeks before reaching out to complainants.

Remember, being in the EMS investigations business means that you are also in the customer service business as well. It took a long time for me to become comfortable with this concept, but it is valid and should not be seen as a hindrance.

A COVER-UP IS ALWAYS WORSE THAN THE ORIGINAL INCIDENT

I worked in the emergency ambulance investigation business for over 30 years. An "orchestrated" cover-up didn't happen often, but occasionally one did occur. I'm not talking about a run-of-the-mill incident, where a crewmember falsified a written statement or lied to an investigator. I'm talking about a brazen coordinated effort to conceal the truth. Such a conspiracy sometimes involved multiple people.

When an orchestrated cover-up did occur, the resulting investigation was always top priority, and any subsequent disciplinary action taken, once the investigation complete, which was usually more severe than it would have been had there actually been no cover-up.

For the following reasons, this type of investigation was always my favorite type of investigation to conduct.

- First, there was the actual "act" itself, frequently an overt violation of one or more regulations. Usually an in-your-face act, which was followed by the involved personnel, literally projecting the image that they are too important to have acted improperly, or even being investigated for committing such an act, denying that the incident ever took place, or that they were even involved; in effect daring someone to prove they did anything wrong, thereby projecting their vindication.

- Secondly often this involved a supervisor/manager and/or their very close associates who declare that the incident never occurred, when in fact they know that it did.
- Thirdly because this behavior often rubs off on hard-working, usually dedicated employees, who were not involved in the actual misconduct itself, but because they may have been at the original incident scene, or somewhere related to the incident scene, or even at a non-related location where they overheard all or some of the subjects making incriminating remarks about the incident, they become involved.
- Fourthly, when you dig into the subject's background for this type of a case, you will likely find that the subjects were involved in other of unprofessional conduct, whether it was a singular incident or just the way they normally conducted their day-to-day business. But because they were never challenged along the way, their "behavior" festered to such a degree that they believed that they were/are untouchable.

Why do such cover-ups take place? Besides not wanting to actually admit what they did, in my opinion it simply comes down to one word, P-O-W-E-R. Power can be looked at on various levels:

- The actual power that the involved person has
- The power that the involved person thinks they have
- The perceived power that subordinates believe that the involved person has

These individuals see themselves as being untouchable, either because of their rank, title or their association with other organizational individuals. In most instances, they believe that they have more power than they actually do, and when the cover-up investigation has been completed, it is these personnel who are almost always the ones that get chopped off at the knees, figuratively speaking of course. In addition, other ranking managers are frequently held accountable for the actions of their subordinates, regardless of their lack of knowledge of, or their involvement in the original incident or cover-up attempt. Due to their position in the organization they "should have known" or should have had a policy or procedure or person in place to prevent the incident and resulting cover-up from occurring. Penalties for such a person include a transfer, demotion or even termination of employment. From an investigative point-of-view, I have long been a fan of such action. It sends the appropriate message that managers are ultimately accountable for the actions of their subordinates.

Examples of cover-ups include (but are certainly not limited to):

- Group (subordinate) denial of the allegations because they fear retaliation by a manager or supervisor if they tell the truth.
- A manager, supervisor or associate directing the re-writing of reports and statements, changing, deleting or omitting facts.
- A manager, supervisor or associate not partaking in a mandated training activity but documenting or directing someone else to document that he/she/they did partake in the activity(s).
- A manager, supervisor or associate also not partaking in mandated training but personally documenting, or again pressuring others to document that he/she/they did partake in the activity.
- The pressuring, whether direct or sublimity, of other employees to lie about an incident. (Subliminal pressure depends upon how a manager or supervisor has run their "Command" on a day-to-day basis in the past).
- Directing that certain official documents, reports or statements not be submitted.
- Directing that an official document be changed, altered or destroyed to protect an employee. This can also include that a complete log-book has gone missing, or where pages from a log-book have been ripped out and are missing.

HOW LONG SHOULD IT TAKE FOR AN INVESTIGATION TO BE COMPLETED?

I completely understand the pressure to quickly investigate what occurred, while at the same time maintaining investigative accuracy. Situations like this can literally be like a tug-of-war. The answer to how long an investigation should take to complete involves various combinations of the following twelve factors:

- The severity of the allegations
- The condition of the patient
- The investigative classification
- The source of the complaint
- The case load at the time
- The number of available investigators
- The individual investigator whom the case is assigned to
- Media coverage
- Outside political pressure towards the organization
- Cooperation and availability of the patient and witnesses
- The probable outcome of the investigation
- The process of obtaining all evidence

The severity of the allegations and criticality of the patient's condition are the two major factors. All others are secondary.

From a managerial point-of-view, one of the most important initial things the IU director should do is to assign each new case the proper investigative classification, much the same way that incoming 9-1-1 calls are assigned their proper priority. This classification process will dictate which cases need to receive immediate attention, and which can receive less attention. If a case is assigned a lower classification, it is easier to understand the premise that it will take longer to complete. Lower classification cases will still require "timely-investigative-attention". (There is no excuse for not working on lower classified cases for days, weeks, or months).

Historically the most serious complaints usually involve the death of a patient, or serious patient care violations, and have always been assigned the highest investigative category. Early on in my career my organization called this classification a "major investigation". Once a "major" was declared, a clock started running because the investigative unit had a mandate to prepare a preliminary report within 24-hours. It was expected that the preliminary report would contain all of the verified facts that had been obtained. The preliminary report had to contain dispatch records (both computer records and audio material), employee statements, organizational reports, patient care records, controlled substance records, site visit information as well as subject and witness employee interview records.

The 24-hour mandate was always in play and was always stressful. There were times when several "major investigations" occurred at the same time. One reason was the quantity of "major investigations" was rising. That was because over time complaint types which necessitated the calling of a "major" expanded, resulting in the rise of "majors". Even with the expansion of the cases, the majority of "major investigations" were always closed in a timely fashion.

I recall a case in the 1980's where the person in charge of my organization declared a "major investigation" for an incident involving the malicious removal and disposal of the front bumper of an ambulance while on an assignment. Initially he made multiple calls to the investigative unit demanding that the ambulance bumper be located and returned. A "major investigation" was initiated which subsequently resulted in the bumper being located and returned. While at first glance this incident might not be thought of as a patient care issue, it really was, because the referenced ambulance had to be placed off service for a long period of time, not only because of the investigation, but also because of the subsequent required repairs.

Because of the rising number of "majors" as well as the expanding call types which necessitated that a "major" be called, my Investigative unit quickly gained investigative proficiency. The sheer volume of all of these investigations provided invaluable investigative on-the-job-training. Investigative techniques that were developed because of all of the "majors", were subsequently adapted for use on minor cases as well.

Each "major investigation" required the preparation of a final investigative report which were time consuming to complete. Since there were hundreds of them, in an effort to managerially assist my investigators, I created an investigative report boilerplate, or "shell report". It was both a guide for the investigators, and a starting point for a preliminary or final investigative report. The basic shell report started with about thirty pages of various investigative topics and related sub-topics which included the source and type of the complaint, information about the 9-1-1 ambulance call report (ACR) information fields, audio recordings, investigative techniques, witness interviews, employee interviews as well as investigative findings and recommendations. The premise was that topics which pertained to the current investigation were kept, while topics that didn't pertain were deleted. Once the deletions were complete, the topics that remained became the outline for the referenced report. Once the respective information was entered into the appropriate fields, the report was complete. As new situations developed, more and more topics were entered into the shell report.

I believe that this shell report, although massive in size, positively assisted my investigators during a very difficult period of time. Remember, I am talking about the time period after the demise of typewriters, and when computers went from the 5 1/4-inch discs, to a 3 ½-inch floppy disk system. This was also the time when you couldn't easily buy computer software which would create such a report, either because the software didn't exist, or if it did exist, it was out of the organization's and/or the IU's price range. Whatever the reason, the report shell had to be created "longhand", which is what I did.

NEGATIVE EMS PERCEPTION

This important topic could be a book all by itself. What exactly is negative EMS perception? Why is "negative perception" especially harmful to individual EMS crews, their respective EMS organizations, and the entire EMS profession? Having conducted EMS investigations for as long as I did, I believe I am in a unique position to address why "negative perception" is so harmful.

One day I was riding in a car with two other people. They were discussing the ongoing poor behavior of a third party. At the very same moment, both quoted the phrase, "perception is reality". When I heard them say it together, a bell went off in my head, which immediately placed this topic into perspective for me. Whether factually accurate or not, if perception is reality, when something thought of as being bad occurs, then negative perception is reality as well. And taking this one step further, if the matter is EMS related, then by extension, negative EMS perception is also reality.

When an incident takes place, the person or persons who observe it, whether they are actively involved or just passers-by, primarily use their eyes and ears to absorb it. Their brain puts it all together and makes a split-second decision how to categorize it, either positively, negatively, or neutrally. Once such a decision is made, it is not easy to change their mind about it.

Negative perception plays a big role in the EMS business, both short term and long term. It can involve an operational issue or an investigative issue.

Unfortunately, I believe that the majority of negatively perceived incidents involve matters which never get officially reported. My experience suggests that the number of complaints officially received by an organization over any period-of-time probably represents only about half of the negatively perceived incidents that actually occurred during the same time frame. Thus, the number of complaints received could potentially be doubled. I came to this conclusion because of the number of times complainants and witnesses would reference past negative incidents to me, and after researching them, I determined that they had never been previously reported.

I also believe that that a negatively perceived incident holds far more weight in the minds of the public than positively perceived incidents do. I often heard a complainant or witness reference a past unrelated negatively perceived issue. This happened far more often than a complainant or witness mentioning a past positive incident, although that did occur. In my experience, the overwhelming majority of reported incidents (complaints) which obviously resulted in negative EMS perception, involved "verbal" or "gesture" related incidents", which would fit into the complaint type category of "discourtesy".

When an issue of past negative EMS perception does come up, especially if it is brought up voluntarily without a probative question first being asked, it's an issue that needs to be explored and documented by the assigned investigator. There are three basic reasons for this:

- To determine if the person truly witnessed the event, rather than having heard about it from someone else.
- To be able to properly evaluate all other information which was provided by the same person. Clearly the investigator needs to determine if information about the new incident is tainted in any way because of the person's personal negative perception of an old incident.
- For the knowledge of any organizational legal staff members who might handle any subsequent discipline arising from the investigation. They would not want to put a person on the witness-stand who potentially could go off on a tangent about the past incident without being prewarned about it. I recall such an incident happening to one of my investigators. It wasn't the end of the world, but it did teach us all an important lesson, or at least it taught me one.

A negatively perceived EMS incident could develop any time from the moment the crew gets into their ambulance at the beginning of their assigned tour (shift) until the very end of the tour many hours later.

Vehicle related potential negative perception scenarios

- A parked ambulance on the street with the crew either inside the ambulance, right outside of the ambulance, or even nowhere in sight
- An ambulance parked with the crew members observed to be inside (either the patient compartment or the cab), watching a movie on a personal video screen
- A parked ambulance with one of the crew members sunning them self, by laying on a blanket which is either spread over the hood of the ambulance, or the ground near the ambulance
- An ambulance parked off the street hidden away behind buildings in an obvious attempt not to be easily seen
- An ambulance parked at a location which impedes the flow of traffic, especially during rush-hour
- A moving ambulance being driven erratically, whether on assignment or not
- Inappropriate use of the ambulances warning lights, siren, spotlights or onboard public-address system, whether or not they were on an assignment at the time
- Inappropriate flag, banner, poster or stickers affixed to the ambulance without specific organizational approval

Crew/call location related potential negative perception issues

- The crew's general appearance
- How the crew acts when approaching the location where the patient is located. Specifically, is there a sense of professionalism, urgency and concern, or does the crew appear lackadaisical or disinterested

- The first verbal interaction between the crew and the patient, family members or bystanders (this will determine how the rest of the call will go)
- How the crew interacts with the patient, the patient's family, or other people who are either physically with the patient, or who are on the telephone requesting to speak to one of the crewmembers
- How the crew responds to a request either by the patient or the patient's family to transport the patient to a specific hospital, especially if this request is made before the crew had a chance to examine the patient
- Other issues concerning hospital selection
- An item at the call location broken by the crew, whether accidentally or on purpose
- Any kind of physical incident involving any of the crewmembers
- Any editorial-like comments made by one or both of the crew members pertaining to how much the patient will be billed for the ambulance response, on-scene treatment or transport. (This could be in response to a question being asked, or an attempt by the crew to persuade the patient to refuse medical aid or transport to a hospital)
- Any kind of a verbal incident involving the crew and members of the hospital staff
- How long it took the ambulance to arrive on the scene of the call

Every 9-1-1 call is stressful to the patient, the patient's family, and in many cases, bystanders. After 9-1-1 is activated, every second feels like a minute, and every minute feel like an hour to the callers and bystanders. Therefore, the crew shouldn't be adding to their stress, whether purposely or inadvertently by making inappropriate comments, or misbehaving, either upon arrival or during the call. For the record, I have always recognized that a call can often be stressful for the EMS crew as well.

Combating future negative perception

Beside dealing with this subject organizationally, educationally, and through individual investigations, I developed another method to help address it. During my career, I often had the opportunity to lecture EMTs,

Paramedic's, newly promoted Supervisor's and various ranks of Chiefs, concerning investigations and the investigative process. Since recognizing and dealing with negative perception was so important to me, it was always one of the main topics that I included in my lectures. I would begin by explaining to my audience that negative EMS perception is like standing at a lake shore on a day when there is no wind, thereby causing the water to appear calm and flat, giving off the appearance of its being "as smooth as glass". I would then explain that if you took a rock and threw it up in the air over the water, when it came down, the point of impact between the rock and the water would represent an EMS incident taking place which was perceived negatively. The subsequent ripples extending outwards in every direction from the point-of-impact would equate to not knowing where in real life one of the negative perception ripples would turn up. Finally, I explained that when and where the first ripple hits the shoreline, that represents the point where the negatively perceived incident turned up, and where the ramifications of the negatively perceived incident would become apparent.

To further make my point, I visually presented a listing of "discourtesy" related words, phrases, scenarios, motions and gestures which had been used by actual complainants when either expressing their complaint, or when being interviewed about what they observed. Each example would likely create an immediate negative perception to anyone whether witnessing the incident or hearing about it. I knew that the key was not to just briefly mention negative perception, but to provide example after example, after example, which is what I did, or at least tried to do to in an effort to help "drive the point home".

This part of my lecture was always received the same way. There was not too much reaction when I first began to present the information. But when I began to present brief complaint-scenarios, I would first hear a laugh or chuckle from the audience, but as I continued to present more and more examples, each one being a little more "serious" than the previous one was, the laughing and chuckling always stopped, and the room became quiet. Once I completed the list, which always included saving what I thought was the worst example for last, because of the silence, and the looks on their faces, I knew my audience completely understood what I was talking about. At the conclusion of these lectures, some members of the audience would come up to me and comment how informative this section of the lecture was to them. From time-to-time over the years I would receive phone calls from someone who had attended one of my lectures. They would complement me on my lecture, and then relate the reason for the call, usually a related matter. To this day, I still feel that this method was the best way for me to communicate my point about the pitfalls of negative EMS perception.

The following are some of the words, phrases, body language, gestures and complaint-scenario examples from my lecture:

Negative perception words & phrases

- Belligerent
- Cold and uncaring
- Condescending
- Discourteous
- I was ignored
- I was treated with disrespect
- Inappropriate
- Inhuman and unprofessional
- Insensitive
- It was the words he used
- Less than professional
- Mean and nasty
- Non-compassionate
- Obnoxious
- Portrayed an attitude of not caring
- Rude
- Rude and abrupt
- Rude and disorderly
- Said "don't tell me how to do my job"
- The crew yelled
- Unhelpful
- Unprofessional
- Unsympathetic
- Used foul language
- Verbally abusive
- Very rude

Negative perception complaint scenarios

- The complainant asked the crewmember why she was treating her like a dog. The crewmember replied, "because you are a dog".
- The crewmember called the complainant a "crazy Chinese man".
- The patient told the crew that the straps were too tight. One crewmember responded, "if you wanted comfort you should have taken a bus and not called an ambulance".
- A crewmember told the complainant to get out of the room and then threw something across the room.
- The crew kept asking the patient if he was a citizen and said they would take him to "INS" (Immigration and Naturalization Service).
- One crewmember said, "why don't you learn to speak English".
- When the crew arrived, they knocked on the complainant's door. The complainant asked who was there. One crewmember answered, "UPS", the other answered, "Pizza Hut".
- One crewmember said, "you don't speak English, you have to speak English in this country".
- Upon arrival one crewmember sarcastically commented, "I know you didn't call us for this".
- When the crew arrived, one asked, "why are you calling 9-1-1 at 11:00 o'clock at night".
- One crewmember said to the other crewmember, "give me the gloves that I use to knock out patients".
- One crewmember asked the patient who had attempted suicide why he chickened out.
- One crewmember made overtures toward two female patients. He later telephoned one of them at home to see how she was doing.
- The complainant said that when they arrived at the hospital their rude comments continued. At one point one crewmember said to the second crewmember he should have worked for the Sanitation Department rather than for EMS. He commented, "they pay a lot better and are doing the same job, hauling garbage". He then looked at the patient and both crewmembers laughed.
- The complainant, who watched from a second-floor window, said that it "appeared" that the crew was discourteous to an elderly oriental female. The complainant said that he/she couldn't hear

what was said but his impression was based upon their gestures (body language).

- A crewmember "gestured" by crossing his fingers in response to the patient commenting "I hope I die".
- The complainant was advised by two people who were on the scene that the crew was making fun "imitating" the patient as she was gasping for air.
- The crew appeared to be "annoyed" that they were there. As the complainant was talking, the crew were rolling their eyes as though they didn't care about the patient.
- One of the crew was "mimicking" the complainant's facial expressions and was making fun of the patient.

The one I saved for last

- The complainant, who was a relative of the patient, asked the crew what hospital they were going to take the patient to. One crewmember matter-of-factly responded, "what difference does it make, he's dead already".

During my lecture, I also mentioned that occasionally complainants would report that when they advised the crew that they intended to make a complaint, one or both crewmembers would comment, "go ahead and make a compliant, nothing will happen". I happily explained to my audience while shrugging my shoulders at the same time, that when this happened, for some reason, a more intense investigation would always occur, including potentially and professionally challenging the crewmember(s) about their statement.

Other ways of addressing the issue of negative EMS perception

If the individual causes or types of reported negatively perceived incidents aren't addressed operationally by your organization, (as a follow up to an investigation) you can be sure that will be a rise in future complaints, involving various complaint types, both discourtesy and more serious ones) which will be problematic in several ways.

How can negative EMS perception be addressed operationally? Here are some direct and indirect methods:

- By direct line supervision
- During recertification education
- Using employee evaluations
- By examining past complaints for any identifiable trends
- Having the investigative unit conduct "overt" surveillances
- By examining the background of employees who are the subject of the complaints
- By examining workload (number of responses by each ambulance by tour)
- Examination of downtime between assignments
- Examining hiring practices
- Examining staffing levels

Negative EMS perception is an important issue which continually needs to be monitored and addressed both by the investigative unit on a case by case basis, and the organization in a variety of ways. Ignoring the subject simply is a recipe for disaster.

THE MEDIA

Unlike others in the EMS business, I never thought of the media as the enemy. I always believed if they had an EMS story, good, bad or indifferent, they should report it, and in my neck-of-the-woods they usually did, literally hundreds and hundreds and hundreds of times over the years.

However, in the early days of my organization's growth, there were ongoing issues where information was being leaked-out to certain local media outlets, as well as to certain politicians. Because of this issue, our organization was forced to adopt a need-to-know information policy. This meant that it was important to limit the number of people that had direct access to information. It simply came down to two important issues; security and confidentiality. Remember this was long before the invention of smart phones, so the process of leaking information was very different back then than it would be today. The information that was being leaked included computer printouts of 9-1-1 assignments, as well as various official documents. This activity actually began before I arrived and continued for many years, lasting through a number of organizational administrations.

One of my cardinal rules has always been that members of the Investigative Unit (IU) including its director, should never be dealing directly with the media. The two don't mix.

It's not a matter of being afraid of the media, and it's not a matter of having an investigation scrutinized, it's a matter of having media-savvy professionals handle all press inquiries. The EMS organization's administrative staff should designate a person to handle the media, This person could be referred to as the "media liaison", or "public information officer", The IU's only involvement should be to provide the "media liaison" with information about the incident(s) or matter(s) which are being inquired about, so that the inquiry can be officially dealt with, hopefully in an expeditious, accurate and honest fashion. Additionally, whatever information is provided by the IU to the "media liaison" should be clearly documented by the IU director or investigator who provided it. This documentation should include a narrative if the information was provided verbally, and copies of any written, audio or visual documentation that was provided. I recommend this because you never want anyone to be able to say that information which was provided to the media by the "media liaison", was part of information which was originally collected and presented by the IU was inaccurate. All that I am saying here is that the IU should protect itself. Hopefully this protective documentation will never be needed.

The media should never be lied to. Once they have learned that they have been lied to, or even suspect it, both the person who they feel lied, as well as the EMS organization itself are likely to become future "targets" for increasingly intense media scrutiny.

During my EMS investigative working years, with one exception, I never had to talk directly with anyone from the media, which was fine with me. There was, however, a one-time incident during the early 1980's when a local television news reporter called to file a complaint about the way that one of her family members had been treated by EMS. I don't recall any of the particulars of the actual complaint, or its final disposition, however I do know that the complaint was processed just like any other complaint would have been at the time, with the exception of an "FYI-notification" to our organization's "media liaison" about the complaint.

During the worst of times, media inquiries involving my organization occurred multiple times a week, requiring the IU to provide information about current or past investigations, or initiate new investigations into new matters that we had not previously been made aware of. Additionally, there was a period of years where one individual media outlet was surveilling certain on-duty EMS personnel, which included visually recording their work-related activities.

Back then media inquiries occurred at an impossible pace, which made most investigations more stressful than they had to be. You had to be there to understand how bad it was. This continued for years and years, and it afforded me the opportunity to observe different "media liaisons" at work. They all had very different operating styles, and obviously different "marching orders". They each dealt with the media differently. I won't mention who had what style, but I can offer a listing of the basic styles that I observed, as well as my opinion as to which style worked the best, strictly from an investigative point-of-view. The three basic "media liaison" working styles that I observed were:

- The "media liaison" often said nothing about the matter at hand and referred inquiring reporters elsewhere (outside of the organization), for an official response.
- The "media liaison" towed-the-company-line, meaning they were instructed specifically what to say, and that's what they did, they said nothing more, nothing less.
- The "media liaison" answered the reporter's questions and was also able to explain what had occurred and was even able to discuss the rationale of why an event or series of events had taken place. This method did occasionally result in a story not being reported because the organizational media liaison person was allowed enough latitude to explain things to the reporter. In my opinion, again only from an investigative point-of-view, this last style was the most beneficial. I say this because over time, it was this method of interaction that lead to less frequent investigative involvement by the Investigative Unit (IU), which in-turn allowed the IU to concentrate on other investigative business. The "media liaisons" who handled media inquiries this way know who they are, and should know how personally appreciative I was, and still am to this day.

There are many "buzz-words" or buzz-phrases" that the media often uses in their print headlines or electronic banners to sensationalize a particular

EMS story, or a series of EMS related stories. Any of these words or phrases suggest negativity. Here is a partial alphabetical listing containing some of the "buzz-words" and "buzz-phrases" that I have seen used:

- abandoned
- abuse
- abused
- accuse
- a dispatch delay
- ambulance arrives late
- ambulance corps need help fast
- ambulance crew caught
- ambulance delays
- ambulance failed to meet response times
- ambulance mishaps
- ambulance system fails
- an overlooked crisis
- answers sought
- apologize
- asthma patient dies
- attrition
- baby's death
- baby dies
- backlog
- beleaguered
- billed for ambulance ride
- blamed
- bosses sorry
- broken
- broken system
- call volume brings uptick in response times
- change in EMS leadership required
- cheating
- city runs out of ambulances
- communications failures and confusion
- could have been saved…
- confusion in call center
- concerns voiced over ambulance response

- council questions city's fire based EMS plans
- county questions ambulance response time and procedures
- cover-up
- critical
- criticized
- dangerous
- defend
- dispatch flap
- editorial…
- embattled
- EMS billing agency mistakenly….
- EMS crisis
- EMS debate revived
- EMS inconsistent
- EMS official charged
- EMS response time
- EMS staffing issues
- EMS struggles
- EMT charged with stealing
- EMT suspended
- examined
- falls short
- family blames
- father questions ambulance response time
- fear reigns
- flawed
- grieving
- honcho
- inadequate delays
- inquest
- inquest into death of a patient
- investigation/possible discipline
- issues known for years
- issues with long EMS response times
- is the ambulance service in crisis
- kickback
- lawsuit: EMS got lost
- lazy

- leakers
- long troubled
- long wait
- medic busted
- multiple ambulance delays linked to deaths
- new information in delayed response to injured child
- officials question promotion of paramedic with history of complaints
- officials tight-lipped
- outraged
- paramedic accused
- paramedic suspended
- patchwork
- patient death inquiry
- probe
- probed
- problematic
- questionable
- report faults
- response is the focus of…
- response time questioned
- response time slipping
- scandal
- scandalously bad
- scheme
- scrutinized
- shedding light
- shock
- slow response times
- someone is going to die
- son blames ambulance
- stealing
- string of deaths
- suspended
- sweeping overhaul
- tampered
- times still lagging
- to be disciplined

- turns deadly
- unatoned
- unexpectedly high ambulance bill
- unhappy
- unprepared
- walkout
- watchdog panel
- widow to sue
- woman dies at hospital after ambulance doesn't show up
- woman dies waiting for ambulance
- worries
- 9-1-1 crisis

When a bad complaint is received, no matter the source, there is always the possibility that one or more local media outlets will pick up the story and "run with it". If the story is sensational enough, it is also possible that the national media might report on it as well, but thankfully that is rare. Usually most EMS related stories will only be reported locally and have a short lifespan. However, the short lifespan could be extended if other local media outlets "pick the story up" and run with it for a day or two themselves.

Additionally, the more EMS related stories a particular media outlet reports on, the more the public who become aware of the reports will begin to believe that there is an overall EMS problem, whether it's true or not. And the more the public becomes aware of what the particular media outlet has been reporting, the more the public is likely to contact this particular media outlet to report other negative incidents that they are aware of. In addition, and most importantly, the longer the media coverage continues, the more likely it is that the subject matter of their questioning will expand and shift from the individual incidents themselves to other areas of the respective EMS organization. Remember, if your organization is connected to the local Fire Department, they too are likely become media targets as well, because in this business, no one is immune.

In addition, the more questions that the media asks will usually mean the more questions that local politicians will ask the organization. And the more questions that local politicians ask will translate into more investigative related questions being asked by the top echelon of the organization both to organizational supervisors as well as the director of the Investigations Unit.

Sometimes it can appear that the media along with an individual politician are working together regarding EMS related negative stories. I can't comment on that. However, in my area there was a time period in the 1980's where this did appear to be the case. There were two politicians that held different positions, and who at different times were always being quoted or interviewed when there was a negative EMS related story. Reflecting back, I don't think these politicians were really in "cahoots" with the media, it was more of a situation of their never having seen a microphone that they didn't want to talk into syndrome, a political phenomenon that certainly continues today, ad-nauseum.

I have always been curious about EMS related media coverage outside of my jurisdiction. Having conducted EMS investigations for as long as I did, I was obviously very familiar with the local media coverage. During the latter part of my investigative career, and even to this day, I research EMS related news stories on a daily basis. As of the date that I wrote this, I have reviewed over 1700 out-of-my-area articles, many of which relate to issues that I have raised in this book. These articles include news stories from numerous locations, throughout the United States and around the world.

At one time, I foolishly believed that the types of complaints that I was investigating were unique to my city, but I learned that this premise isn't true. Most of the news stories that I have come across during my research pertain to the exact same type of cases which I had investigated throughout my investigative career, such as delayed ambulance responses, patient care complaints, theft of patient property and drug related issues (just to name a few). In recent years, a good number of the news stories have also dealt with Medicare/Medicaid fraud issues.

Clusters of media stories

From time to time during my EMS media research I noted various "clusters" of news stories. By "clusters" I mean multiple and continuous media stories most originating from one news source about one individual EMS service or organization, generally over a time period of six months to two or more years. The period of time can vary, but what it comes down to is too many negative stories about one EMS organization over a relatively short period of time is a bad thing for the organization.

While each "cluster" originates from one media source, some stories can also be picked up by other area media sources. Researching these "clusters" of news stories was important to me because during the 1980's and early 1990's, there were times when my EMS organization was on the "receiving end" of such "cluster attacks". To me, each cluster wave seemed to last forever. They didn't, but it sure felt that way at the time.

Not only do these cluster attacks involve new news stories, they include rehashing previously reported stories, sometimes with only a miniscule amount of new information. They can also include combinations of past stories meshed together. They can also include (depending upon the source), editorials from the newspapers, and recaps from the television media. Such editorials or recaps reiterate past stories, and they are usually combined with the theme that personnel changes at the top of the respective EMS organization are required. As an example, I recently came across a non-local article that rehashed forty recent problematic 9-1-1 calls, with twelve of them specifically identified. The article called for major changes within the referenced organization. It's a fair bet that this type of negative coverage will continue until a personnel change at the targeted EMS organization takes place.

If/when there is a subsequent EMS organizational change of personnel, it is likely that after taking credit for the change, and possibly even interviewing the replacement, a "honeymoon" period may occur where the negative media coverage from the particular source will completely stop or will become very sporadic. However, even after making a change at the top, if the EMS organization doesn't make other necessary changes, or doesn't appear to be solving internal problems and issues, the honeymoon period will quickly come to an abrupt halt, and you can be sure that the media coverage will begin again, more than likely turning into a new "cluster attack". I have seen at least two EMS organizations whom over time have been the subject of multiple cluster attacks by the media, and just recently as I am putting the finishing touches on this book, I found one organization that has been the subject of three such attacks.

Another negative result of these "clusters" is in addition to the continuous media coverage, it is likely that "jump-on-the-bandwagon complaints" will be received by the investigative unit. What I mean is if the media coverage wasn't there, these complaints probably wouldn't have been filed. But because of public awareness brought on by the continuing coverage, additional complaints will come in.

Probably the most important lesson to be learned in this section is the longer a cluster attack continues the wider the media's questions will become. When I say widen, I mean moving away from individual complaint related stories and getting into more and more organizational areas and issues. The following is a partial topical listing of wide-ranging cluster attack topics that I have seen:

- Managerial employee or supervisor's credentials for the job
- Ambulance siren issues
- Sick leave issues
- Vendor issues
- How much overtime has been paid out either to an individual EMT, Paramedic, EMS Supervisor or Firefighter
- Fallout over a suspended EMT, Paramedic, EMS Supervisor or Firefighter
- EMT, Paramedic, EMS Supervisor or Firefighter charged with fraud
- Sibling issues within the organization
- Social Media issues
- Issues about overtime for organizational mechanics
- Reserve fleet issues
- Patients transported by fire truck rather than by ambulance
- Organizational staffing issues
- Votes of no confidence
- Sexual assault allegations at organizational facilities or vehicles being investigated
- Investigation into ambulance fires to look at possible sabotage
- Prescription fraud issues
- How fast is EMS/FD where you live?
- EMS helicopter policy issues
- The total number and locations of ambulance stations within the organization's jurisdiction, and plans to build more or move existing ones
- Locations of ambulance station and fire houses
- Issues with personnel assigned to ambulance stations and fire houses
- Arrests of Fire Department and EMS personnel (on duty and off duty)

So, as you can see, media cluster related questions or issues can be much more wide-ranging than normal media questions or issues should be. Each time the questions widen, the worse it becomes for the organization.

THE ZEBRA PRINCIPLE

I was made aware of this principle many years ago, by a small, but distinguished group of people who worked in a certain field office. I didn't know about it for many years, and when I started to hear about it, I didn't pay very much attention to it, in fact I initially dismissed it. But over time I realized that there seemed-to-be some truth to it, so I thought I would pass it along here.

First and foremost, using the term zebra in this context is not meant to be racial, demeaning or anything close to that. Far from it. The principle simply involves "repetitive behavior" and suggests that where someone is the subject of a complaint or investigation which can't be proven, and especially if the subject employee(s) had been involved in previous similar cases, the current case should be closed out as being unsubstantiated. It also suggests that it is likely that in the future, the same employee will be the subject of another investigation or complaint, likely similar in nature, and then, with a little bit of investigative luck, that case might be able to be proven. What this principle comes down to is to:

- Treat each case individually,
- Completely investigate each case honestly,

- Treat the subject employees with your usual professionalism,
- If you can't prove a case, don't worry, close it out, it because down-the-line there will likely be another similar case involving the same employee(s) to investigate.
- The principle involves behavioral repetitiveness.

Over the years, the zebra principle became so engrained into my work that to this day all sorts of people that I interacted with during my career continue to send me pictures, video's and toy replica zebras.

THE USE OF DRONES IN EMS INVESTIGATIONS

Let me start this section off again by saying that I'm not a lawyer, so what I am suggesting here is solely from an investigative point-of-view. If you use, or plan to use drones with video capabilities for investigative purposes, you should run the idea past your organizational attorney's first for various legal reasons. These reasons include:

- Employee rights, both on and off duty
- What to do when non-organizational employees are discovered to be involved
- Privacy issues
- HIPPA (Health Insurance Portability and Accountability Act) issues
- Documentation of activities that become potentially criminal
- Safeguarding of evidence
- Chain of custody issues

I can envision Drones being used for the following investigative purposes:

- Surveillances, both moving and stationary, including location confirmations, and visual sighting of subject ambulance crews *
- Delivering investigative related equipment to investigators in the field
- Obtaining items in the field and transporting them back to the Investigative Unit

- Delayed response investigations (traffic and construction visual survey's)
- Ambulance Station Audits (exterior and roof)
- Firehouse Audits (exterior and roof)
- Sick Leave Abuse investigations
- Compensation Abuse investigations

*The use of drones will not replace the need for field investigators to conduct surveillances, but as a tool they will certainly enhance them in a number of ways.

INVESTIGATIVE VITAL SIGNS

As you should know, in the world of EMS there are vital-signs that are routinely used for patient diagnosis. They include:

- Body Temperature
- Pulse Rate
- Respiratory Rate
- Blood Pressure

Each of the aforementioned vital-signs has a designated informational range where "normal" patient vital-sign results should fall within. If vital-sign numbers are higher or lower, (abnormal), that information will help to provide clues as to what might be wrong with the patient.

Similarly, in the EMS investigative field there are eight sets of statistical "investigative vital-signs" that can provide varying degrees of analytical diagnosis of an organization, either individually or as a group. Four vital signs originate directly from the investigative unit while the other four originate from the organization. The vital signs can be examined individually or blended together. They are:

- Call Volume (an organizational number)
- Response Time (an organizational number)
- Call Times (an organizational number)
- Re-availability time (an organizational number)
- Complaint Volume (an investigative unit number)

- Complaint Types (an investigative unit number)
- Complaint Spikes (an investigative unit number)
- Employees with multiple complaints spikes (an investigative unit number)

Call Time

"Call time" includes the following segments; Police processing time, EMS (Fire) processing time, (in some locations there can be a combination of these into one emergency call center thereby having only one processing time), time, on-scene time (which includes actually locating the patient), travel time to a hospital, and hospital time.

Re-availability Time

Re-availability time deals with the issue of once an ambulance departs the hospital after having completed their transport of the patient, one of three items will occur which will also have an effect on how quickly the ambulance can actually get back into service:

- The ambulance immediately goes back into service,
- The ambulance travels to a particular geographic area before it can go back into service,
- The ambulance returns to an ambulance station or supply depot, so the crew can either restock medical supplies, clean up the ambulance, or change uniforms before going back into service.

Call Volume

"Call volume" by itself is basically an "it-is-what-it-is" figure. There were "x-number" of medical related calls received for a specific period-of-time. These "x-number" of calls can then be broken down by call type, medical priority, time-of-day, the day-of-the-week or in many other ways. At a certain point, a rise in call volume if left alone will lead to a rise in response time, which in turn will likely lead to a rise in complaint volume.

Response Time

- What is the overall response time for all levels (priorities) of calls?
- What is the overall response time to the most serious medical calls?
- Does the response time for these calls meet the established response time targets? If they do, that means an organization is doing well. If they don't, that's trouble. Even if an organization is meeting their goals, constant examination of response time figures is required to look for clues that suggest while things might appear to be ok today, tomorrow's figures probably won't be acceptable and will likely require a fix of some sort.

If over time, call volume is somewhat steady, or generally within its normal highs and lows, it's a somewhat simple figure to deal with. If call volume rises year after year, and all-of-a-sudden is constantly moving above its own average, that's going to be a problem, certainly for the organization, and to a lesser extent for the investigative unit. Some of the areas that an organization will have to look at to fix the problem, include:

- Hiring additional personnel
- Reviewing the locations where ambulances respond from
- Additional response vehicles
- Examining work tour structure
- Revamping preventive maintenance
- Revising the replacement cycle of response vehicles
- Building new ambulance stations
- Relocating existing ambulance stations
- Supplies (purchases, distribution and storage)

Making it simple, "response time" data will include fast responses and slow responses, however the overwhelmingly majority of the responses will fall somewhere in the middle, which in the world of statistics is referred to as "normal distribution". Occasionally some data is not "normally distributed" (in the middle). Something happens where one call or a number of calls are skewed away from the middle in the wrong direction. This skewing (moving away from the middle) creates what is referred to in the business as "outliers", and after some degree of organizational examination, some, or all of these "outliers" are likely to be removed from the official data pool and are not included as part of the final response time figures. This process of course makes the final figures look better than they actually are. The process cleanses them so-to-speak. I have always been against this. To me, even if the total number of outliers removed would only result in a miniscule numerical change in the overall number, it is the "perception" that the numbers are being manipulated that has always been problematic to me. There should be no adjustments of response time data at all, by anyone, no matter what unusual circumstances of any individual calls there might have been. Because of the adjustments, it is my belief that the investigative unit (IU) should never be directly or indirectly involved in any type of data adjustments, or for that matter in directly obtaining any of the three numbers (call time, call volume or response time). When needed, the IU should obtain the numbers from the proper organizational source. I recommend this because you never know down-the-road if or when the issue of how response time numbers are adjusted and/or obtained might come up, which could very possibly get into the arena of falsification of the figures. The IU can't be part of that. The IU has to remain "pure-as-the-wind-driven-snow" (thank you John Delventhal). By not removing "outliers", this will likely keep the response time figures minutely higher, however, I prefer to say that it will keep the response time figures "honest".

I believe that whatever the actions were that caused certain calls to be labeled as "outliers", something did happen, and since that "something" was actually dealt with on the day or days of occurrence, and even if it took days to actually complete and close out the calls, they should be included in the response time calculations, and not be discarded. I guess that's because I'm from the "tell-it-like-it-is" school of thought, win-lose-or-draw". I am sure that I am in the minority on this one.

Complaint Volume

Complaint volume is similar to call volume. Complaint volume is simply the total number of complaints that are received during a specified period-of-time. There can be no cleansing of these numbers, they are-what-they-are. Once you have developed the total number of complaints for a particular period of time, you need to compare it to past numbers of a similar time frame and then measure any changes either up or down.

Complaint Type

Complaint type simply refers to the subject-matter of individual complaints. Usually an individual complaint will consist of one or more call types, such as patient care, delay, or missing patient property. Remember, complaint type numbers will never match complaint volume numbers for any given time period because many complaints encompass more than one complaint type.

Complaint Type Spikes

Another investigative barometer involves complaint type spikes. You and your organization need to define what such a spike is numerically. Is it just a "number", is it an "average" number or is it a "percentage" number? Whatever you choose, you need to determine how high and how long such spikes are allowed to get to before alarm bells go off. You can monitor all of your complaint types or you can follow a combination of the most serious along with ones that are received most often. I recommend following all of them, but if you must be selective, I then recommend using the following eight complaint types:

- Delayed response complaints
- Delayed response complaints associated with a patient death
- Patient care complaints
- Patient care complaints associated with a patient death
- Hospital selection complaints
- Misconduct complaints
- Missing patient property
- Discourtesy complaints

You may wonder why I included discourtesy complaints as they seem to be so different from the other complaint types that are on the list. It is a "unique" barometer and I included it for the following three important reasons:

- It is likely that this is the category that you will receive the most complaints about

- If left unchecked, it is likely to morph into other more serious complaint types
- If the number keeps going up, not only is it likely that there is an issue of lack of supervision in the street, it may also involve a lack of training, the age of the workforce and/or hiring standards

Employees with multiple complaints associated with them

If the overall number of employees with multiple complaints is rising, or if the number of employees remains relatively the same, but their individual complaint numbers are rising, this is an indication of a systemic problem that requires immediate attention.

INTERNAL ORGANIZATIONAL INVESTIGATIVE NOTIFICATIONS

As the Director of my Investigative Unit, over the years I instituted a number of important rules. One of the most important was what we called the "no-surprise-rule". It simply meant that should any unusual incident occur, be it a new complaint or a serious or unusual incident, my investigators all knew that I had to be made aware of it immediately. Not tomorrow, not next week, but today, immediately, right now. Or as my old boss and mentor would say, "mach schnell", a German term which translates to "make it quick". There was no "wiggle-room". It didn't matter if I was on duty or off duty. It didn't matter if I was on vacation, I needed to be sure that if any of my investigators became aware of such an incident, they would notify me immediately. If for some reason they were unable to actually reach me, they were also instructed to notify my superior, and were told to document the notification.

The reason that I needed to know what occurred was so that I could make a timely "protective" determination as to what the next course of action would be. The action might be nothing, it might be something that could wait until the next business day, or it might be something that required me to make an immediate notification, either electronically, by phone, or in person, depending upon the degree of severity. I always preferred making in-person notifications. The point is, I was not leaving anything to chance, my investigators knew that, and my superiors knew that as well. Calling a superior at three o'clock in the morning to make such a notification, was not the most pleasant thing to do, however for everyone's longevity, it was the proper investigative thing to do.

If this type of situation occurred during the workday, I would always walk to, or drive to my superior's office and advise them verbally, and share any information, documentation or evidence that I had been able to gather up to that point. I wanted to be able to look them in the eye as I was explaining the situation to make sure they understood it.

If my superior was temporarily unavailable, I would advise the respective secretary or assistant that I needed to speak with him/her as soon as they became available. If I didn't get a callback in a reasonable amount of time, I would either call the secretary again, or return back to my superiors' office, knowing that there are times when messages don't get passed along immediately. If the matter was important enough, I would call/text my superior advising them that the matter was urgent (if it was) and that I needed to speak to him/her immediately. After receiving a message like that and knowing my managerial track-record, they would usually quickly become available for me quickly.

Another reason for this rule to be in place was certain types of notifications that my superior would have to make. The longer my original notification took to complete, the longer my superior's notifications would take as well. While I always looked out for myself and the IU, I also always tried to look out for my superior(s) as well.

Complementing the "no surprise rule" was the "document-document-document" rule. This was required at the investigator level, at the director's level and at the superior's level. Every call, every notification, every conversation, every notification attempt requires some level of documentation. The documentation rule was meant to protect everyone, the investigators, the director, and the organization.

Not following this simple notification rule could result in disciplinary action, a transfer, a demotion, a suspension or a termination. I have seen non-compliance with this rule ruin peoples' careers and reputations, even if they were a stellar employee prior to the incident. When this happens, I scratch my head in amazement, because the rule is so simple and is easy to follow. I always wonder if not following it was due to laziness, burnout, lack of respect, or something else.

THE EMS INVESTIGATIVE UNIT - RECOGNITION AND HISTORY

There is a lot of pride in the EMS profession. I have seen it first-hand. EMTs have it, Paramedics have it, EMS Supervisors have it, Firefighters have it, Police Officers have it, and hospital staffs have it as well. There is usually a special recognition program in place when someone from one of these aforementioned groups does something note-worthy, or is involved in an incident where a life or lives are saved. Such a recognition program is absolutely warranted.

I have always believed that there should also be some sort of official yearly recognition for the Investigative Unit (IU) and its staff. It would help counteract burnout and enhance investigations and morale. Investigators won't get their picture taken or have an article written about them in a newspaper like EMTs, Paramedics, Firefighters or Police Officers do, so when they do something special, and although EMS investigators will likely be involved in multiple serious cases per year, and any one of which could have major ramifications for the IU and the organization, they are generally not recognized. And recognition is important. I'm not just talking about a supervisor scribbling the words "good job" in red ink on the top page of an investigative report, which my boss did in the late 1970's and early 1980's. This recognition should be formal, something permanent, something that will forever remain with the individual investigator, and etched into IU history. Various ways of accomplishing this goal are as follows:

- Investigator of the year
- Investigation of the year - (patient care)
- Investigation of the year - (misconduct)

By keeping the number of annual awards to a minimum keeps the importance of the recognition to a maximum. I suggest that one recognition award be targeted to a patient care related investigation, as that is what an EMS organization should be dedicated to.

A second recognition should be misconduct related, as it encompasses a broad spectrum of case types, and is often a springboard for involved employees to become involved in more serious complaints. One such misconduct related investigation that comes to mind was the ambulance bumper incident that I previously referenced. I am not suggesting a program that presents awards for everyone and everything, as is frequently done today in children's sports.

You could possibly work the presentation of the IU awards into an existing yearly organizational recognition program. However, there are too many negatives to do it that way, which include confidentiality and stigmatizing issues. It is probably better to keep the presentation/ceremony away from the organizational ceremony and conduct it in-house (within the IU).

How you develop the criteria for this recognition depends upon a number of factors:

- The staffing level of the IU
- The volume of complaints/investigations
- The number of complaint types

The most of important issue to include in the criteria, is that the recognition should not be about finding the subject crewmember(s) guilty or innocent, it should be about the quality of the investigation itself, and how the final disposition(s) were arrived at. One year the award might go to an investigation where the allegations were substantiated, while the next year it might go to one where the allegations were unable to be substantiated. The final disposition doesn't matter, it's the "art of the investigation" that I am talking about, and yes there is an art to investigations.

I prefer the category of investigation of the year, over investigator of the year. Yes, the officially assigned investigator will ultimately receive the recognition, as will any investigators which provided assistance, but by making it about the investigation, the spotlight is focused on the quality of the investigative process. Doing so makes the award more prestigious. Not only do I suggest that the referenced investigator who is being honored receive a plaque, I also recommend a prominently displayed, permanently mounted wall plaque located within the investigative unit's office space which would historically document each years' award winners. I would place it somewhere where it would be easily visible to all that enterer the IU's offices, possibly near the visitors sitting area.

For both the wall plaque as well as the individual investigation/ investigator's plaque, you should list each investigation by the complaint type and the recognized investigator's name. Some case related information may be required for the official presentation, but you need to remember that HIPPA considerations must be followed.

VIDEO, VIDEO, VIDEO

If you are an EMS investigator today, you should give thanks to the abundance of available surveillance video available, especially in big cities. Video was not available to me during the first half of my career. When video did start to become available, and helped to solve a case, it was like receiving an early Christmas gift. Video gradually became available, although availability was nothing like it is today. Whether you are talking about personal video or municipal related video, today video is everywhere.

I would be remiss if I didn't discuss video without mentioning smart-phone-video. Three quarters of all Americans now own a smart phone which translates into an enormous pool of potential video evidence. There are various ways to obtain smart-phone-video:

- **With A Complaint**
  There is nothing better for an investigator to hear when receiving a complaint, when the complainant volunteers' information that they also have video of the incident and are willing to share it. If they don't volunteer that they have any video corroboration, the investigator must ask the complainant if he/she has any or knows of anyone who does. (This question and answer should be documented).

- **Searching the Incident Area**
  Searching an incident area is also known as canvassing. How was evidence found in the old days (pre-video)? By canvassing the area. The same canvassing techniques can be employed today when you are searching for video. The same kind of documentational rules apply as in any other kind of canvass. This simply means sending investigators to the incident location to look for video sources.

- **By Accident**
  This doesn't happen often, but when it does this type of a discovery is always memorable. An investigator at the scene may overhear two strangers talking about the incident and one takes out their smart-phone and shows the other person a video. It might pertain to the current case or even a matter that the investigative unit is not aware of yet.

I again need to reference my legal disclaimer here, I'm not a lawyer and this is one of those issues that you should run by your organization's legal department to determine what rule and regulations need to be followed when obtaining video, both surveillance video and smart-phone video. I was once instructed by my boss to carry release forms with me, and anytime I planned to shot video or take photographs on private property, I first had to get a release form signed by the owner of the property. I understand why I was advised to do this, and in thinking back, it didn't really hamper my investigations like I originally thought that it might. Getting the release signed forced me to seek out the property owner, and sometimes it worked out that the property owner had information which was helpful to the investigation.

HUMOROUS SURVEILLANCE STORY

An investigator, who never worked for me, but whom I am familiar with and whom I greatly admire, once employed a cleverly devised smoke-and-mirror overt technique simply by using a telephone. During the midnight tour the investigator would randomly call ambulance stations or the dispatch center requesting to speak with the on-duty supervisor. When the supervisor came to the phone the investigator would ask the ambulance supervisor if Inspector Niebowitz (fictitious person) had been there. The on-duty supervisor would always answer no. The investigator would then request that the on-duty supervisor have Inspector Niebowitz call him when he arrived. Sometime later the investigator would call back disguising his voice, and identified himself as Inspector Niebowitz, asking if there were any messages for him. The on-duty supervisor would tell him to call the investigator. This was done so cleverly and "just often enough" that many people believed there was a real Inspector Neibowitz who was out-and-about watching them. The bogus investigator ruse was effective enough that according to the investigator, complaints would drop, and ambulance status-signal compliance would rise in the areas where this occurred.

IT'S ALL A MATTER OF SEMANTICS

In the very beginning of this book I mentioned the word semantics. "It's all a matter of semantics" is a true phrase in the investigative world. Words and sentences must be chosen carefully and used in the proper context. By this I mean it is important that investigators completely understand patients and witnesses and vice versa. An investigator that I worked with many years ago used the phrase "It's all a matter of semantics" often, and even printed out a three-foot-long banner with the saying printed on it, pictured below. This banner remained on the wall of the investigative unit's office for many years (and it is still around today). As situations arose, it was often referred to. It reminded investigators to pay attention to exactly recall what was said or written. It also survived the IU being relocated thru a number of different offices over time. Unfortunately, this investigator is no longer with us and I do miss him, but the meaning of his banner will always be with us.

UNTESTED INVESTIGATIVE TECHNIQUES USED FOR PRIORITY CASES

One of my early mentors advised me that during the investigation of a "hot" case, I should not employ any investigative activity or technique which I hadn't been utilized previously. He suggested this to me after such a matter was brought up during an administrative hearing where the union representative who represented the subject crewmembers raised an objection to a specific investigative activity utilized. From then on, I tried never to introduce a new investigative activity during a "hot" case. By doing this, it made for smoother investigations.

SITE VISIT (ADDENDUM)

Although I addressed site visits in my first book, I wanted to provide two examples which I believe illustrate how important site visits can be during an investigation. I believe that the information which was uncovered would never have been discovered had it not been for the site visits. Both examples pertained to allegations of delayed ambulance responses, one occurred during daylight hours, and one occurred after dark.

Example #1

The daylight site visit revealed that the subject building address did exist with the house number permanently affixed to the front wall of the building (private residence) which was facing the street. The building itself was set back more so than most residences would normally be. However, the address numbers were located directly below a small three-sided awning, which was likely placed there in an attempt to "enhance" the numbers. Whatever the original reason for the canopy was, the site visit and weather records revealed that at the time that the subject call occurred, there was a combination of bright sunlight which caused a shade condition under the canopy which directly affected anyone's ability to be able to read the address numbers from a distance. The shadow "optically" caused the address numbers to be almost completely hidden. In fact, you literally had to walk up to the numbers and be within a few feet of them to be able to actually read them. Even if you were sitting in an ambulance by the curb in the vicinity of the address numbers, you still would not have been able to read the numbers. One of the crewmembers would have had to get out of the ambulance to read the numbers,

I have come to learn that this is a country wide issue. I recently came across this sign in another state which addresses the same issue.

Example #2

This evening site visit revealed that the subject address did exist, again with the house numbers permanently affixed to the front of the premises. The referenced location consisted of a number of attached residences, but the site-visit also revealed that the intercom system for the subject residence was not operational. While investigators were there, all of the intercoms were tested, and all worked with the exception of the subject residence intercom. It was also determined that when the ambulance crew arrived, they did ring many different intercoms in an attempt to locate the patient.

Both examples provide information as to why there was a delay in making patient contact, however, the developed information did not excuse the crew's failure to make a more concerted attempt to locate their patient.

MISSING PROPERTY ADDENDUM

I also covered missing patient property and related issues in my first book, but I wanted to add one brief thought about the subject here. Throughout my career when I was interviewing a patient or a witness for a missing property complaint, I often heard them say that one of the crewmembers was observed looking around the room where the patient was located. They did not appear to be admiring the furnishings, but rather seemed to be "looking" for something. For some reason, that statement always remained in my head. A few years ago, I was in a situation where a family member required medical assistance so 9-1-1 was activated. The local Police arrived followed by an ambulance. As I watched from afar, (which is what I do best), I observed the "look" in action. One of the ambulance personnel was looking all around. I wasn't worried as there were too many people in the house for something to happen, but after 30 plus years I finally did get to see the "look" in action, and finally understood what witnesses had been telling me for years.

A WORD ABOUT AUDITS

If your organization has authorized audits of any type, whether it's the more traditional definition of audits such as review of documentation, employee credentials, testing materials, or a broadened definition, such as complete facility and vehicle inspections, it is likely that sometime in the past there were one or more situations, behaviorally driven, which resulted in your organization being embarrassed, fined, or reprimanded, and being placed on some sort of probation.

As in investigations, there should be published official organizational audit guidelines which list the parameters of what the audits encompass. These guidelines should outline the auditor's power, and by the same token provide lines-in-the-sand that the auditors should never cross. I say this because when you are conducting an audit, instead of investigating a case from an office desk, you are conducting the investigation out in the field, at a location where the auditors (investigators) are the guests. You can think of it as going into someone else's house to conduct the audit. Those being audited aren't going to be happy that you are there, and they are going to be looking for anything that the auditors are doing wrong as potential leverage to counteract the final results of the audit might be. Audits can involve any of the following:

- Contraband material
- Alcohol or drugs
- Inappropriate postings on station walls or lockers
- Educational testing and training records
- Documents that are required to be completed in the field
- Billing based upon documents that are completed in the field
- Items that were purchased by your organization
- State mandated patient care related supplies
- Items that are being stored for future or past use
- Medical supplies or narcotic related issues
- Equipment that is required to be on individual ambulances, fire trucks or other response vehicles
- Gasoline purchases and distribution
- Vehicle mileage issues
- Toll issues
- Partial or complete inspections of organizational facilities
- Ensuring that all personnel who are signed in are actually at work and are working
- Timekeeping/Attendance/Lateness records
- Proper disposal of relinquished items

What I am primarily talking about in this section are organizational facility inspection type audits. The audits include, but are not limited to:

- Ambulance Stations

- Fire Houses
- Educational facilities
- Storage facilities
- Maintenance facilities

How are audits selected?

Locations to be audited can be selected as a result of a particular case (for cause auditing), or they can be selected randomly (random auditing). When dealing with a random selection, a computer program which selects the audit site, is probably the best option. The only question is who controls the computer program. Strictly from a "check and balance" point-of-view, it would be better for someone outside of the investigative unit (IU) to control it. The positive is that by having someone else from the Organization make the selection, it takes any negativity about the selection process away from the IU. The negative is that an additional person is now in the audit loop, and there is always the possibility that this person could "tip-off" someone at the subject location that the auditors are coming. Locations that are about to be audited can't have advance notice that the auditors are coming. If a location finds out ahead of time that they are about to be audited, you can be sure that the auditors won't find anything wrong when they arrive. And if they know you are coming, that means that you have a serious leak somewhere in the auditing/investigative chain that needs to be immediately addressed. Such leaks, which are hopefully nonexistent, are not difficult to locate.

There are two important facility related issues that must be addressed:

- The first is that for facility inspections, you are leaving the confines of the investigative unit's offices and are going to a particular facility. It is of the utmost importance that the audit team conducts themselves professionally. Those auditors that are actually going inside of the facility must do so professionally, like they would if there were in their own office. Any auditors that remain outside of the facility must do the same. Both the inside auditors and outside auditors must have a way to communicate with each other. Auditors must act appropriately at all times.

- The second issue pertains to evidence and contraband. If you leave evidence behind, or don't document any contraband that was found, it's a very problematic issue. If you do this, there is no need for audits and if that happens people will say that the auditors are in cahoots with those being audited, and it is my opinion that they wouldn't be wrong in feeling that way.

The leader of the audit/inspection team must possess the highest level of integrity. Whatever the subject of the audit is, all related items must be counted and documented. If you come across contraband, whether or not it is part of the audit in progress, it must be officially dealt with. Contraband is going to be defined by your organization's rules and regulations.

What am I talking about? If any contraband is discovered during the course of an audit, it must be documented, photographed secured and removed. It is likely that official notifications will have to be made from the audit site, especially if the contraband requires the response or notification of an authorized outside agency. If contraband is not handled this way, then audits are a waste of time.

If the employees who are the subject of the audits see that contraband is being overlooked, this will lead to:

- Worse future behavior by the employees at the audit location as well as other locations (because this type of word spreads fast).
- Accusations that the people who conduct the inspections are in cahoots with the employees, and once this is what people believe, the cause is lost because such audits are meaningless and those conducting the audits, in my opinion, could and should lose their jobs.

I can't emphasize enough how important it is to be on the "up-and-up" where audits are concerned.

DATABASE-DATABASE-DATABASE

The Merriam-Webster Dictionary partially defines "database" as a usually large collection of data organized especially for rapid search and retrieval (as by a computer). That definition is the basis for this section and the following sections of this book.

In the beginning of my career as there were no computers, and therefore there were no databases. When there were computers, initially there was no databases, so for a good number of years investigative answers had to be obtained manually or by memory.

WHAT SHOULD THE DIRECTOR OF THE INVESTIGATIVE UNIT DO WHEN A SERIOUS STATISTICAL SPIKE IS IDENTIFIED?

There very well may come a point-in-time when your statistics will reveal something that demands immediate attention, sometimes by the investigative unit, sometimes by the organization, and sometimes by both. My immediate non-legal recommendation is akin to what my investigative policy always was, to "do something with everything". By following that simple rule, not only are you protecting yourself and the Investigative Unit (IU), you are also protecting the organization.

However, you need to be careful that you are not seen as "crying wolf", because if that occurs, you will lose your effectiveness. You should take a pragmatic reporting approach which is primarily meant to protect the investigative unit as well as the organization.

Let me explain. You should already be routinely preparing a number of monthly, quarterly and yearly statistical reports. For the most part, these routinely-shared stats should be somewhat broad, housekeeping type stats, not investigative technique or personnel related specific stats, and they should be shared as part of a professionally presented report (see section 5), or in the case of an emergency, during a one-on-one meeting.

If there is any type of in-person or telephone discussion between the IU director and the recipient about the stats in general, or even more importantly about an individual stat, that information too should be documented by the IU director. This documentation is completed to protect both the director and the investigative unit. By documenting this information, down-the-road it can never be said that the I.U. director knew about certain information but didn't notify anyone in the organization. Copies of the submitted stats along with the director's notes will go a long way to prove that the information was properly forwarded. If the administrator who receives the information from the director doesn't pass the information along, or more importantly doesn't act upon it, the IU director should be safe because there is proof that the proper notifications were made. Hopefully this is documentation will never be needed. Thankfully, I never needed it, but I always thought of it as a type of personal insurance policy.

It should go without saying that prior to presenting any statistical reports, the director must review them to determine if there are any developing issues that either need to be flagged for the organizational administrator, or internally acted upon by the IU in an investigative fashion, or both. In most cases, spikes don't occur overnight, they grow at their own unique pace. Trends appear first, and if left unchecked, they turn into spikes. As you move forward in this area, the IU director and the organizational hierarchy need to be on the same page when it comes to defining what the words spike and trend really mean. Your definition of what constitutes a spike must be realistic, otherwise people will be doing nothing but chasing spikes all day ling. Spikes can be measured in numbers, averages and/or percentages.

Examples of issues that could be derived from stats would be:

- A continuing rise in the overall number of complaints received throughout the total response area.
- A significant rise in the number of complaints received in specific geographic portions of the organization's response area.

- A significant upward spike of a specific complaint type.
- A significant rise in the number of complaints associated with one or more employees.
- While reviewing "response time" stats you identify a significant rise, whether it's an initial rise, or part of a continuing rise, either involving the overall response area, or only a particular geographic portion of the response area. (Response time stats are not primarily an IU issue and should be continually monitored by the organization, whose issue it is).
- A rise in "call volume", which by itself is probably not an issue for the investigative unit, because this information should be picked up by organizational personnel. Planning for weather and holiday related rises are also issues primarily for the organization rather than for the IU.

WHY INPUT SO MUCH INFORMATION INTO YOUR DATABASE?

Investigations by nature are time consuming and repetitive. Entering investigative information into the database is even more time consuming and repetitive. However tedious one may think it is, in the long run it will be well worth the investigative time and effort. The same attention to detail that investigators normally have when they conduct investigations should carry over into their data-basing. No shortcuts should be taken to ensure accuracy and continuity.

If complaint information that was supplied to the hierarchy of your organization, whether it is subsequently released to the public, or only used in-house, if the information is later determined to be inaccurate or flawed for any reason, it will be very difficult, if not impossible for any new information ever to be completely trusted.

When I say document everything, I mean document every fact that was uncovered during the investigation as well as all of the investigative techniques that were utilized into the investigative unit's database. The bulk of the information should be entered by utilizing a combination of check boxes and drop-down-menus. Only a minimal amount of "narrative" information should be used. If information is properly documented in the database, the investigation unit will be able to show off its "investigative productivity." Investigators should be proud of the investigative work that they do. Also, if there is ever talk about investigator layoffs, the available database documentation could hopefully circumvent some, or all them.

The question always comes up if so much "additional information" is entered into the database, can't it be obtained by outsiders? To answer this, let me repeat what I said in my original book. I am not an attorney. This book is not meant to dispense any legal advice, so you will have to get the answer to this question from your organization's attorney. I have always tried to examine this issue from the point of view of an investigator who documented everything, and who conducted investigations with integrity. By thinking that way, I have never understood what the problem would be if outsiders obtained this information from the database as it would be available in individual case folders anyway. The only answers to this issue that I was able to come up with that which had any kind of a negative connotation were as follows:

- Embarrassment by the organization's hierarchy over the number of complaints received, especially the most serious complaints
- Determining that the organization knew that a problem existed and did little or nothing to correct it
- Fear by the organization's hierarchy that their jobs might be in jeopardy
- The fear of negative media stories
- The fear of legal judgments brought against your organization
- A determination by others, usually outsiders, that the organization was not doing enough to correct poor behavior, whether by investigation, pro-actively, educationally, or via the disciplinary process

Potentially there is so much investigative work that can go into one investigation, and obviously not every investigative activity is required for every investigation. Some investigative activities can be conducted in the office, but many must be conducted in the field. Wherever or whatever investigative activities are conducted for a particular investigation, they are important, and take up valuable "investigative time" and therefore should be fully documented. I also recommend that the time spent conducting individual investigative field activities should also be accurately documented. This information can be very helpful when the issue of staffing levels of the investigative unit arises.

If investigative work is properly documented, no one will ever be able to point a finger and say that the investigation was shoddy. As an example, if one investigator spends five 8-hour days conducting a particular surveillance, that's 40 investigative hours used just on the one case. If there were two investigators involved, that's 80 investigative hours used, if four investigators were involved, that's 160 hours. These numbers, which only involve one investigation, are substantial numbers, which need be documented. This is true even if the surveillance itself only gets a one paragraph mention in your final investigative report. When you calculate all surveillance numbers for a year, the total number of hours will surprise and should impress you. Imagine if you include this number in a year-end report, and compare it to previous years, the higher ups in your organization will have no choice but to be impressed.

In the case of a surveillance where multiple investigators are utilized, the investigator to whom the case is assigned should be the only one who physically enters surveillance related information into the database. On the other hand, surveillance reports that go into the case folder can be prepared by individual investigators who were part of the surveillance. That way you are sure that the information that is entered is accurate. It is of the utmost importance that these numbers be accurate.

The surveillance information that is entered into the database should include all of the dates of the surveillance's, the time spent conducting the surveillance's each day, any specialized equipment that was used, the identification of the vehicles that were used, (some sort of an ID number identification would suffice), and the number and identification of any investigators that were involved in the surveillance. When calculating investigative time that is spent on a surveillance, the issue of "travel time" to and from the surveillance location will come up. It is probably easier to lump the travel time into the surveillance time, and just qualify the surveillance time figure by saying it includes travel time to and from surveillance locations.

Throughout my EMS investigative career, I always created monthly and yearly statistics, charts and graphs, which pertained to EMS complaints and investigations. In the early years, the stats were simply a listing of very general complaint types and numbers which were either hand-written or typed onto a sheet of paper. But as time went on the stats developed into more formal charts and graphs that visually answered many questions. I kept fine-tuning them, and fine-tuning them and fine-tuning them, and eventually I got to a point where at any time I would be able to immediately answer almost any investigative question relating to EMS complaints and investigations that might arise. If I couldn't answer a question immediately, I usually could obtain the answer quickly by using one or more of my specialized reports. And if that didn't work, I would have a new program created to address the issue-at-hand.

Over time it also got to a point where I could often accurately predict when certain complaint types were likely to rise, or to drop for any given period-of-time. One simple example was that delayed ambulance response complaints would always spike upwards during the summer, primarily due to the hot weather. You may think that this is something that anyone should have known about without being told. I would agree with you, but I do recall in the early years of my organization, one of its highest-ranking officials (whom I will not identify), stated to the press that he didn't know that it got so hot during the summer. By stating this, he was suggesting that the hot weather either caused or was partially to blame for the ongoing response time problems within the organization that were occurring. This summer hot weather-related delayed response spike appears more dramatic when compared to response time figures for the rest of the year, with the exception of spikes during and after a snow-storm, or heavy rain storm, or on New Year's Eve, Christmas and July Fourth.

I was always proud of all the stats, information and graphs that I prepared. The majority of them were investigative related, some were investigator related, some were operationally related, and some were for specialty situations which weren't routinely shared. These stats should be divided into four separate categories:

- One group of stats and information would be for the entire investigative unit (IU) staff to routinely utilize as "investigative-tools" on a case by case basis. As an example, they can include the subject employee complaint histories, as well as past complaints received for the incident location.
- A second group of stats and information would be for the IU Director to use to produce routine monthly, quarterly, yearly and decade reports. These are generally investigative related statistics to be shared with whomever oversees the IU and hopefully for his/her bosses.

- A third group of stats and information would be for the IU Director to use to monitor investigations, complaint trends, individual investigators and the investigative unit as-a-whole, on a monthly, quarterly and yearly basis.
- A fourth group of specialty stats/reports would be for "unique-queries" by the IU Director. This type of report is only obtained and reviewed when a specific issue, a related issue or a related series of issues develop. If such a unique issue comes up during an investigation and there is no database query available, one should be prepared, so if the same issue arises again, the IU director will be ready.

WHAT INVESTIGATIVE INFORMATION SHOULD BE DATABASED?

The database should include both the initial complaint information, as well as any additional information that was developed during the course of the investigation. Data fields should be sub-divided as follows:

Technical Receipt Information

- Indication if the matter was a complaint (received externally) or if it was a self-generated investigation
- The source of the complaint; telephone, letter, walk-in, governmental complaint reporting system, media, self-generated investigation or other
- The investigative unit's assigned case number
- The assigned investigative classification of the case. This would either be an internal investigation (the most serious), a referral investigation (a case that is referred to one of your organization's commands for investigation would be an internal referral, or to an outside agency, which would be an external referral), or an information and intelligence case (databased only). A case classification can change during the course of an investigation, so you should allow space for more than one investigative classification entry. The date(s) that any classification changes occurred should also be documented

- Indication that a particular complaint was a duplicate complaint to one that was already received
- Any related external identification numbers
- The date, time, and day of the week that the incident occurred
- Indication if the call was the subject employees first call of the shift, last call of the shift or one of the middle calls of the shift.
- Indication what shift (midnight, day or evening) the incident occurred on
- The location of the incident (as listed in the 9-1-1 computer printout(s) of the assignment)
- The official geographic location of the incident. (If your organization divides up their response area into geographic locations)
- The zip code of the incident location (this is another way of dividing up your resoinse area geographically)
- The unique computer-generated identifying number(s) associated with the subject
- 9-1-1 call(s). This includes any related duplicate 9-1-1 calls. This can be complicated if the incident scene was a moving scene rather than a stationary scene
- The call type/priority of the call(s) associated with the investigation, include any upgrades and downgrades
- The official response time for the 9-1-1 calls associated with the investigation, no matter what the allegation is
- Indication if the call location is a designated "sensitive location". (See sensitive locations)
- It is possible that two or more complaints for the same location or event can be received. Both will have to be investigated and special care will have to be taken so there is no confusion as to what information pertains to each of the complaints.

Investigator related

- The identity of the investigator who was assigned the case
- The identity of any other investigators who assisted in any phase of the investigation

Case related

- The date and time that the complaint was initially received, either by the investigative unit, or elsewhere within your organization
- The identify the IU staff member, communications or Ambulance Station Supervisor who initially received the complaint
- The date and time that the investigative unit received the complaint (if the complaint was initially received elsewhere)
- The date that the case was assigned to an investigator
- The assigned investigative classification of the case (internal investigation, preliminary review case, referral investigation, or an information and intelligence case)
- The date and time that the case was received by the investigation unit
- The date, time and location if the complaint was received by anyone other than the investigative unit
- The date and time that the assigned investigator made initial follow-up contact with the complainant after being assigned the case
- The dates and times of any additional contacts with the complainant
- The dates and times of all contacts with the patient (if the patient was not the complainant)
- The full name and address (including zip code) and e-mail address of the complainant
- The full name and address (including zip code) and e-mail address of the patient
- The full name and address (including zip code) and e-mail address of all individual witnesses
- The dates and times of all contacts with witnesses
- Asking and documenting the complainant, patient and witnesses if they have, or are aware of any cell phone video if the incident being complained about
- The date of birth of the patient. (If a particular employee is involved in multiple complaints and you have determined that an employee integrity test is in order you will want to know if there is a particular age patient that is favored by the subject employee, so that you can select the proper aged person for an integrity test)

- The original allegations (complaint types)
- Additional specific issues which were identified and investigated by the investigator during the course of the investigation. (These are separate from original allegations)
- Subject employee(s) identification (name and shield number
- Subject employee(s) assigned work location
- If the employee(s) were not working at their assigned location, the location that ther worked out of for the subject call
- If the incident involved a field unit, the identity of the unit
- Indication if there was an "observer" riding on the subject ambulance
- Indication if the patient expired (usually the complainant will indicate that they believe the patient expiring was related to the incident that the complaint was made about)
- Indication if the patient was injured while in the care of EMS emergency responders (usually the complainant will indicate this was a factor in their making the complaint)
- Indication if any civilian was injured during the subject call
- Indication if any of the crew members were assaulted or injured while on the assignment
- Indication if any organizational reports were prepared directly pertaining to the incident
- Recent organizational photos of the subject employees (If older organizational photos are maintained, there are situations where they too may be needed)
- Indication whether involved employees are subjects or witnesses. An employee that is initially considered to be a witness can become a subject during the course of an investigation, and an employee that is initially thought to be a subject can turn out to be a witness. If this occurs, you must update the status change in the case folder as well as the database. It is the final status that is most important
- Indication whether any of the involved employees were restricted, modified or suspended from duty as a direct result of the referenced investigation
- Documentation of any referrals (including individual referral numbers) related to the case (either within your organization or to an authorized outside agency)

- Indicate if the matter was classified as a workplace violence incident
- Any related media coverage
- The date that the case was closed by the assigned investigator

Complaint types

In addition to listing all of the normal complaint types that your investigative unit follows, make sure to include the following "unusual" types:

- Lapse of certification case - employee
- Lapse of certification case - supervisor who oversees the certification program
- Falsification of certification paperwork
- Patient care-working above an employee's level of certification
- Patient care-working below an employee's level of certification
- Falsification of an Ambulance Call Report (ACR)
- Ambulance chasing (general)
- Ambulance chasing (specific)
- Hospital selection, quid-pro-quo situations
- Hospital selection, non quid-pro-quo situations

Miscellaneous

- Information if the assigned investigator officially discussed the case with anyone (include name, as well as the date, time and location of discussion)
- Information documenting any subsequent outside inquiries into the incident
- Information if a copy of the final report was sent to any authorized external agency, and who authorized it
- Documentation of any notifications (internal or external) pertaining to the subject investigation that were made
- For missing patient property complaints, list each individual missing item, the approximate worth of each item, where and when each item was last seen. Indicate if any or all of the missing property was recovered, and if so, who was it recovered by and

where and when was it recovered. (If the missing property was
U.S. Currency, break it down by denominations and indicate how
many of each denomination were involved)

Investigative tools/activities

- Employee certification records
- Work location logbooks
- DMV (Dept. of Motor Vehicles) record checks
- GPS records
- Cell phone records
- Cell phone video
- Cell phone photographs
- Vehicle preventive maintenance records
- Radio repair records
- Technical services records
- EZ-Pass records
- Photo arrays
- Field Interviews
- Site visits
- Employee interviews (subject)
- Employee interviews (witness)
- Audits
- Covert surveillances
- Overt surveillances
- Certification records
- Station logs
- Vehicle mileage logs

DATABASE REPORTS

Database reports will be the foundation of your statistics and graphical
presentations no matter what time-period you are concerned with. It has
been said that stats can be made to say anything you want, however stats
need to be accurate, and prepared without any embellishment what-so-
ever. The numbers are what they are and should not be modified for any

reason. If in a particular month you received ten cases, and closed nine of them, then you closed ninety percent of your cases, a good average most would say. There will, however, always be someone who says ten percent of your cases weren't closed. That is also true, but from my way of thinking, the ninety percent figure of nine cases far outweighs the ten percent figure of one case. There could be many reasons why the one case wasn't closed. It could be because it involved a complex internal investigation that was received during the last week of the referenced month, or even on the last day of the month, which wouldn't have given you enough time to properly investigate it. If you received one hundred cases during the month and closed ninety of them, you still closed ninety percent. But now the ten percent refers to ten open cases. The percentage of the cases remain the same, but now if the same person refers to the ten percent figure, he/she is referring to ten open cases, which might not sound so good to anyone listening. You have to be prepared to hear such comments and be ready to intelligently answer them. One way to do this is to break the ten cases down into investigative classifications (internal investigations, internal/external referrals or information cases). Again, both you and the person making the statement would be right, but common sense would still suggest that your ninety percent figure is much better position to be in than the person who is speaking of the ten percent figure.

FOUR IMPORTANT SOURCES FOR INVESTIGATIVE STATISTICAL INFORMATION

SOURCE #1 - INVESTIGATIVE UNIT'S DATABASE

A properly constructed database is required to properly document:

- Complaints
- Complaint types
- Self-generated investigations
- Investigative activities
- Investigative dispositions
- Complaint trends and spikes
- Investigator activities
- Use of investigative tools and resources

The IU database must have enough available memory both for the short term as well as the long term. My experience has taught me four things regarding this:

- In the ambulance business, employees come and go. Some will certainly make a career out of working for one organization, but this is not true of everyone. An employee can leave an organization, and then can re-appear in a number of different ways. They can do so by re-applying and getting their old job back from your organization, or they can work for a different ambulance service which interacts with your organization, either directly or indirectly. These other ambulance organizations might respond within your organization's response area, so it is important to maintain older complaint records in your database. I have seen organizational employees work for five different area ambulance services over a period of years. In this business if an employee moves around a lot, with a few exceptions it is not always for good reasons. In the EMS business, the IU needs to know about an employee's complaint history no matter whom their employer is or was, as long as their employer's organization interacts with your organization. If there has to be a limit to the databases "memory ceiling", I would recommend 50 years. I base this on employee life spans. Since I make the point that employees come and go and come back in some way in this business, then a fifty-year memory would solve this issue. (I would recommend however that information over the fifty-year limit be separately stored for historical reference purposes).
- You will not be able to remember the particulars of every complaint and investigation, specifically who the involved employees were, as well as nuances which are unique to their respective investigations.
- Historical reference. You may see an upward trend in a particular complaint type in a particular geographic portion of your response area. You should want to know how this occurred and if there were there any earlier warning signs that would have allowed you to deal with it sooner than you did. On the other hand, there are IU statistical reports such as annual case totals where you will want to show off decades of information. To do that I always found that a bar chart works best. Taking this report one step further, adding

the number of investigators assigned to the IU in the case total report going back decades, is also a powerful graph, and can serve a number of useful investigative related purposes.

- Additionally, there are IU statistical reports such as annual complaint totals and types which can easily and professionally display decades of information.

SOURCE #2 - PERSONNEL (HUMAN RESOURCES) DATABASE INFORMATION

To be able to produce many of the reports that I reference, the investigative unit's database needs to be "computer-optically" linked to your organization's personnel database. Both databases will contain information that some of the investigative unit's (IU) reports will require. Some personnel information is needed for individual cases, some will be needed for employee profiles and some will be needed when developing complaint trends. This should become clearer when I get into these reports why this information is important. No information that originates in the IU's database should get transposed into the personnel database. In other words, the linking of the two databases is for information to travel in one direction only, from the personnel database to the IU's database. The basic information required from the personnel database is as follows:

- The full name of all employees
- Employee shield numbers (past and present) and/or organizational identification numbers (as of the date of the incident which is under investigation)
- The employees original date of appointment
- Indication if an employee is a "rehire", (a person who was a past employee, who left the organization, and was subsequently rehired) the dates of the subject employee's past employment periods)
- Employees date of birth (solely to determine the subject employee's age on the date of the incident that is under investigation)
- Partial or full social security number
- Historical dates and titles of employees (date hired, date assigned to specific work locations, promotional information etc.)

- The assigned work location of employees on the date of the incident that is being investigated
- Historical dates of all prior medical and administrative refreshers attended by employees to date
- Historical dates and types of other educational or re-training
- Dates and explanation of any past short-term assignments that employees have been assigned
- Any other ambulance services that an employee has worked for that your organization is aware of (It is possible that the IU will have more information on this than Human Resources would have).
- Official Organizational employee picture (most recent and past)
- Employee attendance/lateness records

Having this personnel information automatically transferred into the investigative unit's database by computer rather than being manually entered by an investigator will save many hours of investigative work and should keep information errors to a minimum

SOURCE #3 - COMPUTER ASSISTED DISPATCH (CAD) INFOFMATION

Certain stats will only be able to be obtained from your CAD computer information files. This means that the information may have to be entered into the investigative database manually. This information includes, but is certainly not limited to:

- Date of Incident
- Time of incident
- Time of assignment
- The location of the assignment (including any changes of location)
- Call type upgrades or downgrades
- The assignment and time of arrival on the scene of the first medical resource
- Time of arrival of other (non-medical) resources
- The assignment and time of arrival of each additional medical resource

- Time of arrival of other (non-medical) resources
- Identification of other (non-medical) resources
- The time that the patient was transported to the hospital
- Time of arrival at the hospital
- Identity of the hospital that the patient was transported to
- Time that the transporting ambulance(s) cleared from the assignment
- Time that the other ambulance(s) and medical resources cleared from the assignment
- Incident call type (initial and any upgrades or downgrades)
- Crew identification (if CAD is set up to include this information)
- The number, dates, times and call types of past EMS responses to the subject location
- Duplicate assignments for the new investigation as well as for past responses

SOURCE #4 - GLOBAL POSITIONING SYSTEM (GPS) INFORMATION

If GPS is used by your organization for dispatch purposes, this information can provide assistance to the Investigative Unit (IU) in the following areas:

- Location history of where an individual response vehicle or group of response vehicles (ambulance, fire unit, supervisor) were located at the time of dispatch, what their movements were after being dispatched including arrival at the scene, including any stops that were made, and movement after leaving the scene. This information can be helpful during delayed response investigations, missing patient property investigations, as well as certain misconduct investigations.
- The overall movement of one or more vehicles (not necessarily response vehicles) for an entire tour.
- When not on assignment, determining if vehicles were at the location that they were supposed to be at.

TRACKING COMPLAINTS AND INVESTIGATIONS INVOLVING A PATIENT DEATH

The three major complaint types that can usually involve a patient death are:

- Delayed responses
- Patient care
- Hospital selection

It is very important to track complaints/investigations which are associated with patient deaths. Just because a complainant alleges that the patient expired, this does not necessarily mean that there is a connection between the allegations and the death. Hopefully the investigation will make this determination.

FINAL INVESTIGATIVE DISPOSITIONS

It is necessary to document the disposition for each individual allegation as well as any additional issues which were identified during the investigation. (You should address them in the same order that you listed them in the beginning of your final investigative report). The dispositions should be broken down into specific investigative descriptive terms, and then be used to indicate the involvement of each employee, whether subject or witness, in the investigation.

I recommend using the following seven terms to accomplish this:

- **Substantiated-A (wrong-doing noted)**. All original "allegations" and all identified "additional issues" have been proven by the investigation to be true.
- **Substantiated-B (no wrong-doing noted)** All original "allegations" and all identified "additional issues" have been proven by the investigator to be true, however no rules, regulations or guidelines were broken, thus, wrong doing was not noted. (An example of this would be a delayed response allegation. If it alleged that the ambulance took six minutes to respond. If the six minutes was within the targeted response time of the respective call type, and the ambulance crew made a good faith effort to respond, then

the complaint would be substantiated, but because it was within the guidelines, no discipline would be recommended).

- **Partially Substantiated-A (wrong-doing noted)** (Some of the original allegations and/or some of the additional issues have been proven by the investigation to be true. This disposition also signifies that one or more of the original allegations and/or one or additional issues were not substantiated.
- **Partially Substantiated-B (no wrong-doing noted)**
- Some allegations/issues are substantiated, others are not. the overall disposition for a case like this is partially substantiated but no discipline is recommended. This disposition also suggests that some sort of discipline is warranted.
- **Unsubstantiated** (the investigation revealed that none of the original allegations or subsequent issues have been proven by the investigation to be true).
- **Unfounded** (the investigation was unable to identify a call or incident that directly pertains to the complaint. The final disposition for a case like this would be unfounded).
- **Duplicate Case** A particular complaint was a duplicate to another previously received complaint or self-generated investigation, whether already in progress, or closed out. The case number of the original case should be cross referenced with the new (duplicate) case, and vice versa.

Whatever "dispositions" and respective definitions that you use, they all must be utilized exactly the same way by all members of the investigative unit. The definition of the terms can't leave any wiggle-room for a misunderstanding. In addition, there should be at least one database report associated with each disposition that is listed above.

SECTION 3

COMPLAINT TYPES

General Complaint Types

"General" complaint types may suffice for basic monthly, quarterly and annual reporting, but there will be many times when this type of data will not provide enough specificity.

The following is a basic listing of twenty-four "general complaint types" that an EMS investigative unit might routinely track in its investigative database:

- Abuse
- ACR/PCR falsification
- Audits
- Billing
- Death in Police custody
- Delay
- Driving
- Documentation
- Drugs
- Equipment malfunctions
- Hoax calls
- Hospital selection
- Inter-agency transfer issue
- Internet related
- Leave abuse
- Misconduct

- Missing patient property
- Off duty misconduct which reflects negatively on your organization which may result in organizational discipline of the referenced employee(s)
- On duty use of unauthorized medical equipment
- Other (catchall category for any allegation that doesn't fit into any of the other existing categories)
- Patient care
- Patient injury
- Personal business
- Theft of organization property

FAMILY OF COMPLAINT TYPES

The "family" of an individual complaint type is a descriptive term that I have never heard anyone else use or reference, but it's something that I continuously thought about during my working years. Instead of just utilizing a broadly defined complaint type, I am linking them to a more specific and informative listing of related sub-complaint types. Often the sub-complaint types themselves are equally or more serious than the original complaint type. Either way they certainly paint a more descriptive picture than the original complaint type did, and they will fine-tune your statistics into a more comprehensive level of specificity. When you are entering a complaint that involves any of the general family of complaint types, your data base should be set up so that once you check off the general complaint type, all related (family) sub-complaint types should automatically appear in a drop-down menu which allows you to easily select as many of them as appropriate. By setting it up this way you will have the option of running either a "general" report or a "specific report, depending upon what your needs are. The following is a listing of ten "family of complaint types" groupings and the number of family of complaint type reports that are associated with each one. I limited the example size just to make the point of how important the family of complaint types are. If you opt not to track them this way, these reports can be combined into database reports as seen in section four.

1. FAMILY OF "PATIENT CARE" COMPLAINTS

We can all agree that patient care complaints are the most serious complaints that an EMS investigative unit investigates. Yes, delays, hospital selection and missing patient property can be equally problematic, but proper patient care is the paramount concern of any EMS Organization. Patient care is also the complaint type that is most likely to have multiple allegations associated with individual complaints. The term "patient care" can literally refer to a multitude of individual serious sub-issues or sub-types. As an example, I am going to use the following patient-care sub-issues to make my point. There are many, many, many more patient-care issues that should be tracked.

First, all "patient care-complaints or investigations should be divided into one of the following two categories:

- Those associated with a patient death
- Those not associated with a patient death

Then you sub-divide them into the following categories:

- Walking a patient from the call location to the ambulance where the patient's condition fits the criteria for utilizing a carrying devise.
- Walking a patient from the ambulance to the emergency room where the patient's condition fits the criteria for utilizing a carrying devise
- Performing patient care out of title (e.g. A member of your organization who works as an EMT, and who is certified elsewhere as a paramedic. While working as an EMT for your Organization, he/she administers a drug that only Paramedics are authorized to administer).
- Using a chair to transport the patient to the ambulance, or into the hospital emergency department when the patient's signs and symptoms call for the use of a stretcher
- Failure to obtain vital signs
- Failure to obtain the proper number of vital signs.
- Failure to document vital signs

- Failure to provide oxygen when required
- Ran out of oxygen during an assignment
- Failure to shock the patient when required
- Ambulance Call Report (ACR) falsification (this includes documenting one action, or a series of actions on the ACR that weren't actually performed
- Ambulance Call Report (ACR) review. ACRs should be reviewed with a "fine-tooth-comb" when conducting a patient care investigation
- Equipment failure
- Failure to administer the proper narcotics

2. FAMILY OF "DELAY" COMPLAINTS

There can be so many causes, that directly or indirectly result in a delayed response. I listed many of them below. There will be some delay cases where there is no obvious reason why the delay occurred, thus the last selection.

Delayed ambulance response complaints should initially be divided into the following two sub-categories:

- Those associated with a patient death
- Those not associated with a patient death

Next sub-divide them into the following "cause related" categories:

- Resource availability
- Geography
- Street construction
- Call receiving error
- Caller error
- Call volume
- Dispatch error
- Crew error
- Personal business
- On-Scene address
- Weather

- Change of shift
- Unable to determine

3. FAMILY OF "ABUSE" COMPLAINTS

First, they should be divided into the following two categories:

- Those associated with a patient death
- Those not associated with a patient death

Next, sub-divide them into the following categories:

- Discourtesy-Offensive behavior. Inappropriate verbal conduct including rude or profane gestures, nasty words including curses. As I alluded to in my original book, "discourtesy" complaints is the complaint type category that is received far more frequently than other complaint types the most. Discourtesy complaints may seem inconsequential, and they are, but these incidents need to be educationally addressed by your organization. If they are not expeditiously tackled, they usually lead to employees receiving more serious complaints down-the-road. Meaning if they are not addressed, the incoming mole-hill can turn into a landslide.
- Physical incidents. An allegation that an employee physically touched/handled a patient/complainant (in a non-sexual manner). This contact may or may not have caused an injury. This complaint type may be a criminal matter, and may have to be investigated elsewhere.
- Sexual incidents. An allegation that an employee was involved in inappropriate sexual contact usually involving a patient. This complaint type may be a criminal matter.
- Inappropriate language, slurs and/or derogatory remarks about a person's sexual orientation, race, ethnicity, religion, gender or disability. It also includes nonverbal bias acts and complaints. These matters are often referred to an organization's EEO Office and are not investigated by the IU.
- Name refusal. Refusal of an employee to provide his/her name when requested.*

- Shield refusal. Refusal of an employee to provide his/her shield identification number when requested.*

   *A written rule must be on your organization's books documenting that employees must comply with such requests.

You can fine tune the definition of any of the "abuse" sub-complaint types to fit your individual needs. Whatever definitions you choose; they must be specific enough so that there can be no misinterpretation when they are used.

4. FAMILY OF "MISSING PROPERTY" COMPLAINTS

First, they should be divided into the following two categories:

- Allegation associated with a patient death. This complaint type becomes even more reprehensible when the missing property belonged to a deceased person
- Allegation not associated with a patient death

Next, sub-divide them into one of the following two categories:

- patient missing property
- non-patient missing property

Then you want to further sub-divide the complaints into one or more of the following:

- Money (document the total amount and currency breakdown by denominations)
- Jewelry (number of pieces and individual descriptions)
- Prescription drugs (number and descriptions)
- Identification cards (identify)
- Wallet and contents (non-money)
- Wallet and contents (including money)
- Item identified as a family heirloom (identify item)
- Medical devise (cane, walker, personal, portable oxygen)

- Dentures
- Clothing
- Other

5. FAMILY OF "DRIVING" COMPLAINTS (VEHICLE OPERATION)

This involves all types of, ambulances, fire apparatus, as well as supervisory and support vehicles.

First, they should be divided into the following two categories:

- Those associated with a patient death
- Those not associated with a patient death

Next, you want to sub-divide them into the following categories:

- Moving vehicle complaints (on assignment).
- Moving vehicle complaints (not on assignment).
- Parked vehicle complaints-not on assignment. (Location)
- Parked vehicle complaints-not in assignment. (Idling pollution)
- Parked vehicle complaints-not on assignment (Idling noise)
- Parked vehicle complaints-on assignment (location)
- Parked vehicle complaints-on assignment (idling)
- Accidents-reported
- Accidents-not reported
- Vehicle lights, siren and/or spotlight issues
- PA misuse (vehicle public address) issues
- Unauthorized person in the ambulance.
- Falsification, either verbally or in writing, of who the driver (operator) of the ambulance or other organizational vehicle was at or around the time of the incident

If your investigative unit routinely conducts vehicle accident investigations, you can add all the related accident investigation scenarios and situations into this section.

6. FAMILY OF "HOSPITAL SELECTION" COMPLAINTS

First, they should be divided into the following two categories:

- Those associated with a patient death
- Those not associated with a patient death

Next you want to do the following:

The family of Hospital Selection complaints is a slightly different concept than the other family of complaint sections. For this category, you are not breaking the complaint type into sub-categories, you are breaking this complaint type down into "requested hospital" versus the hospital that the patient was actually transported to. For each of the two listings, you should utilize a drop-down menu which lists all of the hospitals that your organization transport patients to. Additionally, you should add one additional category, "Request to not be transported to a specific hospital". This is for documenting the allegation where the patient didn't request any particular hospital but did indicate that he/she didn't want to be transported to one specific hospital (usually because of a previous bad experience at that hospital) but was transported there.

7. FAMILY OF "DRUG" (NARCOTICS) COMPLAINTS

First, they should be divided into the following two categories:

- Those associated with a patient death
- Those not associated with a patient death

Then you want to sub-divide into the following categories:

- Drug use (employee)
- Drug tampering (by employee)
- Drug diversion (by employee)
- Drug theft
- Improper drug documentation and related record keeping

8. FAMILY OF "MISCONDUCT" COMPLAINTS

First, they should be divided into the following two categories:

- Those associated with a patient death
- Those not associated with a patient death

Next you want to sub-divide them into the following categories:

- Personal cell phone usage (on duty)
- Use of personal cell phone in lieu of an "organizational issued" communication device for official business
- Camera/video usage (on duty)
- Inappropriate social media use (on duty or organizational related)
- Inappropriate use of organizational computers, cell phones or tablets
- Improper use of organizational equipment/supplies/vehicle for personal use
- Contacting a patient utilizing information officially obtained during a response to a 9-1-1 call. This includes telephone calls, text messages and/or social media
- Crewmember taking a picture of a patient (regardless of the patient's condition)
- Vandalism/altercation of organizational property
- Cheating on an organizational related educational examination (cheating can come in a number of forms in this context. In addition to the actions of one or two employees that I referenced elsewhere in this book, cheating can include some of the following scenarios. Instructors or others handing out the answers prior to the test or at the test, test takers going to the bathroom where they obtain answers by smart phone or by reference material they previously hid there, instructors altering test sheets by erasing and changing an answer or altering "chads").
- Misuse of organizational issued equipment
- Shopping (on duty)
- Being at a location (on duty) banned by the organization
- Visiting friends (rather than being at a proper authorized location) on duty

- Gambling (on duty)
- Eating (without authorization) on duty
- Cooping (in vehicle) on duty
- Being charged/convicted of a crime (on or off duty)
- Subordinate threatening a supervisor
- Falsification of "flag-down" assignment
- Lapse of certification(s)
- Falsification of certification paperwork
- Ambulance chasing issues (The term "ambulance chasing" pertains to lawyers that follow **ambulances** to the emergency room to find clients).
- Crew dispute (verbal incident)
- Crew dispute (physical)
- Incident reported to a supervisor who took no action
- Theft of patient's personal information
- Timekeeping (timesheets) fraud
- Loss of, theft of, or damage to archived records

9. FAMILY OF "BILLING" COMPLAINTS

First you want to divide this into the following two categories:

- Those associated with a patient death
- Those not associated with a patient death

Then you want to sub-divide this into the following five categories:

- Patient transported
- Patient not transported

Next you want to sub-divide again into one of these two categories:

- Billing complaint received within 2 weeks of the date of incident. (This indicates that the matter was significant enough for the complainant to file a complaint prior to being billed).
- Billing complaint received after invoice for service was mailed out to the patient (Usually more than two weeks after the date of

service). This indicates that it was the bill for service motivated that the complainant.

Finally, you want to further sub-divide this into the following five categories:

- Billing (the charges are too high).
- Billing (the complainant believes that there shouldn't be a charge for the ambulance).
- Billing (associated with another complaint type, such as discourtesy, patient care or hospital selection).
- Billing-Oxygen. Billing for oxygen when it was alleged or determined that none was actually administered. (You might think that this is hard to prove, but my experience tells me that when this allegation is made, it is most often true).
- Billing-Identity theft (Billed patient alleges he/she wasn't a patient, and wasn't in an ambulance and wasn't in the area or the city that day
- ambulance and wasn't in the area or the city that day).
- Billing (all other billing related allegations)

10. FAMILY OF "LEAVE ABUSE" INCIDENTS

You want to divide this down into one of the following four categories:

- Sick Leave Abuse.
- Compensation Leave Abuse
- Falsification of Medical Records (Doctor's notes etc)
- Disability Fraud

FAMILY OF COMPLAINT TYPES – RELATED DATABASE REPORTS

The following is a listing of "family of complaint types" reports related to the ten general complaint types previously listed.

1. "FAMILY OF *PATIENT CARE*" COMPLAINT TYPE DATABASE REPORTS

- 1 Numerical breakdown of all <u>patient care</u> sub-complaint types
- 2 Percentage of all patient care sub-complaint types

- 3 # walking a patient from the call location to the ambulance
- 4 % of this complaint type compared to all family of patient care complaint types
- 5 % of this complaint type compared to all other complaint types

- 6 # walking a patient from the ambulance into the ER
- 7 % of this complaint type compared to all family of patient care complaint types
- 8 % of this complaint type compared to all other complaint types

- 9 # of employee performing patient care out of their title
- 10 % of this complaint type compared to all family of patient care complaint types
- 11 % of this complaint type compared to all other complaint types

- 12 # using a stair chair when a stretcher is the proper carrying devise
- 13 % of this complaint type compared to all family of patient care complaint types
- 14 % of this complaint type compared to all other complaint types

- 15 # of using a stretcher when a stair chair is the proper carrying devise
- 16 % of this complaint type compared to all family of patient care complaint types
- 17 % of this complaint type to all other complaint types

- 18 # failure to obtain any vital signs
- 19 % of this complaint type compared to all family of patient care complaint types
- 20 % of this complaint type compared to all other complaint types

- 21 # failure to obtain the proper number of vital signs
- 22 % of this complaint type compared to all family of patient care complaint types
- 23 % of this complaint type compared to all other complaint types

- 24 # failure to document vital signs
- 25 % of this complaint type compared to all family of patient care complaint types
- 26 % of this complaint type compared to all other complaint types

- 27 # failure to administer oxygen when required
- 28 % of this complaint type compared to all family of patient care complaint types
- 29 % of this complaint type compared to all other complaint types

- 30 # of running out of oxygen during an assignment
- 31 % of this complaint type compared to all family of patient car complaint types
- 32 % of this complaint type compared to all other complaint types

- 33 # failure to shock patient when required
- 34 % of this complaint type compared to all family of patient care complaint types
- 35 % of this complaint type compared to all other complaint types

- 36 # of ACR falsifications
- 37 % of this complaint type compared to all family of patient care complaint types
- 38 % of this complaint type compared to all other complaint types

- 39 # of medical equipment failure
- 40 % of this complaint type compared to all family of patient care complaint types
- 41 % of this complaint type compared to all other complaint types

- 42 # failure to administer narcotics when required

- 43 % of this complaint type compared to all family of patient care complaint types
- 44 % of this complaint type compared to all other complaint types

2. "FAMILY OF *DELAY*" COMPLAINT TYPE DATABASE REPORTS

- 1 Numerical breakdown of all delay sub-complaint types
- 2 Percentage of all delay sub-complaint types

- 3 # of delay (non-death) complaints
- 4 % of this complaint type compared to all family of delay complaint types
- 5 % of this complaint type compared to all other complaint types

- 6 # of delay (with a death) complaints
- 7 % of this complaint type compared to all family of delay complaint types
- 8 % of this complaint type compared to all other complaint types

- 9 # of delay (non-death) complaints issue with first responding ambulance
- 10 % of this complaint type compared to all family of delay complaint types
- 11 % of this complaint type compared to all other complaint types

- 12 # of delay (with a death) complaints issue with first responding ambulance
- 13 % of this complaint type compared to all family of delay complaint types
- 14 % of this complaint type compared to all other complaint types

- 15 # of delay (non-death) complaints issue with specialized ambulance
- 16 % of this complaint type compared to all family of delay complaint types
- 17 % of this complaint you compared to all other complaint types

- 18 # of delay (with a death) complaints issue with specialized ambulance
- 19 % of this complaint type compared to all family of delay complaint types
- 20 % of this complaint type compared to all other complaint types

- 21 # of delay (non-death) complaint issue with CFR response
- 22 % of this complaint type compared to all family of delay complaint types
- 23 % of this complaint type compared to all other complaint types

- 24 # of delay (with a death) complaints issue with CFR response
- 25 % of this complaint type compared to all family of delay complaint types
- 26 % of this complaint type compared to all other complaint types

- 27 # of delay (non-death) complaint, issue with supervisor response
- 28 % of this complaint type compared to all family of delay complaint types
- 29 % of this complaint type compared to all other complaint types

- 30 # of delay (with a death) complaint, issue with supervisor response
- 31 % of this complaint type compared to all family of delay complaint types
- 32 % of this complaint type compared to all other complaint types

- 33 # of delay (non-death) complaint, field unit issue (other than first arriving ambulance, specialized ambulance, CFR unit or supervisor)
- 34 % of this complaint type compared to all other family of delay complaint types
- 35 % of this complaint type compared to all complaint types

- 36 # of delay (with a death) complaint, (field unit issue other than first arriving ambulance, specialized ambulance, CFR unit or supervisor)

- 37 % of this complaint type compared to all family of delay complaint types
- 38 % of this complaint type compared to all other complaint types

- 39 # of delay (non-death) complaint dispatcher issue
- 40 % of this complaint type compared to all family of delay complaint types
- 41 % of this complaint type compared to all other complaint types

- 42 # of delay (with a death) complaints dispatcher issue
- 43 % of this complaint type compared to all family of delay complaint types
- 44 % of this complaint type compared to all other complaint types

- 45 # of delay (non-death) complaints 9-1-1 operator issue
- 46 % of this complaint type compared to all family of delay complaint types
- 47 % of this complaint type compared to all other complaint types

- 48 # of delay (with a death) complaints 9-1-1 operator issue
- 49 % of this complaint type compared to all family of delay complaint types
- 50 % of this complaint type compared to all other complaint types

- 51 # delay (non-death) complaint 9-1-1 caller issue
- 52 % of this complaint type compared to all family of delay complaint types
- 53 % of this complaint type compared to all other complaint types

- 54 # delay (with a death) complaint where resources had to wait for the PD to arrive before entry could be made
- 55 % of this complaint type compared to all family of delay complaint types
- 56 % of this complaint type compared to all other complaint types

- 57 # delay (non-death) complaint where resources had to wait for the PD to arrive before entry could be made

- 58 % of this complaint type compared to all family of delay complaint types
- 59 % of this complaint type compared to all other complaint types

- 60 # delay (with a death) hospital diversion issue
- 61 % of this complaint type compared to all family of delay complaint types
- 62 % of this complaint type compared to all other complaint types

- 63 # delay (non-death) hospital diversion issue
- 64 % of this complaint type compared to all family of delay complaint types
- 65 % of this complaint type compared to all other complaint types

- 66 # delay (with a death) change of tour issue
- 67 % of this complaint type compared to all family of delay complaint types
- 68 % of this complaint type compared to all other complaint types

- 69 # delay (non-death) change of tour issue
- 70 % of this complaint type compared to all family of delay complaint types
- 71 % of this complaint type compared to all other complaint types

- 72 # delay (with a death) construction related issue
- 73 % of this complaint type compared to all family of delay complaint types
- 74 % of this complaint type compared to all other complaint types

- 75 # delay (non-death) hospital diversion issue
- 76 % of this complaint type compared to all family of delay complaint types
- 77 % of this complaint type compared to all other complaint types

- 78 # delay (with a death) no identifiable issue
- 79 % of this complaint type compared to all family of delay complaint types
- 80 % of this complaint type compared to all other complaint types

- 81 # delay (non-death) no identifiable issue
- 82 % of this complaint type compared to all family of delay complaint types
- 83 % of this complaint type compared to all other complaint types

3. "FAMILY OF *ABUSE*" COMPLAINT TYPE DATABASE REPORTS

- 1 # breakdown of all <u>abuse</u> sub-complaint types
- 2 Percentage of all abuse sub-complaint types

- 3 # of discourtesy abuse complaints
- 4 % of this complaint type compared to all family of abuse complaint types
- 5 % of this complaint type compared to all complaint types

- 6 # of discourtesy abuse complaints
- 7 % of this complaint type compared to all family of abuse complaint types
- 8 % of this complaint type compared to all complaint types

- 9 # of physical abuse complaints
- 10 % of this complaint type compared to all family of a use complaint types
- 11 % if this complaint type compared to all other complaint types

- 12 # of physical abuse complaints
- 13 % of this complaint type compared to all family of a use complaint types
- 14 % if this complaint type compared to all other complaint types

- 15 # of all sexual abuse complaints
- 16 % of this complaint type compared to all family of abuse complaint types
- 17 % of this complaint type compared to all complaint types

- 18 # of all sexual abuse complaints
- 19 % of this complaint type compared to all family of abuse complaint types
- 20 % of this complaint type compared to all complaint types

- 21 # of language abuse complaints
- 22 % of this complaint type compared to all family of abuse complaint types
- 23 % of this complaint type compared to all other complaint types

- 24 # of language abuse complaints
- 25 % of this complaint type compared to all family of abuse complaint types
- 26 % of this complaint type compared to all other complaint types

- 27 # of name refusal complaints
- 28 % of this complaint type compared to all family of abuse complaint types
- 29 % of this complaint type compared to all other complaint types

- 30 # of name refusal complaints
- 31 % of this complaint type compared to all family of abuse complaint types
- 32 % of this complaint type compared to all other complaint types

- 33 # of shield number refusal complaints
- 34 % of this complaint type compared to all family of abuse complaint types
- 35 % of this complaint type compared to all other complaint types

- 36 # of shield number refusal complaints
- 37 % of this complaint type compared to all family of abuse complaint types
- 38 % of this complaint type compared to all other complaint types

4. "FAMILY OF *MISSING PROPERTY*" COMPLAINT TYPE DATABASE REPORTS

- 1 # breakdown of all <u>missing property</u> (patient and non-patient) sub-complaint type
- 2 Percentage of all missing property sub-complaint types

- 3 # of all missing patient property money complaints
- 4 % of this complaint type compared to all family of missing property complaints
- 5 % of this complaint type compared to all other complaint types

- 6 # of missing money (non-patient) complaints
- 7% of this complaint type compared to all family of missing property complaint types
- 8 % of this complaint type compared to all other complaint types

- 9 # of missing patient jewelry complaints
- 10 % of this complaint type compared to all family of missing property complaints
- 11 % of this complaint type compared to all other complaint types

- 12 # of missing jewelry (non-patient) complaints
- 13 % of this complaint type compared to all family of missing property complaint types
- 14 % of this complaint type compared to all other complaint types

- 15 # of missing patient prescription drugs complaints (including controlled substances)
- 16 % of this complaint type compared to family of missing property complaint types
- 17 % of this complaint type compared to all other complaint types

- 18 # of missing (non-patient) prescription drugs (including controlled substances)
- 19 % of this complaint type compared to family of missing property complaint types
- 20 % of this complaint type compared to all other complaint types

- 21 # of missing patient ID cards
- 22 % of this complaint type compared to family of missing property complaint types
- 23 % of this complaint type compared to all other complaint types

- 24 # of missing (non-patient) ID cards
- 25 % of this complaint type compared to family of missing property complaint types
- 26 % of this complaint type compared to all other complaint types

- 27 # of missing patient wallet and its contents (non-money) complaints
- 28 % of this complaint type compared to family of missing property complaint types
- 29 % of this complaint type compared to all other complaint types

- 30 # of missing (non-patient) wallet and its contents (non-money) complaints
- 31 % of this complaint type compared to family of missing property complaint types
- 32 % of this complaint type compared to all other complaint types

- 33 # of missing patient wallet and its contents including money
- 34 % of this complaint type compared to family of missing property complaint types
- 35 % of this complaint type compared to all other complaint types

- 36 # of non-patient missing wallet and its contents including money complaints
- 37 % of this complaint type compared to family of missing property complaint types
- 38 % of this complaint type compared to all other complaint types

- 39 # of missing patient family heirloom complaints
- 40 % of this complaint type compared to family of missing property complaint types
- 41 % of this complaint type compared to all other complaint types

- 42 # of missing (non-patient) family heirloom complaints
- 43 % of this complaint type compared to family of missing property complaint types
- 44 % of this complaint type compared to all other complaint types

- 45 # of missing patient medical devise
- 46 % of this complaint type compared to family of missing property complaint types
- 47 % of this complaint type compared to all other complaint types

- 48 # of missing (non-patient) medical devise
- 49 % of this complaint type compared to family of missing property complaint types
- 50 % of this complaint type compared to all other complaint types

- 51 # of missing patient dentures
- 52 % of this complaint type compared to family of missing property complaint types
- 53 % of this complaint type compared to all other complaint types

- 54 # of missing (non-patient) dentures
- 55% of this complaint type compared to family of missing property complaint types
- 56 % of this complaint type compared to all other complaint types

- 57 # of other missing patient property
- 58 % of this complaint type compared to family of missing property complaint types
- 59 % of this complaint type compared to all other complaint types

- 60 # of other missing (non-patient) property
- 61 % of this complaint type compared to other family of missing property complaint types
- 62 % of this complaint type compared to all other complaint types

- 63 # of missing patient property issues determined to have been perpetrated prior to the ambulance's arrival

- 64 % of this complaint type compared to other family of missing property complaint types
- 65 % of this complaint type compared to all other complaint types

- 66 # of missing property issues (non-patient) perpetrated prior to the ambulance's arrival
- 67 % of this complaint type compared to other family of missing property complaint types
- 68 % of this complaint type compared to all other complaint types

5. "FAMILY OF *DRIVING*" COMPLAINT TYPE DATABASE REPORTS

- 1 # breakdown of all <u>driving</u> sub-complaint types
- 2 Percentage of all driving sub-complaint types

- 3 # of moving vehicle while not on assignment complaints
- 4 % of this complaint type compared to family of driving complaint types
- 5 % of this complaint type compared to all other complaint types

- 6 # of moving vehicle while on assignment complaints
- 7 % of this complaint type compared to family of driving complaint types
- 8 % of this complaint type compared to all other complaint types

- 9 # of parked vehicle location complaints while not on assignment
- 10 % of this complaint type compared to family of driving complaint types
- 11 % of this complaint type compared to all other complaint types

- 12 # of parked vehicle location complaints while on assignment
- 13 % of this complaint type compared to family of driving complaint types
- 14 % of this complaint type compared to all other complaint types

- 15 # of parked vehicle idling/pollution complaints while not on assignment
- 16 % of this complaint type compared to family of driving complaint types
- 17 % of this complaint type compared to all other complaint types

- 18 # of parked vehicle idling/pollution complaints while on assignment
- 19 % of this complaint type compared to family of driving complaint types
- 20 % of this complaint type compared to all other complaint types

- 21 # of parked vehicle idling/noise complaints while not on assignment
- 22 % of this complaint type compared to family of driving complaint types
- 23 % of this complaints type compared to all other complaint types

- 24 # of parked vehicle idling/noise complaints while on assignment
- 25 % of this complaint type compared to family of driving complaint types
- 26 % of this complaint type compared to all other complaint types

- 27 # of reported accidents while not on assignment
- 28 % of this complaint type compared to family of driving complaint types
- 29 % of this complaint type compared to all other complaint types

- 30 # of reported accidents while on assignment
- 31 % of this complaint type as compared to family of driving complaint types
- 32 % of this complaint type as compared to all other complaint types

- 33 # of unreported accident while not on assignment
- 34 % of this complaint type as compared to family of driving complaint types

- 35 % of this complaint type as compared to all other complaint types

- 36 # of unreported accidents while on assignment
- 37 % of this complaint type as compared to family of driving complaint types
- 38 % of this complaint type as compared to all other complaint types

- 39 # of siren usage complaints while not on assignment
- 40 % of this complaint type as compared to family of driving complaint types
- 41 % of this complaint type as compared to all other complaint types

- 42 # of siren usage complaints while on assignment
- 43 % of this complaint type as compared to family of driving complaint types
- 44 % of this complaint type as compared to all other complaint types

- 45 # of PA usage complaints while not on assignment
- 46 % of this complaint type as compared to family of driving complaint types
- 47 % of this complaint type compared to all other complaint types

- 48 # of PA usage complaints while on assignment
- 49 % of this complaint type as compared to family of driving complaint types
- 50 % of this complaint type as compared to all other complaint types

- 51 # of unauthorized passenger in ambulance complaints while not on assignment
- 52 % of this complaint type as compared to family of driving complaint types
- 53 % of this complaint type as compared to all other complaint types

- 54 # of unauthorized passenger in ambulance complaints while on assignment
- 55 % of this complaint type as compared to family of driving complaint types
- 56 % of this complaint type as compared to all other complaint types

- 57 # of falsification of who the organizational vehicle driver was
- 58 % of this complaint type compared to family of driving complaints
- 59 % of this complaint type compared to other complaint types

- 60 # of allegations that an organization vehicle caused but was not involved an accident
- 61 % of this complaint type compared to family of driving complaints
- 62 % of this complaint type compared to all other complaint types

- 63 # of allegations reckless or dangerous driving
- 64 % of this complaint type compared to family of driving complaints
- 65 % of this complaint type compared to all other complaint types

- 66 # of allegations excessive speed
- 67 % of this complaint type compared to family of driving complaints
- 68 % of this complaint type compared to all other complaint types

- 69 # of allegations of wrong way driving
- 70 % of this complaint type compared to family of driving complaints
- 71 % of this complaint type compared to all other complaint types

- 72 # driving policy violations
- 73 % of this complaint type compared to family of driving complaints
- 74 % of this complaint type compared to all other complaint types

- 75 # of allegations of using cell phone while driving
- 76 % of this complaint type compared to family of driving complaints
- 77 % of this complaint type compared to all other complaint types

- 78 # of allegations of smoking, drinking alcohol, drug use while driving
- 79 % of this complaint type compared to family of driving complaints
- 80 % of this complaint type compared to all other complaint types

- 81 # of allegations of driving on a boardwalk, through a park or other restricted areas
- 82 % of this complaint type compared to family of driving complaints
- 83 % of this complaint type compared to all other complaint types

- 84 # of allegations of traffic signals, road sign violations
- 85 % of this complaint type compared to family of driving complaints
- 86 % of this complaint type compared to all other complaint types

- 87 # of allegations of availability signal violations
- 88 % of this complaint type compared to family of driving complaints
- 89 % of this complaint type compared to all other complaint types

- 90 # of allegations of parking/standing in front of liquor stores or known drug or prostitution locations
- 91 % of this complaint type compared to family of driving complaints
- 92 % of this complaint type compared to all other complaint types

6. "FAMILY OF *HOSPITAL SELECTION*" COMPLAINT TYPE DATABASE REPORTS

- 1 # breakdown of all <u>hospital selection</u> sub-complaint types

- 2 Percentage of all hospital selection sub-complaint types

- 3 # request hospital "A" patient transported to hospital "B" complaints
- 4 % of this complaint type as compared to family of hospital selection complaint types
- 5 % of this complaint type as compared to all complaint types

- 6 # request hospital "A" patient transported to hospital "C" complaints
- 7 % of this complaint type as compared to family of hospital selection complaint types
- 8 % of this complaint type as compared to all complaint types

- 9 # request hospital "B" patient transported to hospital "A" complaints
- 10 % of this complaint type as compared to family of hospital selection complaint types
- 11 % of this complaint type as compared to all other complaint types

- 12 # request hospital "B" patient transported to hospital "C" complaints
- 13 % of this complaint type as compared to family of hospital selection complaint types
- 14 % of this complaint type as compare to all other complaint types

- 15 # request hospital "C" patient transported to hospital "A" complaints
- 16 % of this complaint type as compared to family of hospital selection complaint types
- 17 % of this complaint type as compared to all other complaint types

- 18 # request hospital "C" patient transported to hospital "B" complaints
- 19 % of this complaint type as compared to family of hospital selection complaint types

- 20 % of this complaint type as compared to all other complaint types

- 21 # requested not to be transported to hospital "A", but was transported there anyway
- 22% of this complaint type as compare to family of hospital selection complaint types
- 23 % of this complaint type as compared to all other complaint types

- 24 # requested not to be transported to hospital "B" but was transported there anyway
- 25 % of this complaint type as compared to family of hospital selection complaint types
- 26 % of this complaint type as compared to all other complaint types

- 27 # requested not to be transported to hospital "C" but was transported there anyway
- 28 % of this complaint type as compared to family of hospital selection complaint types
- 29 % of this complaint type as compared to all other complaint types

Note: All hospitals that your organization transports patients to must be listed in this section. I only listed three hospitals (A, B, C).

7. "FAMILY OF *DRUG*" COMPLAINT TYPE DATABASE REPORTS

- 1 # breakdown of all <u>drug</u> related sub-complaint types
- 2 Percentage of all drug sub-complaint types

- 3 # of employee drug use
- 4 % of this complaint type as compared to family of drugs complaint types

- 5 % of this complaint type as compared to all other complaint types

- 6 # of employee drug tampering (ambulance, ambulance station, organization drug storage area)
- 7 % of this complaint type as compared to family of drug complaint types
- 8 % of this complaint type as compared to all other complaint types

- 9 # of drug breakage
- 10 % of this complaint type as compared to family of drug complaint types
- 11 % of this complaint type as compared to all other complaint types

- 12 # of drug related documentation
- 13 % of this complaint type as compared to family of drugs complaint types
- 14 % of this complaint type as compared to all other complaint types

- 15 # of drug usage cases
- 16 % of this complaint type as compared to family of drugs complaint types
- 17 % of this complaint type as compared to all other complaint types

8. "FAMILY OF *MISCONDUCT*" COMPLAINT TYPE DATABASE REPORTS

- 1 # breakdown of all misconduct complaint types
- 2 Percentage of all misconduct sub-complaint types

- 3 # of personal cell phone usage on duty
- 4 % of this complaint type as compared to family of misconduct complaint types

- 5 % of this complaint type as compared to all other complaint types

- 6 # use of a personal cell phone in lieu of officially issued communications equipment
- 7 % of this complaint type as compared to family of misconduct complaint types
- 8 % of this complaint type as compared to all other complaint types

- 9 # use of cell phone camera/camera/video on duty without authorization – including selfies with patients
- 10 % of this complaint type as compared to family of misconduct complaint types
- 11 % of this complaint type as compared to all other complaint types

- 12 # inappropriate social media usage
- 13 % of this complaint type as compared to family of misconduct complaint types
- 14 % of this complaint type as compared to all other complaint types

- 15 # Contacting a previous patient utilizing information officially obtained during a previous response to a 9-1-1 call
- 16 % of this complaint type as compared to family of misconduct complaint types
- 17 % of this complaint type as compared to all other complaint types

- 18 # inappropriate use of officially issued tablet/computer
- 19 % of this complaint type as compared to family of misconduct complaint types
- 20 % of this complaint type as compared to all other complaint types

- 21 # vandalism by employee of organizational issued equipment
- 22 % of this complaint type as compared to family of misconduct complaint types
- 23 % of this complaint type as compared to all other complaint types

- 24 # cheating on organizational related tests
- 25 % of this complaint type as compared to family of misconduct complaint types
- 26 % of this complaint type as compared to all other complaint types

- 27 # shopping while on duty
- 28 % of this complaint type as compared to family of misconduct complaint types
- 29 % of this complaint type as compared to all other complaint types

- 30 # visiting while on duty
- 31 % of this complaint type as compared to family of misconduct complaint types
- 32 % of this complaint type as compared to all other complaint types

- 33 # of gambling while on duty
- 34 % of this complaint type as compared to misconduct complaint types
- 35 % of this complaint type as compared to all other complaint types

- 36 # unauthorized meal while on duty
- 37 % of this complaint type as compared to family of misconduct complaint types
- 38 % of this complaint type as compared to all other complaint types

- 39 # cooping in vehicle

- 40 % of this complaint type compared to family of misconduct complaint types
- 41 % of this complaint type compared to all other complaint types

- 42 # cooping other than vehicle
- 43 % of this complaint type compared to family of misconduct complaint types
- 44 % of this complaint type compared to all other complaint types

- 45 # arrested while on duty
- 46 % of this complaint type compared to family of misconduct complaint types
- 47 % of this complaint type compared to all other complaint types

- 48 # arrested off duty
- 49 % of this complaint type compared to family of misconduct complaint types
- 50 % of this complaint type compared to all other complaint types

- 51 # transporting a patient to a particular hospital for a quid pro quo
- 52 % of this complaint type compared to family of misconduct complaint types
- 53 % of this complaint type compared to all other complaint types

- 54 # time-sheet fraud
- 55 % of this complaint type compared to family of misconduct complaint types
- 56 % of this complaint type compared to all other complaint types

- 57 # being at a location which is prohibited by the organization
- 58 % of this complaint type compared to family of misconduct complaint types
- 59 % of this complaint type compared to all other complaint types

- 60 # subordinate threatening a supervisor
- 61 % of this complaint type compared to family of misconduct complaint types

- 62 % of this complaint type compared to all other complaint types

- 63 # falsification of "flag-down" assignment
- 64 % of this complaint type compared to family of misconduct complaint types
- 65 % of this complaint type compared to all other complaint types

- 66 # ambulance chasing issues
- 67 % of this complaint type compared to family of misconduct complaint types
- 68 % of this complaint type compared to all other complaint types

- 69 # information reported to a supervisor who took no action
- 70 % of this complaint type compared to family of misconduct complaint types
- 71 % of this complaint type compared to all other complaint types

- 72 # theft of patient personal information
- 73 % of this complaint type compared to family of misconduct complaint types
- 74 % of this complaint type compared to all other complaint types

- 75 # loss of, or damage to archived records
- 76 % of this complaint type compared to family of misconduct complaint types
- 77 % of this complaint type compared to all other complaint types

- 78 # crew dispute (on duty)
- 79 % of this complaint type compared to family of misconduct complaint types
- 80 % of this complaint type compared to all other complaint types

- 81 # crew fight (on duty)
- 82 % of this complaint type compared to family of misconduct complaint types
- 83 % of this complaint type compared to all other complaint types

9. "FAMILY OF *BILLING*" COMPLAINT TYPE DATABASE REPORTS

- 1 # breakdown of all <u>billing</u> complaint types
- 2 Percentage of all billing sub-complaint types

- 3 # of all billing complaints charges are too high
- 4 % of this complaint type compared to family of billing complaint types
- 5 % of this complaint type compared to all other complaint types

- 6 # of billing complaints associated with another (non-billing) complaint
- 7 % of this complaint type compared to family of billing complaint types
- 8 % of this complaint type compared to all other complaint types

- 9 # of billing, no oxygen but oxygen was billed for
- 10 % of this complaint type compared to family of billing complaint types
- 11 % of this complaint type compared to all other complaint types

- 12 # billing complaints associated with identity theft
- 13 % of this complaint type compared to family of billing complaint types
- 14 % of this complaint type compared to all other complaint types

- 15 # of billing complaints received after an invoice for service was sent
- 16 % of this complaint type compared to family of billing complaint types
- 17 % of this complaint type compared to all other complaint types

- 18 # of billing complaints received within two weeks of service
- 19 % of this complaint type compared to family of billing complaint types
- 20 % of this complaint type compared to all other complaint types

- 21 # of billing complaints-other
- 22 % of this complaint type compared to family of billing complaint types
- 23 % of this complaint type compared to all other complaint types

10. "FAMILY OF *LEAVE*" COMPLAINT TYPE DATABASE REPORTS

- 1 # breakdown of all <u>leave</u> complaint types
- 2 Percentage of all leave sub-complaint types

- 3 # of sick leave abuse
- 4 % of this complaint type compared to leave abuse complaint types
- 5 % of this complaint type compared to all other complaint types

- 6 # of sick leave document falsification
- 7 % of this complaint type compared to leave abuse complaint types
- 8 % of this complaint type compared to all other complaint types

- 9 # of compensation leave abuse
- 10 % of this complaint type compared to leave abuse complaint types
- 11 % of this complaint type compared to all other complaint types

- 12 # of compensation documentation falsification
- 13 % of this complaint type compared to leave abuse complaint types
- 14 % of this complaint type compared to all other complaint types

- 15 # falsification of time records
- 16 % of this complaint type compared to leave abuse complaint types
- 17 % of this complaint type compared to all other complaint types

Reports for all of the complaint types that you follow, not just the samples that are listed above can be set up this way.

SECTION 4

INVESTIGATIVE REPORTS

The following is a listing of 543 investigative reports which I developed over time. Why did I come up with so many reports? My experience taught me that in the world of EMS investigations, many unusual questions will be asked, or unusual situations arise where such information is required. Such questions or issues may only come up once, or the issue may be repetitive. Either way the Investigative Unit (IU) needs to be prepared. Remember, the more years of information that is entered into the IU database will result in more informative reports and statistics.

Each of the following reports will fall within one or more of the following 46 categories:

- age
- ambulance chasing
- ambulance stations
- audits
- call types
- calls of shift
- calls of tour
- cases
- certifications
- complainants
- complaints
- complaint sources
- complaint types
- database reports

- dates
- employee history
- employee interviews
- employee rank
- employees with multiple complaints
- false ambulance call report
- final dispositions
- geographic areas
- guideline changes
- hoax 9-1-1 calls
- investigations
- investigative activities
- investigative classifications
- investigative management
- investigative reports
- investigators
- notifications
- observers
- on-assignment versus non-assignment complaints and investigations
- past responses to a particular location
- patient death related complaints and investigations
- patient injuries related complaints and investigations
- patients
- preventive maintenance records
- radio repair records
- regular time versus overtime complaints and investigations
- referrals
- sensitive locations
- surveillances (covert and overt)
- time
- traffic sheet related reports
- witnesses

The subject key word or words in the title of each of the individual reports have been *italicized* to indicate what category or categories they belong to.

In addition, there are up to four managerial uses that each report falls under. I have made a notation under each report what its usage is for.

Managerial Usage	Code
Investigators	1
Director of Investigations-Routine	2
Director of Investigations-Special Circumstances	3
Director of Investigations-Investigative Management	4

1   TOTAL *COMPLAINTS*

This is a basic but important report as "complaints" are what any EMS Investigative Unit is all about. It is a building block for many other reports. This report only includes complaints.
Code 2, 4

2   TOTAL *SELF-GENERATED INVESTIGATIONS*

Self-generated "investigations" are also important. They document that your Investigative Unit is proactive, and doesn't always wait for a complaint to be received if an incident or situation is brought to the unit's attention without an actual complaint being received. This is also a basic building block report. This report only includes self-generated investigations.
Code 2, 4

3   TOTAL *CASES*

This building block report combines the totals from the first two reports listed above and it forms the basis for many other reports. This report includes both complaints and self-generated investigations.
Code 2, 4

4   TOTAL *SELF-GENERATED*-MEDIA (TELEVISION) *INVESTIGATIONS*

The number of self-generated "investigations" which are initially based upon a media television report. This report only includes self-generated investigations.
Code 2, 4

5   **TOTAL *SELF-GENERATED*-MEDIA (RADIO) *INVESTIGATIONS***

The total number of self-generated "investigations" which are initially based upon a media radio report. This report only includes self-generated investigations.
Code 2, 4

6   **TOTAL *SELF-GENERATED*-MEDIA (NEWSPAPER) *INVESTIGATIONS***

The total number of self-generated "investigations" which are initially based upon a media newspaper report. This report only includes self-generated investigations.
Code 2, 4

7   **TOTAL *SELF-GENERATED*-MEDIA (INTERNET) *INVESTIGATIONS***

The total number of self-generated "investigations" which are initially based upon a media related internet report. This report only includes self-generated investigations.
Code 2, 4

8   **TOTAL *SELF-GENERATED INVESTIGATIONS* WHERE A SUBSEQUENT *COMPLAINT* IS RECEIVED**

This is a housekeeping type of report where the information generated is interesting from an investigational/managerial point of view. This can show how proactive the Investigative Unit is. This report only includes self-generated investigations.
Code 4

9   **TOTAL *SOCIAL MEDIA COMPLAINTS***

This report is the hot report of the past few years. It involves social media "complaints", both on-duty and off-duty postings, and will usually, but not always, be work related. This report only includes complaints.
Code 2, 3, 4

10 **TOTAL *SOCIAL MEDIA INVESTIGATIONS***
This report involves social media related self-generated investigations, both on-duty and off-duty postings, and will usually, but not always, be work related. This report only includes self-generated investigations.
Code 2, 3, 4

11 **TOTAL *SOCIAL MEDIA CASES***
This involves both social media complaints and investigations. This report includes both complaints and self-generated investigations.
Code 2, 3, 4

12 **TOTAL *ANONYMOUS SOURCE COMPLAINTS***
This is a "complaint" that is initially based upon an "anonymous source". This can include a caller who is reluctant to supply their name, or a photo or video which is received without any of the sender's information. Even though you don't technically have an actual complainant, (someone that you can interview, someone who can testify), an anonymous complaint should be thought of as a trackable source, therefore it should be included in the "sources" that you track. I have seen some investigative policies around the country that preclude initiating an investigation based upon an anonymous source. I strongly disagree with that line of thinking. I addressed this topic in my original book. This report includes only complaints.
Code 2, 3, 4

13 **TOTAL *CASES* CLOSED AS *DUPLICATES***
This is a housekeeping report. Total number of all "cases" (both complaints and self-generated investigations) closed as being a "duplicate" of another case which was previously received by the Investigative Unit. It is very important to document all the information from the newest complaint that is being closed out and merged into the open case. This report includes both complaints and self-generated investigations.
Code 4

14 **TOTAL NUMBER OF *COMPLAINTS* BY *INVESTIGATIVE CLASSIFICATIONS***
This is a managerial type of report. It will list "complaints" by their investigative classification. This report only includes complaints.
Code 2, 4

15 **TOTAL NUMBER OF *INVESTIGATIONS* BROKEN DOWN BY *INVESTIGATIVE CLASSIFICATIONS***
This is a managerial type of report. It will list investigations by their investigative classification. This report only includes self-generated investigations.
Code 2, 4

16 **TOTAL NUMBER OF ALL CASES BY *INVESTIGATIVE CLASSIFICATION***
This is a managerial type of report. This report tally's the total number of the following "Investigative case classifications":
• Internal Investigations
• Preliminary Investigations (will ultimately be upgraded or downgraded)
• Referrals
• Information & Intelligence
This report includes both complaints and self-generated investigations.
Code 2, 3, 4

17 **PERCENTAGE OF *COMPLAINTS* BY *INVESTIGATIVE CLASSIFICATION***
The percentage of complaints broken down by investigative classification. This report only includes complaints.
Code 2, 3, 4

18 **PERCENTAGE OF *SELF-GENERATED INVESTIGATIONS* BY *INVESTIGATIVE CLASSIFICATION***
The percentage of all investigative case classifications compared to each other. This answers the question; what percent of the investigative workload involve the most serious cases versus the less serious cases. This report includes only self-generated investigations.
Code 2, 3, 4

19 **PERCENTAGE OF ALL *CASES* BY *INVESTIGATIVE CLASSIFICATION***

The percentage of all cases by investigative classification compared to each other. This report includes both complaints and self-generated investigations.

Code 2, 3, 4

20 **TOTAL NUMBER OF *COMPLAINTS* BROKEN DOWN BY *COMPLAINT TYPE***

This is another managerial report. It displays how many complaints or each complaint type that you track, were received during a particular time frame. This report only includes complaints.

Code 2, 3, 4

21 **TOTAL NUMBER OF *SELF-GENERATED INVESTIGATIONS* BROKEN DOWN BY *COMPLAINT TYPE***

Total number of "self-generated investigations" broken down by "complaint type". This report displays the number of investigations that pertain to high priority assignments versus lower priority assignments. This report only includes self-generated investigations.

Code 2, 3, 4

22 **TOTAL NUMBER OF *CASES* BROKEN DOWN BY *COMPLAINT TYPE***

This report lists case types for all cases. It includes both complaints and self-generated investigations.

Code 2, 3, 4

23 **PERCENTAGE OF *COMPLAINTS* BY *COMPLAINT TYPE***

This is a managerial report listing all of the complaints that were received and how they broke down into individual complaint types. This report only includes complaints.

Code 2, 3, 4

24 PERCENTAGE OF *INVESTIGATIONS* BY *COMPLAINT TYPE*

This is a managerial report noting all of the investigations broken down by complaint type. This report only includes self-generated investigations.

Code 2, 3, 4

25 PERCENTAGE OF *CASES* BY *COMPLAINT TYPE*

This managerial report notes all cases broken down by complaint type. This report includes both complaints and self-generated investigations.

Code 2, 3, 4

26 *CHIEF'S* REPORT – IN (NUMBER)

The total number of items that were "referred" to the Investigative Unit by the top-ranking Chief of your Organization. (If you don't have a top Chief, then change the report name to Executive Manager incoming top report). This report includes only complaints.

Code 2, 4

27 *CHIEF'S* REPORT – OUT (NUMBER)

The total number of items "referred" by your Investigative Unit to the top-ranking Chief of your Organization. (If you don't have a top chief, then change the title of this report to Executive Manager outgoing report). This report includes both complaints and self-generated investigations.

Code 2, 4

28 *CHRONO* REPORT

This housekeeping report is a chronological listing of case numbers which were entered; or were supposed to be entered into the investigative unit's database between any two dates. The sole purpose of this report is for "check and balance" purposes, specifically to make sure that all the assigned cases within the referenced time-period were actually entered into the database. By reviewing this report, you can determine which cases numbers weren't entered into the database, simply by looking for missing case numbers. This report should contain both complaints and self-generated investigations.

Code 2

29 **TOTAL *CASES* WHERE *COMPLAINT TYPES* ARE COMPARED TO THE AVERAGE *AGE* OF *SUBJECT EMPLOYEES***

This is an important reference report when you are examining complaint trends. For each "complaint type" that you track, this report will display what the average age of the associated subject employees are. One of the many things that this may show you is that the organization may have to put more age-specific educational emphasis into their training programs. It can also provide information for specific complaint types, what age employees might be more likely to be involved. A bar graph and line chart would work well for this report. This report should include complaints and self-generated investigations.
Code 3, 4

30 **TOTAL *COMPLAINTS* COMPARED TO TOTAL *SYSTEM RESPONSES***

Total number of "complaints" received compared to the total number of system ambulance responses for the same time-period. If the number of complaints is high, this report will make them appear smaller. This is a legitimate comparison because it is a logical assumption that the more calls an organization does, the more complaints it will receive. Some of the information for this report is obtained from your CAD (computer aided dispatch) System. There may be areas that an EMS organization may have to address internally to stop or steady the rise in complaints. This report only includes complaints.
Code 3, 4

31 **TOTAL *INVESTIGATIONS* COMPARED TO TOTAL *SYSTEM RESPONSES***

Total number of investigations received compared to the total number of system ambulance responses for the same time-period. This report only includes self-generated investigations.
Code 3, 4

32 **TOTAL *CASES* COMPARED TO TOTAL *SYSTEM RESPONSES***

Total number of "cases" as compared to the total number of system ambulance responses for the same time-period. If the number of complaints is high, this report will make them appear smaller. This is a legitimate comparison because it is a logical assumption that the more calls an organization does, the more complaints it will receive. Some of the information for this report is obtained from your CAD (computer aided dispatch) System. There may be areas that an EMS organization may have to address internally to stop or steady the rise in complaints. This report includes complaints and self-generated investigations.

Code 3, 4

33 TOTAL *COMPLAINTS* COMPARED TO *SYSTEM RESPONSES*, FOR ONE SPECIFIC *GEOGRAPHIC AREA*

This complaint related report allows a specific geographical segment of the organizational response area to be examined. This report only includes complaints.

Code 3, 4

34 TOTAL *SELF-GENERATED INVESTIGATIONS* COMPARED TO *SYSTEM RESPONSES* FOR ONE SPECIFIC *GEOGRAPHIC AREA*

This self-generated related report allows a specific geographical segment of the organizational response area to be examined. This report only includes self-generated investigations.

Code 3, 4

35 TOTAL *CASES* INVOLVING *SYSTEM RESPONSES* FOR ONE *GEOGRAPHIC AREA*

This case related report allows a specific geographical segment of the organizational response area to be examined. This report includes both complaints and self-generated investigations.

Code 3, 4

36 AVERAGE NUMBER OF *COMPLAINTS* COMPARED TO THE AVERAGE *SYSTEM RESPONSE TIME*

This can be an important report, that probably won't be used often. It is one of the reports that should be created just in case it is ever required. This report only includes complaints.

Code 3, 4

37 AVERAGE NUMBER OF *COMPLAINTS* RECEIVED

This report will provide you with the average number of "complaints" that were received for a given time-period. This is an important report and can be used to calculate any time periods that you want. This report should only include complaints.
Code 2, 3, 4

38 AVERAGE NUMBER OF *SELF-GENERATED INVESTIGATIONS* INITIATED

This report documents the average number of self-generated investigations for a particular time period. This report should only include self-generated investigations.
Code 2, 3, 4

39 AVERAGE NUMBER OF *CASES* RECEIVED

This report documents the average number of cases received for a designated time period. This report includes both complaints and self-generated investigations.
Code 2, 3, 4

40 *COMPLAINTS* INITIALLY RECEIVED BY YOUR EMS ORGANIZATION

The number of complaints that were originally received by your organization, not by the investigative unit. It used for complaint management purposes only. If the Investigative Unit is routinely not open 24-hours a day, a fool-proof procedure must be in place that deals with complaints received during non-business hours. Usually these complaints will be received via telephone. However, this procedure is set-up, it should become a trackable complaint source. This report only includes complaints.
Code 4

41 TIME IT TOOK *COMPLAINTS* THAT WERE ORIGINALLY RECEIVED BY THE EMS ORGANIZATION TO REACH THE INVESTIGATIVE UNIT

This report is related to the previous report. It documents the time that it took for "complaints" that were initially received within the organization but outside of the investigative unit to actually reach the investigative unit. you must determine whether to use calendar days or business days to calculate the information. If the complaint is "routine" it should never take more than three days (weekend plus a one-day holiday) to reach the IU. In the previous report, I mentioned that a procedure needs to be in place for this topic. The off-duty complaint receipt procedure must include an immediate IU on-call notification if the complaint is a serious one requiring some sort of immediate IU attention. This report only includes complaints. Code 4

42 **TOTAL BREAKDOWN OF ALL *COMPLAINTS* BY THEIR *FINAL DISPOSITION***

How all complaints stack up based upon their respective final dispositions. (Substantiated-A, Substantiated-B, Partially Substantiated-A, Partially Substantiated-B, Unsubstantiated, Unfounded or Duplicate Case). This report should include only complaints. Code 3, 4

43 **TOTAL BREAKDOWN OF *SELF-GENERATED* *INVESTIGATIONS* BY *FINAL DISPOSITION***

How all self-generated investigations compare to each other up based upon their respective final dispositions. (Substantiated-A, Substantiated-B, Partially Substantiated-A, Partially Substantiated-B, Unsubstantiated, Unfounded or Duplicate Case). This report should include only self-generated investigations. Code 3, 4

44 **TOTAL BREAKDOWN OF *CASES* BY *FINAL DISPOSITION***

How all cases compare to each other up based upon their respective final dispositions. (Substantiated-A, Substantiated-B, Partially Substantiated-A, Partially Substantiated-B, Unsubstantiated, Unfounded or Duplicate Case). This report should include both complaints and self-generated investigations. Code 3, 4

45 **PERCENTAGE OF** *COMPLAINTS* **BY** *COMPLAINT TYPE* **AND BY** *FINAL DISPOSITION*
The percentage of each individual "complaints", complaint type, and related final dispositions. This report only includes complaints.
Code 3, 4

46 **PERCENTAGE OF** *SELF-GENERATED INVESTIGATIONS* **BY** *COMPLAINT TYPE* **AND BY** *FINAL DISPOSITION*
The percentage of each individual "self-generated investigation" by complaint type, and related final dispositions. This report only includes self-generated investigations.
Cade 3, 4

47 **PERCENTAGE OF** *CASES* **BY** *COMPLAINT TYPE* **AND** *FINAL DISPOSITIONS*
The percentage of each case's complaint type by final dispositions. This report includes both complaints and self-generated investigations.
Code 3, 4

48 **PERCENTAGE BREAKDOWN OF** *REFERRALS* **OUT (CASES) - BY** *FINAL DISPOSITION*
The percentage of "outgoing referrals" by their final disposition. This report should include both complaints and self-generated investigations.
Code 2, 3, 4

49 **TOTAL BREAKDOWN OF** *REFERRALS* **OUT (***CASES***) - BY** *COMPLAINT TYPE*
The number of "outgoing referrals" broken down by their respective complaint types. This report should include both complaints and self-generated investigations.
Code 2, 3, 4

50 **PERCENTAGE OF** *REFERRALS* **OUT (***CASES***) - BY** *COMPLAINT TYPE*

The percentage of "outgoing referrals", broken down by their respective complaint types. This report should include both complaints and self-generated investigations.

Code 2, 3, 4

51 **TOTAL NUMBER OF** *COMPLAINTS* **BROKEN DOWN BY** *GEOGRAPHIC AREA*

If your organization breaks down its total ambulance response area into geographic areas or zones, (e.g. north sector, east sector, south sector and west sector), it would be helpful to know which sectors yield the highest number of "complaints". If you don't have a geographic area breakdown, depending upon how large your response area is, you could use 5-digit zip codes to accomplish this. This report should include only complaints.

Code 2, 3, 4

52 **TOTAL** *SELF-GENERATED INVESTIGATIONS* **BY** *GEOGRAPHIC AREA*

If your organization breaks down their total ambulance response area into geographic zones, such as north sector, east sector, south sector and west sector, it would be helpful to know which sectors yield the highest number of "investigations". If you don't have a geographic area breakdown, you could use 5-digit zip codes to accomplish this. If one geographic zone generates a much higher number than the other sectors, you need to find out why This report should only include self-generated investigations.

Code 2, 3, 4

53 **TOTAL** *CASES* **BY** *GEOGRAPHIC AREA*

If your organization breaks down their total ambulance response area into geographic zones, such as north sector, east sector, south sector and west sector, it would be helpful to know which sectors yield the highest number of "cases". If one geographic zone generates a much higher number than the other sectors, you need to find out why This report should include both complaints and self-generated investigations.

Code 2, 3, 4

54 **PERCENTAGE OF** *COMPLAINTS* **BY** *GEOGRAPHIC AREA*

If your organization breaks down the total ambulance response area into geographic zones, such as north sector, east sector, south sector and west sector, it would be helpful to know which sectors yield the highest percentage of "complaints". This report should only include complaints.

Code 2, 3, 4

55 **PERCENTAGE OF** *SELF-GENERATED INVESTIGATIONS* **BY** *GEOGRAPHIC AREA*

If your organization breaks down the total ambulance response area into geographic zones, it would be helpful to know which sectors yield the highest percentage of "self-generated investigations". This report should only include self-generated investigations.

Code 2, 3, 4

56 **PERCENTAGE OF** *CASES* **BY** *GEOGRAPHIC AREA*

If your organization breaks down the total ambulance response area into geographic zones, it would be helpful to know which sectors yield the highest percentage of "cases". This report should include both complaints and self-generated investigations.

Code 2, 3, 4

57 *COMPLAINT TYPES* **BROKEN DOWN BY** *GEOGRAPHIC AREA (COMPLAINT* **RELATED)**

Total number of "complaint types" broken down by geographic area, complaint related. If one geographic zone generates a much higher number than the other sectors, you need to find out why This report should include only complaints.

Code 2, 3, 4

58 *COMPLAINT TYPES* **BROKEN DOWN BY** *GEOGRAPHIC AREA (SELF-GENERATED INVESTIGATIONS* **RELATED)**

Total number of "complaint types" broken down by geographic area, self-generated investigations related. If one geographic zone generates

a much higher number than the other sectors, you need to find out why This report should only include self-generated investigations.
Code 2, 3, 4

59 *COMPLAINT TYPES* BROKEN DOWN BY *GEOGRAPHIC AREA (CASES* RELATED)

Total number of "complaint types" broken down by geographic area, case related. If one geographic zone generates a much higher number than the other sectors, you need to find out why This report should include both complaints and self-generated investigations.
Code 2, 3, 4

60 *SELF-GENERATED INVESTIGATIONS - INVESTIGATIVE CLASSIFICATIONS* BROKEN DOWN BY *GEOGRAPHIC AREA*

This is another important geographic managerial area report. If one geographic zone generates a higher number of self-generated investigations than the other sectors, you need to find out why. This report compares the related investigative classifications. This report includes only self-generated investigations.
Code 2, 3, 4

61 TOTAL NUMBER OF *COMPLAINTS* BROKEN DOWN BY *SENSITIVE LOCATIONS*

Total number of "complaints" broken down by "sensitive location" (school, theatre, prisons, or construction sites, just to name four). You could break "specific location" down into hundred different ways, but to be most effective, it should only include your primary problem area or areas. (See sensitive locations later on in this book). This report should only include complaints.
Code 2, 3, 4

62 TOTAL NUMBER OF *INVESTIGATIONS* BROKEN DOWN BY *SENSITIVE LOCATIONS*

This is another important sensitive location report. This report should only include self-generated investigations.
Code 2,3 4

63 **TOTAL NUMBER OF *CASES* BROKEN DOWN BY *SENSITIVE LOCATIONS***

This is another important sensitive location report. This report should include both complaints and self-generated investigations.
Code 2,3 4

64 **TOTAL NUMBER OF *SENSITIVE LOCATION COMPLAINTS* BROKEN DOWN BY *GEOGRAPHIC AREA***

This is another important report where "sensitive location complaints" are broken down into your organization's "geographic area". This report should include only complaints.
Code 2, 3, 4

65 **TOTAL NUMBER OF *SENSITIVE LOCATION INVESTIGATIONS* BROKEN DOWN BY *GEOGRAPHIC AREA***

This is another important "sensitive location" report which are broken down by "geographic area". This report should include only self-generated investigations.
Code 2, 3, 4

66 **TOTAL NUMBER OF *SENSITIVE LOCATION CASES* BROKEN DOWN BY *GEOGRAPHIC AREA***

This is another important "sensitive location investigations" which are broken down by "geographic area". This report should include both complaints and self-generated investigations.
Code 2, 3, 4

67 **PERCENTAGE OF *SENSITIVE LOCATION COMPLAINTS* BROKEN DOWN BY *GEOGRAPHIC AREA***

An important "sensitive location" report. This report only includes complaints.
Code 2, 3, 4

68 PERCENTAGE OF *SENSITIVE LOCATION INVESTIGATIONS* BROKEN DOWN BY *GEOGRAPHIC AREA*

This is the percentage of "sensitive location investigations" which are broken down by "geographic areas". This report should include only self-generated investigations.

Code 2, 3, 4

69 PERCENTAGE OF *SENSITIVE LOCATION CASES* BROKEN DOWN BY *GEOGRAPHIC AREA*

Another important "sensitive location" report. It is broken down by geographic area. This report includes both complaints and self-generated investigations.

Code 2, 3, 4

70 TOTAL NUMBER OF *SENSITIVE LOCATION COMPLAINTS* BROKEN DOWN BY *CALL TYPE*

"Sensitive locations" are problematic because they can generate a high number of similar complaints. This report provides information regarding sensitive locations, if there is a particular call type being complained about more so than others, and if so, what geographic area is it occurring in. This report only includes complaints.

Code 2, 3, 4

71 TOTAL NUMBER OF *SENSITIVE LOCATION INVESTIGATIONS* BROKEN DOWN BY *CALL TYPE*

This is another important sensitive location report. This report includes only self-generated investigations.

Code 2, 3, 4

72 PERCENTAGE OF *SENSITIVE LOCATION COMPLAINTS* VERSUS OTHER *COMPLAINTS*

This is another important report in the sensitive location series of reports. It compares sensitive location complaints versus non sensitive location complaints. This report should include only complaints.

Code 2, 3, 4

73 **NUMBER OF** *NON-ASSIGNMENT* **VERSUS** *ON ASSIGNMENT COMPLAINTS*

Total number of complaints where the subject employees were on assignment versus on-duty but off assignment. This is a subject to keep an eye on, and depending upon the numbers, that may have to be taken up with your organization. This should only include complaints.

Code 4

74 **PERCENTAGE OF** *NON-ASSIGNMENT* **VERSUS** *ON ASSIGNMENT COMPLAINTS*

The percentage of complaints that involved a non-assignment situation versus on-duty and on-assignment situation. This is a subject to keep an eye on, and depending upon the numbers, that may have to be taken up with your organization. This report includes only complaints.

Code 4

75 **NUMBER OF** *NON-ASSIGNMENT* **VERSUS** *ON ASSIGNMENT INVESTIGATIONS*

Total number of "investigations" involving non-assignments versus investigations that involve actual assignments. This is a subject to keep an eye on, and depending upon the numbers, that may have to be taken up with your organization. This report should include only self-generated investigations.

Code 4

76 **PERCENTAGE OF** *NON-ASSIGNMENT* **VERSUS** *ON ASSIGNMENT INVESTIGATIONS*

What is the overall percentage of non-assignment versus on assignment cases? This is a subject to keep an eye on, and depending upon the numbers, that may have to be taken up with your organization. This report should include only self-generated investigations.

Code 4

77 **NUMBER OF *NON-ASSIGNMENT* VERSUS *ON ASSIGNMENT CASES***

This issue can become an issue at any time. This report includes both complaints and self-generated investigations.
Code 4

78 **PERCENTAGE OF *NON-ASSIGNMENT* VERSUS *ON ASSIGNMENT CASES***

This issue can also become an issue at any time. This report includes both complaints and self-generated investigations.
Code 4

79 ***COMPLAINANT-PATIENT-WITNESS* REPORT**

If you want to determine if a person has been involved in any previous complaint or investigation, as either a complainant, patient or witness, this is the report to use. This is an important background report. It should include both complaints and self-generated investigations.
Code 1, 2, 3, 4

80 ***COMPLAINANT-PATIENT-WITNESS* BY *COMPLAINT TYPE***

This may tell you if there is a particular complaint type that an individual (complainant, patient or witness) has been involved in. It is unusual for a person (civilian) to be involved in multiple cases unless they are a "frequent flyer". This report should include both complaints and self-generated investigations.
Code 2, 3, 4

81 ***COMPLAINANT-PATIENT-WITNESS* BY *INVESTIGATIVE CLASSIFICATION***

This report is an investigative-managerial tool. You search your records to determine if a particular name was ever a complainant, patient or witness in any case. This report should include both complaints and self-generated investigations.
Code 2, 3, 4

82 **NUMBER OF** *COMPLAINTS* **WHERE THE** *COMPLAINANT* **WAS THE** *PATIENT*

This number is likely to be a high number and is an important report to use. This report only includes complaints.

Code 4

83 **NUMBER OF** *CASES* **WHERE THE** *COMPLAINANT* **WAS THE** *PATIENT*

This can yield important information. This report only includes complaints.

Code 4

84 **NUMBER OF** *CASES* **WHERE THE** *COMPLAINANT* **WAS A** *FAMILY MEMBER*

This report can yield important information. This report only includes complaints.

Code 4

85 **NUMBER OF** *CASES* **WHERE THE** *COMPLAINANT* **WAS A** *FAMILY FRIEND*

This can yield important information. It includes only complaints.

Code 4

86 **NUMBER OF** *CASES* **WHERE** *OTHER* **WAS THE** *COMPLAINANT*

This can also yield important information. This report includes only complaints.

Code 4

87 **PERCENTAGE OF** *COMPLAINTS* **WHERE THE** *COMPLAINANT* **WAS THE** *PATIENT*

This should also be a high number. This is an interesting report. This report only includes complaints.

Code 4

88 **NUMBER OF *COMPLAINTS* WHERE THE *COMPLAINANT* WAS THE *PATIENT* BROKEN DOWN BY *COMPLAINT TYPE***

This can be an important report. This report only includes complaints.
Code 4

89 **NUMBER OF *COMPLAINTS* THAT INVOLVE POSSIBLE *AMBULANCE CHASING* (GENERAL)**

Obviously, for some, ambulance chasing is a lucrative endeavor, otherwise it wouldn't have been around for as long as it has been. It subject is probably a subject that is better handled by others outside of the investigative unit (IU). This report only includes complaints.
Code 3, 4

90 **NUMBER OF *INVESTIGATIONS* THAT INVOLVE POSSIBLE *AMBULANCE CHASING* (GENERAL)**

As noted, ambulance chasing is a lucrative endeavor, otherwise it wouldn't have been around for as long as it has been. It is probably a subject that is better handled by others rather than by investigative unit (IU). The IU may be requested to provide information on this topic from time-to-time to whomever handles this. This report includes only self-generated investigations.
Code 3, 4

91 **NUMBER OF *CASES* THAT INVOLVE POSSIBLE *AMBULANCE CHASING* (GENERAL)**

Ambulance chasing is probably a subject that is better handled by others rather than by investigative unit (IU). The IU may be requested to provide information on this topic from time-to-time to whomever handles this. This report includes both complaints and self-generated investigations.
Code 3, 4

92 **NUMBER OF *COMPLAINTS* THAT INVOLVE POSSIBLE *AMBULANCE CHASING* (INTERNAL)**

This report differs from the ones above in that it involves specific employees. Their involvement can be that they provide a lawyer's business card to a patient or a patient's family, or they provide patient

information either directly to a lawyer, or through a middleman, a more serious matter). This report only includes complaints.
Code 3, 4

93 NUMBR OF *INVESTIGATIONS* THAT INVOLVE POSSIBLE *AMBULANCE CHASING* (INTERNAL)

This report differs from the ones above in that it includes specific organizational employees. Their involvement may be that they provide a lawyer's business card to a patient or to a patient's family, or they provide patient information either to a lawyer, or to a middleman. This is the one topic where it is likely that there will be more investigations related cases rather than complaint related cases. This report includes only self-generated investigations.
Code 3, 4

94 PERCENTAGE OF *CASES* THAT INVOLVE POSSIBLE *AMBULANCE CHASING* (BOTH INTERNAL AND EXTERNAL) VERSUS THOSE THAT DO NOT

This is an important managerial report. This report includes both complaints and self-generated investigations.
Code 3, 4

95 INTERNAL *REFERRAL* REPORT

Total number of cases "referred" to internal commands within your organization. This report should include both complaints and self-generated investigations.
Code 2, 3, 4

96 EXTERNAL *REFERRAL* REPORT

Total number of cases "referred" to authorized outside agencies outside of your organization. This report should include both complaints and self-generated investigations.
Code 3, 4

97 *COMPLAINT* RELATED *REFERRALS* VERSUS TOTAL *COMPLAINTS*

Percentage of "complaints" which are referred to internal commands within your organization compared to the number of cases that were

not referred for the same time-period. This report should include only complaints.
Code 3, 4

98 *REFERRALS* VERSUS TOTAL *INVESTIGATIONS*
Percentage of investigations which are "referred" to internal commands within your organization compared to the number of "investigations which are received for the same time-period. This report should include only self-generated investigations.
Code 3, 4

99 *REFERRALS* VERSUS TOTAL *CASES*
This is an important tracking report. This report includes both complaints and self-generated investigations.
3, 4

100 **EXTERNAL** *NOTIFICATIONS* **REPORT**
Total number of "notifications" (not referrals) made to authorized outside agencies by the investigative unit. Generally, these notifications are linked to certain specific allegations. This report should include both complaints and self-generated investigations.
Code 3, 4

101 **INTERNAL** *NOTIFICATIONS* **REPORT**
Simply how many investigative related notifications did the investigate unit make within the organization? This should include both complaints and self-generated investigations.
Code 3, 4

102 *CASE* **RECAP REPORT - NARRATIVE**
This is a tool for the Director of the Investigative Unit as well as for individual investigators. This report should list most of the information that an investigator entered into the database involving one particular case. This report should include both complaints and self-generated investigations.
Code 1, 2, 3, 4

103 *CASE* RECAP REPORT – CODING

This is a tool for the Director of the Investigative Unit as well as for individual investigators. This report should list most, if not all the information that an investigator entered into the database concerning one particular case divided up into sections, using coding numbers, similar to a medical coding worksheet. This report should include both complaints and self-generated investigations.

Code 3, 4

104 THE *EVERYTHING CASE* REPORT (*CASES*)

This is a proof-reading tool as well as an informational tool for the investigator. It will document all information that was entered for one specific case, whether the information was entered by the use of check boxes, drop-down-menus or a narrative form. This should include both complaints and self-generated investigations.

Code 1, 2, 3, 4

105 *DATES* REPORT

This is a timeline of events that directly pertains to one individual case. It includes:

- Date of incident
- Date of complaint received by your organization (not the Investigative Unit)
- Date that the complaint was received by the Investigative Unit (Or the date of a self-generated investigation being created)
- Date assigned
- Date that the complainant was originally contacted by the assigned investigator
- Dates that the complainant was re-contacted by the assigned investigator
- Date of patient interview (if different than the complainant)
- Date of witness interviews
- Date of related investigative activities
- Dates any internal or external related case numbers were received
- Date that the case was closed
- Dates of all related administrative hearings and/or court appearances

This report should include both complaints and self-generated investigations.
Code 1, 2, 3, 4

106 *COMPLAINT SOURCE* REPORT - NUMBER

This is the number of complaints received from any of the internal or external complaint sources that the investigative unit tracks. They can include but are not limited to:

- Telephone
- Mail
- E-mail
- Municipal complaint intake system
- 9-1-1
- The media
- Politicians
- Walk-ins
- Organizational field supervisors
- State Department of Health (DOH)
- Local Police agencies
- Other

Probably the most important of all of the sources to track is the municipal complaint intake system source. If your area has such a system in place, it is important to make sure that all matters which are received this way get "appropriate" and "timely", "documented" investigative attention. I have witnessed instances where such items were received by the organization, and either sat on someone's desk, or remained in their computer before being forwarded to the investigative unit or were initially sent to the wrong person. Sometimes it took a month or more to actually reach the IU.

I believe that people generally don't have any faith that their complaint will be acted upon in the municipal arena, so when you add in an internal delay to the matter that is being complained about, it makes the complainant feel even worse, and it reinforces their negative feelings about their complaint.

For all cases, especially ones that involve the local Municipal Complaint Intake System, I always instructed my investigators to make immediate contact with the complainant, and to advise them their complaint was just received by the investigative unit (IU), and the investigation has started. (I also instructed my investigators to document whatever occurred timewise prior to our receiving the complaint). By immediately biting the bullet and advising that the complaint was just received by the IU, and by admitting that there was some sort of a processing delay by others, this will likely help forge a professional relationship between the complainant and the investigator.

This report should only include complaints.
Code 1, 2, 3, 4

107 *COMPLAINT SOURCE* REPORT- PERCENTAGE

This is the percentage of total complaints that were received from each of the individual complaint sources that you track. This report should only include complaints.
Code 2, 3, 4

108 *INVESTIGATIVE CLASSIFICATION* CHANGE REPORT - *COMPLAINTS*

This report should show how many complaints had their investigative classifications changed at some point during the investigation. This report should only include complaints.
Code 3, 4

109 *INVESTIGATIVE CLASSIFICATION* CHANGE REPORT - *INVESTIGATIONS*

This report should show how many investigations had their investigative classification changed at some point during the investigation. This report should include only self-generated investigations.
Code 3, 4

110 *INVESTIGATIVE CLASSIFICATION* **CHANGE REPORT-PERCENTAGE - CASES RELATED**

It should show the percentage of cases whose "investigative classifications" were changed at some point during the investigation. This report should include both complaints and self-generated investigations.

Code 4

111 *EMPLOYEE INVESTIGATIONAL HISTORY* **REPORT**

This report involves one individual employee and should contain a historical listing of all matters the employee has been involved in, indicating whether they were subjects or witnesses in prior IU cases. It should also include internal organizational reports, commendations, employment dates, promotional information, training information, and any available information regarding the employee current and past assigned work location(s). Some information for this report will have to be obtained from your Human Resources or Personnel Department computers via a computer link. This is an important report when starting a new investigation. It provides the investigator with important background information for employee(s). While this information is important, it should only be used as background information. Even if the employee was the subject of prior complaints of the same type, the new investigation can only concern itself with the facts you develop during the new investigation. You can't just say the subject employee is guilty based upon the employee's complaint history. This is also an important report if you are trying to determine if the employee is a candidate for an integrity test (a subject that I addressed in my first book). This report should include both complaints and self-generated complaints

Code 1, 2, 3, 4

112 **TOTAL** *CASES* **CLOSED**

This is a "traffic sheet" report. It reflects the total number of cases which were closed by the investigative unit, both in total and by individual investigator. This report should include both complaints and self-generated investigations.

Code 2, 3, 4

113 *CASES* CLOSED BY *INVESTIGATOR*

This is another "traffic sheet" related report. It reflects the total number of cases which were closed by each individual investigator for a reference time period. This also documents the unit's investigative productivity. This should include both complaints and self-generated investigations.

Code 2, 3, 4

114 *EMPLOYEE INTERVIEWS - COMPLAINT* RELATED

Total number of complaint related employee interviews, broken down by subject and witness. This is a tool for the director of investigations to determine how many interviews took place over a specific period-of-time to provide Information concerning the staffing level of the Investigations Unit. This report should include only complaints.

Code 3, 4

115 NUMBER OF *SUBJECT EMPLOYEE INTERVIEWS* VERSUS THE NUMBER OF *WITNESS EMPLOYEE INTERVIEWS* - COMPLAINT RELATED

This is an important investigative managerial report. This report includes only complaints.

Code 3, 4

116 NUMBER OF SUBJECT EMPLOYEE INTERVIEWS VERSUS THE NUMBER OF WITNESS EMPLOYEE INTERVIEWS – CASES RELATED

This is another important investigative managerial report. This report includes both complaints and self-generated investigations.

Code 3, 4

117 PERCENTAGE OF *SUBJECT EMPLOYEE INTERVIEWS* VERSUS *WITNESS EMPLOYEE INTERVIEWS* – COMPLAINT RELATED

This is an important investigative managerial report. This report only includes complaints.

Code 3, 4

118 PERCENTAGE OF *COMPLAINTS* THAT REQUIRE *EMPLOYEE INTERVIEWS* VERSUS THOSE THAT DO NOT

This is an important stat. It should only include complaints. This report only includes complaints.
Code 3, 4

119 *EMPLOYEE INTERVIEWS - INVESTIGATIONS* RELATED

This is also an important stat. It provides the total picture of employee interviews. It includes only self-generated investigations.
Code 3, 4

120 PERCENTAGE OF *SUBJECT EMPLOYEE INTERVIEWS* VERSUS *WITNESS EMPLOYEE INTERVIEWS* – *INVESTIGATIONS* RELATED

This is an important investigative managerial report. This report includes only self-generated investigations.
Code 3, 4

121 *EMPLOYEE INTERVIEWS* – *CASES* RELATED

An important report. This report includes both complaints and self-generated investigations.
Code 3, 4

122 PERCENTAGE OF *CASES* THAT REQUIRE *EMPLOYEE INTERVIEWS* VERSUS THOSE THAT DO NOT

This is an interesting fact to know. This report should include both complaints and self-generated investigations.
Code 3, 4

123 *EMPLOYEE INTERVIEWS* VERSUS NUMBER OF *INVESTIGATORS*

This is another of my very favorite charts. Total number of employee interviews broken down by subject and witness, "compared" to the number of investigators assigned to the investigative unit. This report should include both complaints and self-generated investigations.
Code 3, 4

124 *EMPLOYEE INTERVIEWS (COMPLAINT RELATED) - TIME*

An important tracking report. This report includes only complaints.
Code 3, 4

125 *EMPLOYEE INTERVIEWS (INVESTIGATIONS RELATED) - TIME*

Total time spent by the investigative unit as a whole, and by individual investigators conducting employee interviews. It should be broken down by "subject" interviews and "witness" interviews. If more than one investigator is involved in a particular interview, all should be included in this time stat. This is a tool for the director of investigations to determine how long these activities take and to make a case for additional investigators. This report should include only self-generated investigations.
Code 3, 4

126 *EMPLOYEE INTERVIEWS (CASES RELATED) - TIME*

This is an important tracking report, It includes both complaints and self-generated investigations.
Code 3, 4

127 *EMPLOYEE INTERVIEWS BY INVESTIGATIVE CLASSIFICATIONS – COMPLAINT RELATED*

The bulk of your employee interviews should usually involve "internal investigations" (the most serious level of investigative classification). However, it is reasonable to conduct interviews involving less serious cases and then refer the case. It should be broken down by "subject" interviews and "witness" interviews. This report should include only complaints.
Code 3, 4

128 *EMPLOYEE INTERVIEWS BY INVESTIGATIVE CLASSIFICATIONS -INVESTIGATIONS RELATED*

The bulk of your employee interviews should usually involve "internal investigations" (the most serious level of investigative classification). However, it is reasonable to conduct interviews involving less serious cases and then refer the case. It should be broken down by "subject"

interviews and "witness" interviews. This report should include only self-generated investigations.
Code 3, 4

129 *EMPLOYEE INTERVIEWS* BY *INVESTIGATIVE CLASSIFICATIONS – CASES* RELATED

This is a listing of all cases requiring employee interviews, broken down by investigative classifications. This report should include both complaints and self-generated investigations.
Code 3, 4

130 *EMPLOYEE INTERVIEWS* BY *COMPLAINT TYPE - (COMPLAINT* RELATED)

This helps to determine which complaint types result in the most employee interviews. It should be broken down by "subject" interviews and "witness" interviews. This report should include only complaints.
Code 3, 4

131 *EMPLOYEE INTERVIEWS* BY *COMPLAINT TYPE - (INVESTIGATIONS* RELATED)

This helps to determine which complaint types result in the most employee interviews. It should be broken down by "subject" interviews and "witness" interviews. This report should include only self-generated investigations.
Code 3, 4

132 *EMPLOYEE INTERVIEWS* BY *COMPLAINT TYPE – (CASES* RELATED)

This helps to determine which complaint types result in the most employee interviews overall. It should be broken down by "subject" interviews and "witness" interviews. This report should include both complaints and self-generated investigations.
Code 3, 4

133 **PERCENTAGE OF *EMPLOYEE INTERVIEWS* BY *COMPLAINT TYPE* – (*COMPLAINT* RELATED)**
This report will reflect the percentage of employee interviews broken down by all complainant types which are tracked by the IU. This report should include only complaints.
Code 3, 4

134 **PERCENTAGE OF *EMPLOYEE INTERVIEWS* BY *COMPLAINT TYPE* – (*INVESTIGATIONS* RELATED)**
This report will reflect the percentage of employee interviews broken down by all complainant types which are tracked by the IU. This report should include only self-generated investigations.
Code 3, 4

135 **PERCENTAGE OF *EMPLOYEE INTERVIEWS* BY *COMPLAINT TYPE* – (*CASES* RELATED)**
This report will reflect the percentage of employee interviews broken down by all complainant types which are tracked by the IU. This report should include both complaints and self-generated investigations.
Code 3, 4

136 **NUMBER OF *COMPLAINT* RELATED *EMPLOYEE INTERVIEWS* BROKEN DOWN BY *AMBULANCE STATION***
This report will identify a particular ambulance station which may require special attention either by the Investigative Unit or by the organization because of the unusual number of complaints. This report should only include complaints.
Code 3, 4

137 **NUMBER OF *INVESTIGATIONS RELATED EMPLOYEE INTERVIEWS* BROKEN DOWN BY *AMBULANCE STATION***
This report will identify if there is a particular ambulance station that may require special attention either by the Investigative Unit or by the organization because of the unusual number of investigations related interviews. This report should include only self-generated investigations.
Code 3, 4

138 **NUMBER OF *CASES* RELATED *EMPLOYEE INTERVIEWS* BROKEN DOWN BY *AMBULANCE STATIONS***

This report will identify if there is a particular ambulance station that may require special attention either by the Investigative Unit or by the organization because of an unusual number of case related interviews. This report should include both complaints and self-generated investigations.

Code 3, 4

139 **PERCENTAGE OF *CASES* RELATED *EMPLOYEE INTERVIEWS* BROKEN DOWN BY *AMBULANCE STATIONS***

This report will identify if there is a particular ambulance station that may require special attention either by the Investigative Unit or by the organization because of tan unusual number of case related interviews. This report should include both complaints and self-generated investigations.

Code 3, 4

140 *SITE VISITS - COMPLAINT RELATED*

Total number of site visits related to individual complaints. This report should include only complaints.

Code 2, 3, 4

141 *SITE VISITS - INVESTIGATIONS RELATED*

Total number of site visits related to individual investigations. This report should include only self-generated investigations.

Code 2, 3, 4

142 *SITE VISITS – CASES RELATED*

Total number of site visits related to individual investigations. This report should include both complaints and self-generated investigations.

Code 2, 3, 4

143 PERCENTAGE OF *CASES* REQUIRING *SITE VISITS*

Percentage of cases that require site visits versus those that do not. This report should include both complaints and self-generated complaints.
Code 2, 3, 4

144 *SITE VISITS – TIME – CASES* RELATED

Total time spent by the investigative unit as a whole, and by individual investigators when conducting investigative site visits. (If more than one investigator is involved in a particular site visit, all should be included in this time stat). This is a tool for the director of investigations to determine how long these activities take and to make a case for additional investigators. This report should include both complaints and self-generated investigations.
Code 3, 4

145 *FIELD INTERVIEWS - COMPLAINT* RELATED

Total number of complaint related field interviews conducted by the IU. This report should include only complaints.
Code 2, 3, 4

146 *FIELD INTERVIEWS - INVESTIGATIONS* RELATED

Total number of investigations related field interviews conducted by the IU. This report should include only self-generated investigations.
Code 2, 3, 4

147 *FIELD INTERVIEWS - CASES* RELATED

Total number of cases related field interviews conducted by the IU. This report should include both complaints and self-generated investigations.
Code 2, 3, 4

148 PERCENTAGE OF *CASES* REQUIRING *FIELD INTERVIEWS*

The percentage of cases that require field interviews compared to the number of cases that do not. This report should include both complaints and self-generated investigations.
Code 3, 4

149 *FIELD INTERVIEWS - TIME*

Total time spent by the investigative unit as a whole and by individual investigator, when conducting investigative field interviews. If more than one investigator is involved in case related field interviews, all should be included in this time stat. This is a tool for the director of investigations to determine how long these activities take and to make a case for additional investigators. This report should include both complaints and self-generated investigations.
Code 3, 4

150 *EVIDENCE COLLECTIONS - COMPLAINT* RELATED

The total number of "complaint" related evidence collections. This report should include only complaints.
Code 2, 3, 4

151 *EVIDENCE COLLECTION - INVESTIGATIONS* RELATED

The total number of "investigations" related evidence collections by the IU. This report should include only self-generated investigations.
Code 2, 3, 4

152 *EVIDENCE COLLECTION – CASES* RELATED

The total number of "cases" related evidence collections by the IU. This report should include both complaints and self-generated investigations.
Code 2, 3, 4

153 **PERCENTAGE OF** *CASES* **THAT REQUIRE** *EVIDENCE COLLECTIONS*

The percentage of "cases" that require evidence collections versus those cases that do not. This report should include both complaints and self-generated investigations.
Code 2, 3, 4

154 *EVIDENCE COLLECTION - TIME*

Total time spent by the investigative unit as a whole as well as by individual investigators regarding evidence collections. If more than one investigator is involved in evidence collection, all should be included in this time stat. This is a tool for the director of investigations

to determine how long these activities take and to make a case for additional investigators. This report should include both complaints and self-generated investigations.
Code 3, 4

155 TOTAL NUMBER OF *AUDIO RECORDINGS - COMPLAINT* RELATED

The number of "complaint" related audio recordings (review and re-recordings of 9-1-1 related phone-calls, ambulance radio transmissions and dispatch telephone conversations) which were conducted. (In my initial book, I referred to these as "tape-searches"; which is a historical term referring to a time when original audio was recorded onto reel-to-reel magnetic tape, which an investigator had to search through to find the required information). This report should include only complaints.
Code 2, 3, 4

For historical purposes, I placed a picture of a reel-to-reel audio reproducer here.

156 TOTAL NUMBER OF *AUDIO RECORDINGS - INVESTIGATIONS* RELATED

The number of "investigations" related audio recordings (review and re-recordings of 9-1-1 related phone-calls, ambulance radio transmissions and dispatch telephone conversations) which were conducted. This report should include only self-generated investigations.
Code 2, 3, 4

157 TOTAL NUMBER OF *AUDIO RECORDINGS - CASES* RELATED

The number of "cases" related audio recordings (review and re-recordings of 9-1-1 related phone-calls, ambulance radio transmissions and dispatch telephone conversations) which were conducted. This report should include both complaints and self-generated investigations.
Code 2, 3, 4

158 PERCENTAGE OF *CASES* REQUIRING *AUDIO RECORDINGS* VERSUS THOSE THAT DO NOT

What percentage of cases require audio recordings versus the percentage of cases that don't require them. This report should include both complaints and self-generated investigations.
Code 3, 4

159 *AUDITS* (NON-AMBULANCE) *COMPLAINT* RELATED

Total number of complaint-related non-ambulance audits, such as uniform, paperwork, ACRs or narcotic, which were conducted by the IU. This is a tool for the director of investigations to determine how long these activities take and to make a case for additional investigators. This report should include only complaints.
Code 3, 4

160 *AUDITS* (NON-AMBULANCE) *INVESTIGATIONS* RELATED

Total number of non-ambulance audits "investigations" related, such as uniform, paperwork, ACRs or narcotic, which were conducted by the IU. This is a tool for the director of investigations to determine how long these activities take and to make a case for additional investigators. This report should include only self-generated investigations.
Code 2, 3, 4

161 *AUDITS* (NON-AMBULANCE) *CASES* RELATED

Total number of non-ambulance audits "cases" related, such as uniform, paperwork, ACRs or narcotic, which were conducted by the IU. This is a tool for the director of investigations to determine how long these activities take and to make a case for additional

investigators. This report should include both complaints and self-generated investigations.
Code 2, 3, 4

162 PERCENTAGE OF *CASES* THAT REQUIRE NON-AMBULANCE *AUDITS* VERSUS THOSE THAT DON'T

An interesting audit related stat. It should include both complaints as well as self-generated investigations.
Code 2, 3, 4

163 AMBULANCE *AUDITS COMPLAINT* RELATED

An interesting audit related stat which only involves audits of ambulances. This report only includes "complaints".
Code 2, 3, 4

164 AMBULANCE *AUDITS INVESTIGATIONS* RELATED

Another interesting audit related stat which only involves the audits of ambulances which are related to an investigation. This includes only self-generated investigations.
Code 2, 3, 4

165 AMBULANCE *AUDITS CASES* RELATED

Another interesting audit related stat which only involves the audits of ambulances which are cases related. This includes both complaints and self-generated investigations.
Code 2, 3, 4

166 PERCENTAGE OF *CASES* THAT REQUIRE *AMBULANCE AUDITS* VERSUS THOSE THAT DON'T

Another interesting audit related stat which is related to investigations. This includes both complaints and self-generated investigations.
Code 2, 3, 4

167 *AUDITS - TIME*

The time it took to complete all audits, organized by audit type which were conducted by the IU and by individual investigators. If more than one investigator is involved in a particular audit, all should be

included in this time stat. This report should include both complaints and self-generated investigations.
Code 2, 3, 4

168 **AMBULANCE STATION AUDITS - COMPLAINT RELATED**
This is an important audit report. This report only includes complaints.
Code 2, 3, 4

169 **AMBULANCE STATION AUDITS - INVESTIGATIONS RELATED**
This is also an important audit report. It includes only self-generated investigations.
Code 3, 4

170 **AMBULANCE STATION AUDITS – CASES RELATED**
This is also an important audit report. It includes both complaints and self-generated investigations.
Code 3, 4

171 **AUDITS – ALL (CASES RELATED)**
This report compiles all of the individual audit related reports by subject and incorporates them into one recap type report. Audits can include but are not limited to:
- Employee credentials
- Employee uniforms
- Narcotics
- Time and leave issues
- Equipment on ambulances
- Ambulance Call Report (ACR) reviews
- Activities in and around ambulance stations and fire houses
- Contraband material

This report includes both complaints and self-generated investigations.
Code 3, 4

172 **COMPLAINTS VERSUS INVESTIGATORS REPORT**

This is a comparison between the number of complaints received versus the number of investigators assigned to the IU during a specified period-of-time. This informative report has always been one of my favorite reports. This report should only include complaints.
Code 3, 4

173 *INVESTIGATIONS* VERSUS *INVESTIGATORS* REPORT

This is a comparison between the number of investigations conducted versus the number of investigators assigned to the IU during a particular period of time. This report should include only self-generated investigations.
Code 3, 4

174 *CASES* VERSUS *INVESTIGATORS* REPORT

This is a comparison between the number of cases versus the number of investigators assigned to the IU during a particular period of time. This report should include both complaints and self-generated investigations.
Code 3, 4

175 *TESTIFYING - COMPLAINT* RELATED

Total number of times during a particular time period that investigators were required to testify relative to a complaint. If three investigators were required to testify on one particular case, that should be counted as three times. This is a tool for the director of investigations to determine how many cases involve having investigators testify, to make a case for additional investigators. This report should include only complaints.
Code 3, 4

176 *TESTIFYING - INVESTIGATIONS* RELATED

Total number of times during a particular time period that investigators were required to testify relative to an investigation. If three investigators were required to testify on one particular case, that should be counted as three times. This is a tool for the director of investigations to determine how many cases involve having investigators testify, to make a case for additional investigators. This report should include only self-generated investigations.
Code 3, 4

177 *TESTIFYING – CASES* RELATED

Total number of times during a particular time period that investigators were required to testify relative to a case. If three investigators were required to testify on one particular case, that should be counted as three times. This is a tool for the director of investigations to determine how many cases involve having investigators testify, to make a case for additional investigators. This report should include both complaints and self-generated investigations.
Code 3, 4

178 PERCENTAGE OF *COMPLAINTS* THAT REQUIRE *TESTIFYING* VERSUS THOSE THAT DON'T

This is an interesting stat, especially when answering the question, what does an investigator do. This report only includes complaints.
Code 3, 4

179 PERCENTAGE OF *INVESTIGATIONS* THAT REQUIRE *TESTIFYING* VERSUS THOSE THAT DO NOT

This is an interesting stat, especially when answering the question, what does an investigator do. This report only includes self-generated investigations.
Code 3, 4

180 PERCENTAGE OF *CASES* THAT REQUIRE *TESTIFYING* VERSUS THOSE THAT DO NOT REQUIRE IT

This is an important investigative managerial report. It includes both complaints and self-generated investigations.
Code 3, 4

181 *TESTIFYING – TIME (CASES* RELATED*)*

The amount of time that the investigative unit as a whole as well as individual investigators spent testifying. If more than one investigator is involved in testifying in a particular case, all should be included in this time stat. This report should include both complaints and self-generated complaints.
Code 3, 4

182 *GUIDELINE CHANGE* REPORT (*CASES* RELATED)

This should include any guideline change or creation, specifically if an organizational rule or guideline was changed/created/cancelled as a direct result of a specific investigation. It should list case numbers, complaint type, case priority, descriptions of the old guideline as well as the new guideline. This report should include both complaints and self-generated investigations.
Code 3, 4

183 *GUIDELINE CHANGE* REPORT – PERCENTAGE – (*CASES* RELATED)

The percentage of cases where there was a guideline change, creation, or if an organizational rule or guideline was changed/created/cancelled as a result of a specific investigation. This report should include both complaints and self-generated investigations.
Code 3, 4

184 *EMERGENCY RESPONSES* TO A SPECIFIC LOCATION - *COMPLAINT* RELATED

The number of past emergency responses to a specific address which were related to a complaint. This should include only complaints.
Code 1, 2, 3, 4

185 *EMERGENCY RESPONSES* TO A LOCATION - *INVESTIGATIONS* RELATED

The number of past emergency responses to a specific address which were related to an investigation. This should include only self-generated investigations.
Code 1, 2, 3, 4

186 *EMERGENCY RESPONSES* TO A LOCATION – *CASES* RELATED

The number of past emergency responses to a specific address which were cases related. This should include both complaints and self-generated investigations.
Code 1, 2, 3, 4

187 **ALL *PAST EMERGENCY REPSPONSES* TO A LOCATION FROM *CAD*, (NOT NESESSARILY INVESTIGATION, COMPLAINT OR CASES RELATED)**

The number of all past responses to a specific address according to your computer aided dispatch (CAD) computer. These responses don't have to be related to a complaint or an investigation.
Code 1, 2, 3, 4

188 **PERCENTAGE OF *PAST EMERGENCY RESPONSES* TO A LOCATION WHERE A *COMPLAINT* WAS FILED VERSUS THOSE WHERE NO *COMPLAINT* WAS FILED**

This is an interesting stat when looking for investigative background information. Unless this location qualifies as a "sensitive location", the number should be very small. This should only include complaints.
Code 3, 4

189 ***PAST RESPONSES* TO A LOCATION - *SUBJECT CREW MEMBER***

The number of past responses to a specific address which involve one or both subject crew members. They don't necessarily have to be related to a complaint or investigation.
Code 1, 2, 3, 4

190 ***PAST RESPONSES* FOR A PARTICULAR *PATIENT* BY ONE OR BOTH OF THE SUBJECT *CREW* AT ANY LOCATION**

The location of the calls for this report don't have to be the same as the subject call. It contains both complaints and self-generated investigations.
Code 1, 2, 3, 4

191 ***PAST COMPLAINT* RELATED *RESPONSES* TO A LOCATION BY *COMPLAINT TYPE***

The number of "complaint" related past responses to a specific location by complaint type. This report should only include complaints.
Code 2, 3, 4

192 *PAST INVESTIGATIONS RELATED RESPONSES* TO LOCATION - BY *COMPLAINT TYPE*

The number of investigations related past responses to a specific location by call type. This report should include only self-generated investigations.

Code 2, 3, 4

193 *PAST "CASES" RELATED RESPONSES* TO A LOCATION – BY *COMPLAINT TYPE*

The number of cases related past responses to a specific location by call type. This report should include both complaints and self-generated investigations.

Code 2, 3, 4

194 *PAST COMPLAINT RELATED RESPONSES* TO A LOCATION - BY *INVESTIGATIVE CLASSIFICATION*

The number of "complaint" related past responses to a specific location by investigative classification. This report should only include complaints.

Code 3, 4

195 *PAST INVESTIGATIVE RELATED RESPONSES* TO A LOCATION BY *INVESTIGATIVE CLASSIFICATION*

This is an important background report. The number of 'investigations" related past responses to a specific location by investigative classification. This report should only include self-generated investigations.

Code 3, 4

196 *PAST CASES RELATED RESPONSES* TO A *LOCATION* BY *INVESTIGATIVE CLASSIFICATION*

This is another important background report. The number of 'cases" related, past responses to a specific location by investigative classification. This report should both complaints and self-generated investigations.

Code 3, 4

197 **INVESTIGATOR** *TRAFFIC SHEET*

A traffic sheet documenting an individual investigator's activity between any two dates. This should include open cases (and their status), as well as closed cases. This report should include both complaints and self-generated investigations.
Code 1, 2, 3, 4

198 **INVESTIGATIVE UNIT *TRAFFIC SHEET***

A traffic sheet documenting the Investigative Unit's activity between any two dates. This should include by individual investigator and the unit as a whole, all open cases (and their status), as well as closed cases. This report should include both complaints and self-generated investigations.
Code 1, 2, 3, 4

199 *ASSIGNED CASES - INVESTIGATORS*

This "traffic sheet" related report that will reflect the number of cases that were assigned to each individual investigator during a specific period of time. This report should include both complaints and self-generated investigations.
Code 1, 2, 3, 4

200 *OPEN CASES*

This is another "traffic sheet" related report identifying all of the open cases at a particular time for the investigative unit as a whole. This includes both complaints and self-generated investigations.
Code 1, 2, 3, 4

201 *COMPLAINT* PROCESSING BY INDIVIDUAL *INVESTIGATOR* PRIOR TO ASSIGNMENT

This is also a "traffic sheet" related report. It reflects pre-assignment complaint action that individual IU investigators are involved in prior to a case actually being assigned. I have always believed that if an investigator initially receives and processes a complaint, whether or not this investigator is actually assigned the case, he or she should get credit for receiving and processing the complaint. Receiving and processing a new complaint takes "investigative time", so investigators should receive a stat for it. This report should include only complaints.
Code 2, 3, 4

202 *REFERRALS* TO THE MEDICAL DIRECTOR - *COMPLAINT* RELATED

The number of complaints referred to your organization's Medical Director. This report should only include complaints.
Code 2, 3, 4

203 *REFERRALS* TO THE MEDICAL DIRECTOR - *INVESTIGATIONS* RELATED

The number of investigations referred to the organization's Medical Director. This report should include only self-generated investigations.
Code 2, 3, 4

204 *REFERRALS* TO THE MEDICAL DIRECTOR - *CASES* RELATED

The number of cases referred to the organization's Medical Director. This report should include both complaints and self-generated investigations.
Code 2, 3, 4

205 PERCENTAGE OF *REFERRALS* TO THE MEDICAL DIRECTOR

The percentage of referral cases which were referred to your organization's Medical Director versus all other referrals. This report should include both complaints and self-generated investigations.
Code 2, 3, 4

206 PERCENTAGE OF *COMPLAINT* RELAITED *REFERRALS* VERSUS TOTAL *CASES*

An interesting stat to show what percent of "cases" were referred out for investigation versus what percent were investigated in-house. This only includes complaints.
Code 2, 3, 4

207 PERCENTAGE OF *REFERRALS* (SELF-GENERATED INVESTIGATIONS) VERSUS TOTAL *INVESTIGATIONS*

An interesting stat to show what percentage of "cases" were referred out for investigation versus what percent were investigated in-house. This includes only self-generated investigations.

Code 2, 3, 4

208 *REFERRALS* TO INDIVIDUAL *AMBULANCE STATIONS - COMPLAINT* RELATED

This complaint related report will tell you which ambulance stations require special attention because they routinely receive a higher number of referrals than other stations do. This report only includes complaints.

Code 2, 3, 4

209 *REFERRALS* TO INDIVIDUAL *AMBULANCE STATIONS - INVESTIGATIONS* RELATED

This investigations' related report will tell you which ambulance stations require special attention. This report includes only self-generated investigations.

Code 2, 3, 4

210 *REFERRALS* TO INDIVIDUAL *AMBULANCE STATIONS – CASES* RELATED

This "cases" related report will tell you which ambulance stations require special attention. This report includes both complaints and self-generated investigations.

Code 2, 3, 4

211 *COMPLAINT TYPE SPIKE* REPORT

This report compares the current number of complaints to past complaints of the same complaint type for a specific time frame. Suggested time frames include:

- The current month versus the previous month
- The current quarter versus the previous quarter
- The current half year versus the previous half year
- The current year versus the previous year
- The current decade versus the past decade

A spike can occur for many reasons. Once the spike for the time-period that you are examining becomes larger, continues to rise, this is a sure sign that the situation has become serious.

Once you have identified a serious spike, you should make a written notification to your organization's administration, up the chain-of-command, so that they can take appropriate corrective action. If your past investigations have suggested any reasons for the spike, this information should be relayed as well. By the same token, if you have previously notified your administration of an upward spike, and now the spike seems to be dropping or leveling off, you should notify them of the downward trend. This report should only include complaints. Code 3, 4

212 *SPIKE* REPORT – OTHER (NON-COMPLAINT TYPE) COMPLAINTS RELATED

An interesting stat when looking at investigational trends. This could include a multitude of subjects, from on-scene time, to at-hospital time, to any basic investigative classification. This report only includes complaints.
Code 3, 4

213 *EMPLOYEE PATIENT DEATH* REPORT - *COMPLAINT* RELATED

Total number of all "complaints' which involve an individual employee associated with a patient death allegation. While there are two people assigned to an ambulance, because of a variety of reasons, the same two employees will not always be working together, so both members of a particular crew may not have an equal number of patient death complaints. This report should include only complaints.
Code 2, 3, 4

214 *EMPLOYEE PATIENT DEATH* REPORT - *INVESTIGATIONS* RELATED

Total number of all "investigations" for an individual employee associated with a patient death allegation. This report should include only self-generated investigations.
Code 2, 3, 4

215 *EMPLOYEE PATIENT DEATH* REPORT – *CASES* RELATED

Total number of all "cases" for an individual employee associated with a patient death allegation. This report should include both complaints and self-generated investigations.

Code 2, 3, 4

216 PERCENTAGE OF *CASES* WHICH INVOLVE A *PATIENT DEATH* VERSUS THOSE THAT DON'T

This is an important background report because the percentage of patient death cases should be very low. If the number is not low, or if it starts to rise, this is an indication of a serious problem. This should include both complaints and self-generated investigations.

Code 2, 3, 4

217 PERCENTAGE OF *CASES* WHICH INVOLVE A *PATIENT DEATH* VERSUS THOSE THAT DON'T BY *COMPLAINT TYPES*

This is an important report. While the because the percentage of patient death cases should be very low and breaking them down by complaint types will make them even lower because the numbers are spread out, it is information that needs to be examined. While you will mostly see high priority call types, you will also find some lower priority ones as well. This should include both complaints and self-generated investigations.

Code 2, 3, 4

218 *EMPLOYEE PATIENT INJURY* REPORT - *COMPLAINT* RELATED

Total number of all "complaints" involving an individual employee which are associated with an injury to a patient. This report should include only complaints.

Code 2, 3, 4

219 EMPLOYEE *PATIENT INJURY* REPORT - *INVESTIGATIONS* RELATED

Total number of all "investigations" involving an individual employee, which are associated with an injury to a patient. This report should only include self-generated investigations.

Code 2, 3, 4

220 **EMPLOYEE** *PATIENT INJURY* **REPORT -** *CASES* **RELATED**

Total number of all "cases" involving an individual employee, which are associated with an injury to a patient. This report should include both complaints and self-generated investigations.
Code 2, 3, 4

221 **PERCENTAGE OF** *CASES* **WHICH INVOLVE A** *PATIENT INJURY* **VERSUS THOSE THAT DON'T**

This is an important background report. the percentage of patient injury cases should be very low. If the number is not low, or if it starts to rise, this is an indication of a serious problem. It should include both complaints and self-generated investigations.
Code 2, 3, 4

222 *DAY OF THE WEEK* **REPORT -** *COMPLAINT* **RELATED**

This report will help you determine what day of the week incidents that result in complaints being made occur. It may identify "problem days" that should be examined further. This report only includes complaints.
Code 3, 4

223 *DAY OF THE WEEK* **REPORT -** *INVESTIGATIONS* **RELATED**

This report will help you determine what day of the week incidents that result in complaints being made. It may identify "problem days" that should be examined further. This report only includes self-generated investigations.
Code 3, 4

224 *DAY OF THE WEEK* **REPORT -** *CASES* **RELATED**

This report will help you determine what day of the week a case related incident occurs. the incident day of a case. It may identify "problem days" that should be examined further. This report includes both complaints and self-generated investigations.
Code 3, 4

225 *DAY OF THE WEEK* PERCENTAGE REPORT -
COMPLAINT RELATED

This report will compare each day of the week with respect to day-
of-incidents where complaints are received. This report should only
include complaints.

Code 3, 4

226 *DAY OF THE WEEK COMPLAINT* REPORT (DATE
RECEIVED)

This report will compare each day of the week with respect to how
many complaints are received each day. (This pertains to the day the
complaint was received, not the day of an incident). This report should
only include complaints.

Code 2, 3, 4

227 *DAY OF THE WEEK COMPLAINT* PERCENTAGE
REPORT (DATE RECEIVED)

This report will compare each day of the week with respect to what
days complaints are received on. (This pertains to the day that the
complaint was received, not the day of incident). This report should
only include complaints.

Code 2, 3, 4

228 *DAY/TIME COMPLAINT - COMPLAINT TYPE* REPORT

This will help you determine if there is a time of a particular day-
of-the-week by complaint type, where it likely that an incident will
occur. This report should only include complaints.

Code 3, 4

229 *DAY/TIME EMPLOYEE COMPLAINT* REPORT

This will help you determine if there is a particular day of the week
and time of day that a complaint involving a particular employee is
likely to be received. This report should only include complaints.

Code 3, 4

230 *DAY/TIME GEOGRAPHIC AREA*
REPORT - *COMPLAINTS*

This will help you determine what day of the week and time of the day in each geographic region of your organization's response area complaints are received. This report only includes complaints.
Code 3, 4

231 *RELATIONSHIP TO PAYDAY* REPORT

This is especially important information to know when you are creating employee profiles (missing patient property complaints or drug related matters). It is likely that any employee who is involved in such issues, cannot wait until payday for their next infusion of money, so it is important to know this information. The following could be going on:

- If the issue is only missing money, this underlying cause could be related to gambling, money borrowed from a loan-shark, drug use or personal debt.
- It the issue is theft of organizational drugs (from an ambulance or from the organization's medication narcotic/narcotic reserves), the thefts could be for personal use, for the use of another person, or to sell. The first scenario is the most likely. This report should be calculated in calendar days, and it should include both complaints and self-generated investigations.

Code 3, 4

232 WEATHER REPORT (HISTORICAL)

This will track or document the weather conditions for every complaint or self-generated investigation. This report is particularly useful when examining delayed response complaints. You will probably determine that the weather affects much more than just delayed responses.

If you can't set this up as a program in your database, there are a number of web sites which will provide you with historical weather information that you could utilize. During the winter, snow is certainly an issue. However, an active snowstorm is not the only snow issue. You also need to examine the days immediately following a snowstorm. If there is snow on the roads from a prior storm, this can be a cause for a delay. As much as an active snowstorm can be an issue, rain can also be a factor as well.
Code 1, 2, 3, 4

233 **NUMBER OF *COMPLAINTS* RECEIVED PER DAY BY *WEATHER* CONDITIONS**

This is an interesting ongoing historical stat to determine what the average number of complaints per day compared to weather conditions. You might want to break this down into categories such as:

- 32 Degrees and below
- 33-50 Degrees
- 71-74 Degrees
- 75 Degrees and above
- Snow
- Rain
- Winds over 25 MPH (miles per hour)

This report includes only complaints.
Code 2, 3, 4

234 **AVERAGE *AGE* OF *PATIENT* REPORT – *COMPLAINTS***

This is an important report when researching past complaints to set up an employee integrity test. This should suggest the age range of patient that the subject employee seems to "feel comfortable with" and might continue his behavior with. This report should only include complaints.
Code 3, 4

235 **AVERAGE *AGE* OF *COMPLAINT* RELATED *PATIENTS* BROKEN DOWN BY *COMPLAINT TYPE***

This is an important report when researching past complaints to set up an employee integrity test. This should suggest the age range of patient that the subject employee seems to "feel comfortable with" and might continue his behavior with. This report should only include complaints.
Code 3, 4

236 **AVERAGE *AGE* OF *COMPLAINT* RELATED *PATIENTS* BROKEN DOWN BY *GEOGRAPHIC AREA***

This is an important report when researching past complaints to set up an employee integrity test. This should suggest the age range of

patient that the subject employee seems to "feel comfortable with" and might continue his behavior with. This report should only include complaints.
Code 3, 4

237 TOTAL NUMBER OF *COMPLAINTS* BROKEN DOWN BY *EMPLOYEE RANK* AND *WORKFORCE INFORMATION*

When you are examining "complaints", it is important to know how many employees have had one or more complaints made against them, and what their rank was at the time of each incident. This should be compared to the total number of employees by their rank on the date of the incident. This report should include only complaints.
Code 3, 4

238 TOTAL NUMBER OF *INVESTIGATIONS* BROKEN DOWN BY *EMPLOYEE RANK*

This is an important background report. When you are examining "investigations", it is important to know how many employees were involved in one or more investigations, and what their rank was at the time of each incident. This should be compared to the total number of employees by their rank. This report should only include self-generated investigations.
Code 3, 4

239 TOTAL NUMBER OF *CASES* BROKEN DOWN BY *EMPLOYEE RANK*

This is an important background report. When you are examining "cases", it is important to know how many employees were involved in one or more investigations, and what their rank was at the time of each incident. This should be compared to the total number of employees by rank. This report should include both complaints and self-generated investigations.
Code 3, 4

240 AVERAGE NUMBER OF *COMPLAINTS* BROKEN DOWN BY *EMPLOYEE RANK* AND *TITLE* PERCENTAGE

The average number of "complaints" for each employee rank, and a comparison to the overall percentage of employees in each respective rank. This should be compared to the total number of employees by their rank. This information should change over time. This report should include only complaints.
Code 3, 4

241 AVERAGE NUMBER OF *INVESTIGATIONS* BROKEN DOWN BY *EMPLOYEE RANK* AND *TITLE* AVERAGE

The average number of "investigations" for each employee rank. This should be compared to the total number of employees in each rank and the average number of total employees by rank. This report should only include self-generated investigations.
Code 3, 4

242 AVERAGE NUMBER OF *CASES* BROKEN DOWN BY *EMPLOYEE RANK* AND *TITLE* AVERAGE

The average number of "cases" for each employee rank. This should be compared to the total number of employees in each rank and the average number of total employees by rank. This report should include both complaints and self-generated investigations.
Code 3, 4

243 PERCENTAGE OF *COMPLAINTS* BY *EMPLOYEE RANK* AND *WORKFORCE* TOTALS

A stat to determine the percentage of employees who are associated with complaints broken down by their employee rank. This report only includes complaints.
Code 3, 4

244 PERCENTAGE OF *INVESTIGATIONS* BY *EMPLOYEE RANK*

This is an important background report. This report includes only self-generated investigations.
Code 3, 4

245 PERCENTAGE OF *CASES* BY *EMPLOYEE RANK*

This is an important background report. This report includes both complaints and self-generated investigations.
Code 3, 4

246 TOTAL NUMBER OF *COMPLAINTS* RECEIVED BY *WORK SHIFT*

This is another interesting statistic. The total number of complaints are broken down by the subject employee's work shift. This report should work for two or three work shifts per day. It would not work for a one shift per day system. Knowing this information could result in resources being redistributed. While it would seem logical that there would be a correlation between work shift and call volume, it is also interesting to add complaints into the mix. The number of complaints received per shift will be different. There probably are other unique factors that would come into play. This report is for complaints only.
Code 3, 4

247 TOTAL NUMBER OF *INVESTIGATIONS* BROKEN DOWN BY *WORK SHIFT*

This is another interesting report. This report should only include self-generated investigations.
Code 3, 4

248 TOTAL NUMBER OF *CASES* BROKEN DOWN BY *WORK SHIFT*

This is another interesting report. This report should include both complaints and self-generated investigations.
Code 3, 4

249 NUMBER OF *COMPLAINTS* TOUR 1 (OVERNIGHT TOUR)

This report works if there are two or three work shifts. The number of complaints received which occurred during tour one. This only includes complaints.
Code 3, 4

250 NUMBER OF *COMPLAINTS* TOUR 2 (DAY TOUR)

This report works if there are two or three work shifts. The number of complaints received which occurred during tour two. This only includes complaints.
Code 3, 4

251 NUMBER OF *COMPLAINTS* TOUR 3 (EVENING TOUR)

There must be three work shifts for this one to work. The number of complaints received which occurred during tour three. This only includes complaints.
Code 3, 4

252 PERCENTAGE OF *COMPLAINTS* FOR ALL TOURS

There must be more than one work shift for this one to work. The percentage of complaints that occurred during each tour is compared to each other. This report only involves complaints.
Code 3, 4

253 NUMBER OF *INVESTIGATIONS* TOUR 1 (OVERNIGHT TOUR)

This report works if there are two or three work shifts. The number of investigations involving tour one. This report should include only self-generated investigations.
Code 3, 4

254 NUMBER OF *INVESTIGATIONS* TOUR 2 (DAY TOUR)

This report works if there are two or three work shifts. The number of investigations involving tour two. This report should only include self-generated investigations
Code 3, 4

255 NUMBER OF *INVESTIGATIONS* TOUR 3 (EVENING TOUR)

There must be three work shifts for this one to work. The number of investigations involving tour three. This report should include only self-generated investigations.
Code 3, 4

256 NUMBER OF *CASES* TOUR 1 (OVERNIGHT TOUR)

This is another interesting statistic. The total number of cases broken down by the subject employee's work shift. This report should work for two or three work shifts per day. It would not work for a one shift per day system. Knowing this information could result in resources being redistributed. This report includes both complaints and self-generated investigations.

Code 3, 4

257 NUMBER OF *CASES* TOUR 2 (DAY TOUR)

This is another interesting statistic. The total number of cases broken down by the subject employee's work shift. This report should work for two or three work shifts per day. It would not work for a one shift per day system. Knowing this information could result in resources being redistributed. This report includes both complaints and self-generated investigations.

Code 3, 4

258 NUMBER OF *CASES* TOUR 3 (EVENING TOUR)

This is another interesting statistic. The total number of cases broken down by the subject employee's work shift. This report should work for two or three work shifts per day. It would not work for a one shift per day system. Knowing this information could result in resources being redistributed. This report includes both complaints and self-generated investigations.

Code 3, 4

259 PERCENTAGE OF *INVESTIGATIONS* FOR ALL *TOURS*

There must be two to three work shifts for this one to work. The percentage of investigations involving each tour are compared to the other tours. This report should include both complaints and self-generated investigations.

Code 3, 4

260 *EMPLOYEES* WITH *MULTIPLE COMPLAINTS*, WHO WERE ON *OVERTIME* VERSUS *REGULAR TIME*

For an employee who has received multiple complaints, you want to determine how many occurred during, or immediately following an overtime shift. Sometimes an employee works an overtime shift

prior to their regularly scheduled work shift so you have to be careful when entering this information which is important information. This report could be broken down into whatever forms of overtime your organization has, such as voluntary overtime or forced overtime. This report only includes complaints.
Code 3, 4

261 *EMPLOYEES* WITH *MULTIPLE COMPLAINTS* - PERCENTAGE ON *OVERTIME* VERSUS *REGULAR TIME*

The percentage of employees who were working overtime, versus regular time when involved in an incident that resulted in a complaint being filed. This report should only include complaints.
Code 3, 4

262 NUMBER OF *COMPLAINTS* WHERE *SUBJECT EMPLOYEE* WAS ON *REGULAR TIME*

An interesting investigative stat, when looking into an employee's background. This report only includes complaints.
Code 3, 4

263 PERCENTAGE OF *COMPLAINTS* WHERE *SUBJECT EMPLOYEE* WAS ON *REGULAR TIME*

An interesting investigative stat when looking into an employee's background. This report only includes complaints.
Code 3, 4

264 NUMBER OF *COMPLAINTS* WHERE *SUBJECT EMPLOYEE* WAS ON *OVERTIME*

An interesting investigative stat when looking into an employee's background. This report only includes complaints.
Code 3, 4

265 PERCENTAGE OF *COMPLAINTS* WHERE THE *SUBJECT EMPLOYEE* WAS ON *OVERTIME*

An interesting investigative stat when looking into an employee's background. This report only includes complaints.
Code 3, 4

266 NUMBER OF *INVESTIGATIONS* WHERE *SUBJECT EMPLOYEE* WAS ON REGULAR TIME

An interesting investigative stat when looking into an employee's background. This report includes only self-generated investigations. Code 3, 4

267 PERCENTAGE OF *INVESTIGATIONS* WHERE *SUBJECT EMPLOYEE* WAS ON *REGULAR TIME*

An interesting stat when looking into an employee's background. This report includes only self-generated investigations. Code 3, 4

268 NUMBER OF *CASES* WHERE *SUBJECT EMPLOYEE* WAS ON REGULAR TIME

An interesting stat when looking into an employee's background. This report includes both complaints and self-generated investigations. Code 3, 4

269 PERCENTAGE OF *CASES* WHERE *SUBJECT EMPLOYEE* WAS ON *REGULAR TIME*

An interesting stat when looking into an employee's background. This report includes both complaints and self-generated investigations. Code 3, 4

270 NUMBER OF *INVESTIGATIONS* WHERE *SUBJECT EMPLOYEE* WAS ON *OVERTIME*

An interesting stat when looking into an employee's background. This report includes both complaints and self-generated investigations. Code 3, 4

271 PERCENTAGE OF *INVESTIGATIONS* WHERE *SUBJECT EMPLOYEE* WAS ON *OVERTIME*

An interesting stat when looking into an employee's background. This includes both complaints and self-generated investigations. Code 3, 4

272 **NUMBER OF *COMPLAINTS* WHERE THE *SUBJECT EMPLOYEE* WAS ON *REGULAR TIME* THAT IMMEDIATELY FOLLOWED AN *OVERTIME* TOUR**
This is another valuable report in a series of stats where overtime versus regular time are compared. This report only includes complaints.
Code 3, 4

273 **PERCENTAGE OF COMPLAINTS WHERE THE *EMPLOYEE* WAS ON *REGULAR TIME* THAT IMMEDIATELY FOLLOWED AN OVERTIME TOUR**
This is another valuable report in a series of stats where overtime versus regular time are compared. This report only includes complaints.
Code 3, 4

274 **NUMBER OF *INVESTIGATIONS* WHERE THE *EMPLOYEE* WAS ON *REGULAR TIME* THAT IMMEDIATELY FOLLOWED AN *OVERTIME* TOUR**
This is another important report in a series of stats where overtime versus regular time are compared. This report includes only self-generated investigations.
Code 3, 4

275 **PERCENTAGE OF *INVESTIGATIONS* WHERE THE *EMPLOYEE* WAS ON *REGULAR TIME* WHICH IMMEDIATELY FOLLOWED AN *OVERTIME* TOUR**
This is another important overtime related report. This report includes only self-generated investigations.
Code 3, 4

276 **NUMBER OF *CASES* WHERE THE *EMPLOYEE* WAS ON *REGULAR TIME* WHICH IMMEDIATELY FOLLOWED AN *OVERTIME* TOUR**
This is another important report in a series of stats where overtime versus regular time are compared. This report includes both complaints and self-generated investigations.
Code 3, 4

277 **PERCENTAGE OF *CASES* WHERE THE *EMPLOYEE* WAS ON *REGULAR* TIME WHICH IMMEDIATELY FOLLOWED AN *OVERTIME* TOUR**

This is another important report in a series of stats where overtime versus regular time are compared. This report includes both complaints and self-generated investigations.

Code 3, 4

278 **NUMBER OF *COMPLAINTS* WHERE *SUBJECT EMPLOYEE* WAS ON *REGULAR TIME* BY *AMBULANCE STATION***

This is an important background report. This report only includes complaints.

Code 3, 4

279 **PERCENTAGE OF *COMPLAINTS* WHERE *SUBJECT EMPLOYEE* WAS ON *REGULAR TIME* BY *AMBULANCE STATION***

This is an important background report. This report only includes complaints.

Code 3, 4

280 **NUMBER OF *COMPLAINTS* WHERE *SUBJECT EMPLOYEE* WAS ON *OVERTIME* BY *AMBULANCE STATION***

This is an important background report. This report only includes complaints.

Code 3, 4

281 **PERCENTAGE OF *COMPLAINTS* WHERE *SUBJECT EMPLOYEE* WAS ON *OVERTIME* BY *AMBULANCE STATION***

This is an important background report. This report only includes complaints.

Code 3, 4

282 **NUMBER OF *INVESTIGATIONS* WHERE *SUBJECT EMPLOYEE* WAS ON *REGULAR TIME BY AMBULANCE STATION***

This is an important background report. This report includes only self-generated investigations.
Code 3, 4

283 **PERCENTAGE OF *INVESTIGATIONS* WHERE *SUBJECT EMPLOYEE* WAS ON *REGULAR TIME* BY *AMBULANCE STATION***

This is an important background report. This report includes only self-generated investigations.
Code 3, 4

284 **NUMBER OF *CASES* WHERE *SUBJECT EMPLOYEE* WAS ON *REGULAR TIME* BY *AMBULANCE STATION***

This is an interesting background report which will compare this scenario ambulance station to ambulance station. This report includes both complaints and self-generated investigations.
Code 3, 4

285 **NUMBER OF *COMPLAINTS* INVOLVING THE *FIRST CALL* OF TOUR**

Total number of complaints involving the first call of an employee's tour (shift). This can be an important report when planning an integrity test, or for supervisory purposes. This report should include only complaints.
Code 3, 4

286 **PERCENTAGE OF *COMPLAINTS* INVOLVING THE *FIRST CALL* OF TOUR**

The percentage of complaints involving the first call of an employee's tour (shift). This can be an important report when planning an integrity test, or for supervisory purposes. This report should include only complaints.
Code 3, 4

287 **TOTAL *INVESTIGATIONS* INVOLVING THE *FIRST CALL* OF TOUR**

Total number of investigations involving the first call of an employee's tour (shift). This can be an important report when planning an integrity test, or for supervisory purposes. This report should include only self-generated investigations.
Code 3, 4

288 **PERCENTAGE OF *INVESTIGATIONS* INVOLVING THE *FIRST CALL* OF TOUR**

The percentage of investigations involving the first call of an employee's tour (shift). This can be an important report when planning an integrity test, or for supervisory purposes. This report should include only self-generated investigations.
Code 3, 4

289 **TOTAL *CASES* INVOLVING THE *FIRST CALL* OF TOUR**

Total number of cases involving the first call of an employee's tour (shift). This can be an important report when planning an integrity test, or for supervisory purposes. This report should include both complaints and self-generated investigations.
Code 3, 4

290 **PERCENTAGE OF *CASES* INVOLVING THE *FIRST CALL* OF TOUR**

The percentage of cases involving the first call of an employee's tour (shift). This can be an important report when planning an integrity test, or for supervisory purposes. This report should include both complaints and self-generated investigations.
Code 3, 4

291 **TOTAL *COMPLAINTS* INVOLVING THE *LAST CALL* OF TOUR**

Total number of complaints involving the last call of an employee's tour (shift). This can be an important report when planning an integrity test, or for supervisory purposes. This report should include only complaints.
Code 3, 4

292 PERCENTAGE OF *COMPLAINTS* INVOLVING *LAST CALL* OF TOUR

Percentage of complaints involving the last call of an employee's tour (shift). This can be an important report when planning an integrity test, or for supervisory purposes. This report should include only complaints.

Code 3, 4

293 TOTAL *INVESTIGATIONS* INVOLVING THE *LAST CALL* OF TOUR

Total number of investigations involving the last call of an employee's tour (shift). This can be an important report when planning an integrity test, or for supervisory purposes. This report should include only self-generated investigations.

Code 3, 4

294 PERCENTAGE OF *INVESTIGATIONS* INVOLVING *LAST CALL* OF TOUR

Percentage of investigations involving the last call of an employee's tour (shift). This can be an important report when planning an integrity test, or for supervisory purposes. This report should include only self-generated investigations.

Code 3, 4

295 TOTAL *CASES* INVOLVING THE *LAST CALL* OF TOUR

Total number of cases involving the last call of an employee's tour (shift). This can be an important report when planning an integrity test, or for supervisory purposes. This report should include both complaints and self-generated investigations.

Code 3, 4

296 PERCENTAGE OF *CASES* INVOLVING THE *LAST CALL* OF TOUR

Percentage of cases involving the last call of an employee's tour (shift). This can be an important report when planning an integrity test, or for supervisory purposes. This report should include both complaints and self-generated investigations.

Code 3, 4

297 NUMBER OF *COMPLAINTS* INVOLVING *MIDDLE CALLS* OF TOUR

The number of complaints involving any of the middle calls of an employee's tour (shift).

This report is expected to be a higher number that the first or last call reports because we are generally speaking of multiple calls. This can be an important report when planning an integrity test, or for supervisory purposes. This report should only include complaints.
Code 3, 4

298 PERCENTAGE OF *COMPLAINTS* INVOLVING *MIDDLE CALLS* OF TOUR

The percentage of complaints involving any of the middle calls of an employee's shift (tour). This report is expected to be a higher number that the first or last call reports because we are generally speaking of multiple calls. This can be an important report when planning an integrity test, or for supervisory purposes. This report should only include complaints.
Code 3, 4

299 NUMBER OF *INVESTIGATIONS* INVOLVING THE *MIDDLE CALLS* OF A TOUR

Total number of investigations which involve any of the middle calls of an employee's tour (shift). This can be an important report when planning an integrity test, or for supervisory purposes. This report includes only self-generated investigations.
Code 3, 4

300 PERCENTGE OF *INVESTIGATIONS* INVOLVING *MIDDLE CALLS* OF TOUR

The percentage of investigations which involve any of the middle calls of an employee's tour (shift). This can be an important report when planning an integrity test, or for supervisory purposes. This report includes only self-generated investigations.
Code 3, 4

301 NUMBER OF *CASES* INVOLVING THE *MIDDLE CALLS* OF A TOUR

Total number of cases which involve any of the middle calls of an employee's tour (shift). This can be an important report when planning an integrity test, or for supervisory purposes. This report includes both complaints and self-generated investigations.
Code 3, 4

302 PERCENTGE OF *CASES* INVOLVING *MIDDLE CALLS* OF TOUR

The percentage of cases which involve any of the middle calls of an employee's tour (shift). This can be an important report when planning an integrity test, or for supervisory purposes. This report includes both complaints and self-generated investigations.
Code 3, 4

303 RECAP OF THE *NUMBER/PERCENTAGE* OF *COMPLAINTS, INVESTIGATIONS* AND *CASES* INVOLVING THE *FIRST, LAST* AND *MIDDLE CALLS OF TOUR*

This is a recap report of all of the calls of tour reports listed above. This is an interesting report. This report includes both complaints and self-generated investigations.
Code 3, 4

304 AVERAGE NUMBER OF *COMPLAINTS* FOR *EMPLOYEES* WITH *MULTIPLE COMPLAINTS*

For the employees that have multiple complaints, what is the average number of complaints? You can include complaints no matter how old they might be, or you can set up a specific time period. This report should only include complaints.
Code 3, 4

305 NUMBER OF *EMPLOYEES* THAT HAVE *MULTIPLE COMPLAINTS* COMPARED TO THEIR AVERAGE *AGE*

This report will suggest to you what age group of employees have had more than one complaint against them. The larger the reporting sample the better. This report may also be of assistance to your

organization in the areas of future hiring and education. This report should only include complaints.
Code 3, 4

306 TIME FRAME INVOLVED FOR THE GROUP OF *EMPLOYEES* THAT HAVE *MULTIPLE COMPLAINTS*

This report will provide another perspective into the issue of employees with multiple complaints. In other words, are they recent or are they from long ago? This report should only include complaints.
Code 3, 4

307 NUMBER OF EMPLOYEES THAT HAVE *MULTIPLE COMPLAINTS,* COMPARED TO THEIR RESPECTIVE *COMPLAINT TYPES*

This report will document what the various complaint types are involving employees who have multiple complaints against them. It answers the question, are certain complaint types more likely to involve employees who have multiple complaints lodged against them. This report only includes complaints.
Code 3, 4

308 AVERAGE NUMBER OF DAYS FROM THE DATE OF INCIDENT TO THE DATE WHEN THE *COMPLAINT* WAS ACTUALLY *RECEIVED* (EITHER BY THE ORGANIZATION, OR THE INVESTIGATIVE UNIT)

This is an interesting report. This is one of those reports where you have to decide if you are using calendar days or business days to calculate the information. This report only includes complaints.
Code 3, 4

309 AVERAGE NUMBER OF *DAYS* FROM DATE OF INCIDENT UNTIL *COMPLAINT* IS RECEIVED (BY THE ORGANIZATION OR THE INVESTIGATIVE UNIT) BROKEN DOWN BY *COMPLAINT TYPE*

This is a similar report to the preceding one, but with an important and informative twist. This is one of those reports where you have to decide if you are using calendar days or business days to calculate the information. This report only includes complaints.

Code 3, 4

310 THE AVERAGE NUMBER OF DAYS IT TAKES FOR A *COMPLAINT* TO BE RECEIVED BY *INVESTIGATIVE CLASSIFICATION*

This report answers the question how long does it take for a complaint to be received broken down by investigative classification. We are talking about measuring from the date of incident until the date that the complaint is received either by the IU or the organization itself. This figure should be calculated in calendar days. This report only incudes complaints.

Code 3, 4

311 TOTAL NUMBER OF *COVERT SURVEILANCES - COMPLAINT* RELATED

Total number of complaint-related covert surveillances by the IU over a specific period of time. This report only includes complaints.

Code 2, 3, 4

312 TOTAL NUMBER OF *COVERT SURVEILANCES - INVESTIGATIONS* RELATED

Total number of investigations related covert surveillances over a specific time. This report includes only self-generated investigations.

Code 2, 3, 4

313 TOTAL NUMBER OF *COVERT SURVEILANCES – CASES* RELATED

Total number of cases related covert surveillances over a specific time. This report includes both complaints and self-generated investigations.

Code 2, 3, 4

314 TOTAL *TIME* OF *COVERT SURVEILANCES*

The total time the IU spent conducting covert surveillances. If multiple investigators are involved in a particular covert surveillance, all should be included in this time stat. This report includes complaints and self-generated investigations.

Code 3, 4

315 **TOTAL NUMBER OF** *OVERT SURVEILANCES -* *COMPLAINT* **RELATED**

The total number of overt surveillances by the investigative unit. If multiple investigators are involved in a particular overt surveillance, all should be included in this time stat. This report only includes complaints.
Code 3, 4

316 **TOTAL NUMBER OF** *OVERT SURVEILANCES -* *INVESTIGATIONS* **RELATED**

This report will document the number of overt surveillances which were investigations related. While it may seem unusual, there will be times when overt surveillances should be conducted. It will include only self-generated investigations.
Code 2, 3, 4

317 **TOTAL NUMBER OF** *OVERT SURVEILANCES - CASES* **RELATED**

The total number of overt surveillances by the investigative unit which are case related. If multiple investigators are involved in a particular overt surveillance, all should be included in this time stat. This report includes both complaints and self-generated investigations.
Code 2, 3, 4

318 **TOTAL** *TIME* **OF** *OVERT SURVEILANCES*

The total time the IU spend conducting overt surveillances. If multiple investigators are involved in a particular overt surveillance, each one should be included in this time stat. This report includes complaints and self-generated investigations.
Code 3, 4

319 **TOTAL NUMBER OF** *COVERT* **AND** *OVERT* *SURVEILANCES*

Total number of surveillance's (covert and overt) conducted. This report includes complaints and self-generated investigations.
Code 2, 3, 4

320 TOTAL *TIME* OF *COVERT* AND *OVERT SURVEILANCES*
The total amount of time the IU spent conducting both overt and covert surveillances. This report includes both complaints and self-generated investigations.
Code 3, 4

321 TOTAL NUMBER OF *COMPLAINTS* REQUIRING *SURVEILANCES* VERSUS THOSE THAT DON'T
This report will help the IU justify or increase the number of investigators. This report includes only complaints.
Code 3, 4

322 TOTAL PERCENTAGE OF *COMPLAINTS* REQUIRING *SURVEILANCES* VERSUS THOSE THAT DON'T REQUIRE THEM
This is an interesting report involving surveillances. This report will help the IU justify or increase the number of investigators. This report only involves complaints.
Code 3, 4

323 TOTAL NUMBER OF *INVESTIGATIONS* REQUIRING *SURVEILANCES* VERSUS THOSE THAT DO NOT REQUIRE THEM
This is an interesting report involving surveillances. This report involves only self-generated investigations.
Code 3, 4

324 TOTAL PERCENTAGE OF *INVESTIGATIONS* THAT REQUIRE *SURVEILANCES* VERSUS THOSE THAT DON'T
This is an interesting report involving surveillances This report includes both only self-generated investigations.
Code 3, 4

325 TOTAL NUMBER OF *CASES* THAT REQUIRE *SURVEILANCES* VERSUS THOSE THAT DON'T
This is an interesting report involving surveillances. This report involves both complaints and self-generated investigations.
Code 3, 4

326 **TOTAL PERCENTAGE OF *CASES* THAT REQUIRE *SURVEILANCES* VERSUS THOSE THAT DON'T**

This is an interesting report involving surveillances This report includes both complaints and self-generated investigations.
Code 3, 4

327 *CASE LOAD*

This is a traffic sheet related report. It reflects the entire investigative unit's case load as well as individual investigators on one particular date. This would be one of the reports that would work well using bar graphs. This report includes both complaints and self-generated investigations.
Code 1, 2, 3, 4

328 *INVESTIGATOR CASE LOAD* BROKEN DOWN BY *INVESTIGATIVE CLASSIFICATION*

This is a traffic sheet related report. This report includes both complaints and self-generated investigations.
Code 2, 3, 4

329 *INVESTIGATOR CASE LOAD* BROKEN DOWN BY *COMPLAINT TYPE*

This is a traffic sheet related report. This report includes both complaints and self-generated investigations.
Code 2, 3, 4

330 *INVESTIGATOR CASE LOAD* BETWEEN TWO DATES

This is a traffic sheet related report. Individual Investigator case load number between two particular dates. This report includes both complaints and self-generated investigations.
Code 2, 3, 4

331 *PHOTO ARRAYS - COMPLAINTS*

Total number of employee photo arrays (displays) that are complaint related. This report only includes complaints.
Code 2, 3, 4

332 *PHOTO ARRAYS - INVESTIGATIONS*

Total number of employee photo arrays (displays) which are investigations related. This report includes only self-generated investigations.

Code 2, 3, 4

333 **PHOTO ARRAYS - *CASES***

Total number of employee photo arrays (displays) which are cases related. This report includes both complaints and self-generated investigations.

Code 2, 3, 4

334 *PHOTO ARRAYS - TIME*

The time it took to complete and show employee photo arrays (displays) which are cases related. This report includes both complaints and self-generated investigations.

Code 2, 3, 4

335 **PERCENTAGE OF *COMPLAINTS* THAT REQUIRE *PHOTO ARRAYS* VERSUS THOSE THAT DON'T**

This is an investigative management tool. This report only includes complaints.

Code 2, 3, 4

336 **PERCENTAGE OF *INVESTIGATIONS* THAT REQUIRE *PHOTO ARRAYS* VERSUS THOSE THAT DON'T**

This is an investigative management tool. This report includes only self-generated investigations.

Code 2, 3, 4

337 **PERCENTAGE OF *CASES* THAT REQUIRE *PHOTO ARRAYS* VERSUS THOSE THAT DON'T**

Total number of employee photo arrays (displays) which are investigations related. This report includes both complaints and self-generated investigations.

Code 2, 3, 4

338 *DOCUMENTATION REQUESTS* **RECEIVED**

This report identifies the number of documentation requests which were received/processed during a specific period-of-time. A documentation request is a request from anyone outside of the investigative unit (IU) who is authorized to receive the document that they are requesting. The organizations legal staff should provide counsel on this issue. be on board with this issue, so this process can run smoothly and not be time consuming.

Code 2, 3, 4

339 *DOCUMENTATION* **REVIEW**

This catches any document, procedure, or other item that the IU was asked to review, or that the IU reviewed on your own during a specific time period.

Code 2, 3, 4

340 *COMPLAINTS* **WITH** *MULTIPLE COMPLAINANTS*

How many complaints received where there was more than one actual complainant? (The complaints don't have to have been received at the same time). This report only includes complaints.

Code 3, 4

341 *COMPLAINTS* **WITH** *MULTIPLE COMPLAINANTS* **BY** **COMPLAINT** *TYPE*

How many individual complaints received more than one complaint and what were the complaint types. This report only includes complaints.

Code 3, 4

342 **NUMBER OF** *COMPLAINTS* **(OTHER THAN SUBJECT COMPLAINT) RECEIVED FOR THE SAME CALENDAR DATE**

How many other complaints were received for the same day as the subject complaint? This report only involves complaints.

Code 3, 4

343 THE NUMBER OF *SELF-GENERATED INVESTIGATIONS* WHERE A SUBSEQUENT *COMPLAINT* WAS RECEIVED

How many self-generated investigations also had a complaint filed? This report only includes self-generated investigations.
Code 3, 4

344 THE NUMBER OF *SELF-GENERATED INVESTIGATIONS* WHICH HAD A SUBSEQUENT *COMPLAINT* RECEIVED BROKEN DOWN BY *COMPLAINT TYPE*

How many self-generated investigations also had a complaint filed, and of those, what were the complaint types that were involved? This report only includes self-generated investigations.
Code 3, 4

345 *RESOURCE RESPONSE COMPLAINTS*

The number of complaints received broken down by a 1-resource response, a 2-resource response, a 3-resource response, a 4-resource response and a 5-or-more resource response. This report only includes complaints.
Code 2, 3, 4

346 *RESOURCE RESPONSE INVESTIGATIONS*

The number of investigations received broken down by a 1-resource response, a 2-resource response, a 3-resource response, a 4-resource response and a 5-or-more resource response. This report only includes self-generated investigations.
Code 2, 3, 4

347 *RESOURCE RESPONSE CASES*

The number of cases broken down by a 1-resource response, a 2-resource response, a 3-resource response, a 4-resource response and a 5-or-more resource response. This report includes both complaints and self-generated investigations.
Code 2, 3, 4

348 *AMBULANCE STATION - COMPLAINTS*

Not only do you want to know which ambulance station generates the most complaints, you also want to know which generates the least. You also want to know where in the middle other stations stand. If ambulance stations are broken up into "geographic areas", you also want to rate the stations within each individual area. It could be helpful for integrity testing as well as a barometer for supervision. This report only includes complaints.

Code 2, 3, 4

349 *AMBULANCE STATION - INVESTIGATIONS*

Not only do you want to know which ambulance station generates the most investigations, you also want to know which generates the least and where the other stations stand. If ambulance stations are broken up into "geographic areas", you also want to rate the stations within each area. This report includes only self-generated investigations.

Code 2, 3, 4

350 *AMBULANCE STATION CASES*

While you want to know which ambulance station generates the most cases, you also want to know which generates the least and where the other stations stand. If ambulance stations are broken up into "geographic areas", you also want to rate the stations within each area. This report includes both complaints and self-generated investigations.

Code 2, 3, 4

351 *AMBULANCE STATION COMPLAINTS* BROKEN DOWN BY *COMPLAINT TYPE*

Not only do you want to know how many complaints each ambulance station receives, you want to further break them down by call type, such as how many delay complaints or how many patient care complaints. This report only includes complaints.

Code 3, 4

352 *AMBULANCE STATION INVESTIGATIONS* BROKEN DOWN BY *COMPLAINT TYPE*

Not only do you want to know how many investigations each ambulance station is involved with, you want to further break them down by call type. How many delay complaints, how many patient care complaints; etcetera. This report includes only self-generated investigations.

Code 3, 4

353 *AMBULANCE STATION CASES* BY *COMPLAINT TYPE*

You want to know how many cases each ambulance station is involved with, and you will want to further break them down by call type. How many delay complaints, how many patient care complaints; etcetera. This report includes both complaints and self-generated investigations.

Code 3, 4

354 COMPARISON OF ALL *AMBULANCE STATION COMPLAINTS* VERSUS THEIR RESPECTIVE *RESPONSE TIMES* AND *CALL TYPES*

What this means is, if an ambulance station runs four ambulances, then you are comparing each of the four Station ambulances against each other by the number of complaints, by response times and by call type. This report only includes complaints.

Code 3, 4

355 COMPARISON OF *ALL AMBULANCE STATION INVESTIGATIONS* AND THEIR RESPECTIVE *REPONSE TIME* AND *CALL TYPES*

What this means is, if an ambulance station runs four ambulances, then you are comparing each of the four Station ambulances against each other by the number of investigations, by response times and by call type. This report includes only self-generated investigations.

Code 3, 4

356 COMPARISON OF ALL *AMBULANCE STATION CASES* AND THEIR RESPECTIVE *RESPONSE TIME* AND *CALL TYPES*

What this means is, if an ambulance station runs four ambulances, then you are comparing each of the four Station ambulances against each other by the number of investigations, by response times and by call type. This report includes both complaints and self-generated investigations.
Code 3, 4

357 NUMBER OF *COMPLAINTS* RECEIVED ON A CERTAIN DAY BY *COMPLAINT TYPE*

How many complaints were received on a certain calendar day, broken down by complaint type? This report only includes complaints.
Code 3, 4

358 NUMBER OF *SELF-GENERATED INVESTIGATIONS* INITIATED ON A CERTAIN DAY BY *COMPLAINT TYPE*

How many investigations were initiated on a certain calendar day, broken down by complaint type? This report only includes self-generated investigations.
Code 3, 4

359 *CALL VOLUME* VERSUS *COMPLAINT VOLUME* BY *TIME OF DAY*

To some degree there should be a relationship between these two stats. The two numbers will never be the same, and there will be times where one goes up while the other goes down. The way to compare them is by determining their "normal distribution" and then calculate their movement. This report only includes complaints.
Code 3, 4

360 AVERAGE ORGANIZATIONAL *TIME* SPENT *ON SCENE* OF CALL

This is an important stat to know. It involves all past responses organizational wide within a particular time frame. This report will allow you to compare the average on-scene time of the call which is under investigation to this stat.
Code 2, 3, 4

361 AVERAGE *TIME* SPENT *ON THE SCENE* OF A CALL BY *SUBJECT CREW COMPLAINT* RELATED

This will give you an average historical perspective of how long the subject crew spends on the scene of the call, where a complaint is filed, which then allows you to compare it to the call being investigated. This report includes only complaints.

Code 1, 2, 3, 4

362 AVERAGE *TIME* SPENT *ON* THE *SCENE* OF A CALL *BY SUBJECT CREW INVESTIGATIONS* RELATED

This will give you an average historical perspective of how long the subject crew spends on the scene of the call, where a self-generated investigation is initiated, which then allows you to compare it to the call being investigated. This report includes only self-generated investigations.

Code 1, 2, 3, 4

363 AVERAGE *TIME* SPENT *ON* THE *SCENE* OF A CALL BY *SUBJECT CREW CASES* RELATED

This will give you an average historical perspective of how long the subject crew spends on the scene of the call, cases related, which then allows you to compare it to the call being investigated. This report includes both complaints and self-generated investigations.

Code 1, 2, 3, 4

364 AVERAGE ORGANIZATIONAL *TIME* SPENT *ON-SCENE* OF CALL BY *RESOURCE LEVEL - EMT* AMBULANCE

This is an interesting stat involving all EMT related past responses within a particular time frame.

Code 2, 3, 4

365 AVERAGE ORGANIZATIONAL *TIME* SPENT *ON THE SCENE* OF A *CALL* BY *RESOURCE LEVEL - PARAMEDIC* AMBULANCE

This is an interesting stat involving all Paramedic related responses within a particular time frame.

Code 2, 3, 4

366 **AVERAGE ORGANIZATIONAL TIME SPENT ON THE SCENE OF A CALL BY RESOURCE LEVEL - DUAL RESPONSE (BOTH AN *EMT* AMBULANCE AND A *PARAMEDIC* AMBULANCE)**
This is an interesting stat involving both EMT and Paramedic dual responses within a particular time frame.
Code 2, 3, 4

367 **AVERAGE ORGANIZATIONAL *TIME* SPENT *ON-SCENE* OF A CALL BY *RESOURCE LEVEL - SUPERVISOR***
This is an important and interesting stat involving all Supervisor related responses within a particular time frame.
Code 2, 3, 4

368 **AVERAGE ORGANIZATIONAL *TIME* SPENT *ON-SCENE OF CALL* BY *CALL TYPE***
This is an important stat to know. It involves all past organizational responses within a particular time frame. You can compare the on-scene time and the call type of the call which is under investigation to this stat.
Code 2, 3, 4

369 **AVERAGE ORGANIZATIONAL *TIME* SPENT *AT HOSPITAL***
This is an important stat to know. It involves all past organizational responses within a particular time frame. You can compare the at-hospital time of the call which is under investigation to this stat.
Code 2, 3, 4

370 **AVERAGE ORGANIZATIONAL *TIME* SPENT *AT HOSPITAL BY RESOURCE LEVEL - EMT* AMBULANCE**
This is an important investigative stat to know. It involves all past EMT related organizational responses within a particular time frame. You can compare the at-hospital time of the call which is under investigation to this stat.
Code 2, 3, 4

371 **AVERAGE ORGANIZATIONAL** *TIME* **SPENT** *AT HOSPITAL* **BY** *RESOURCE LEVEL - PARAMEDIC* **AMBULANCE**

This is an important stat to know. It involves all past Paramedic related organizational responses within a particular time frame. You can compare the at-hospital time of the call which is under investigation to this stat.

Code 2, 3, 4

372 **AVERAGE ORGANIZATIONAL** *TIME* **SPENT** *AT-HOSPITAL* **BY** *RESOURCE* **LEVEL -** *SUPERVISOR*

This is an important stat to know. It involves all past Supervisor related organizational responses within a particular time frame. You can compare the at-hospital time of the call which is under investigation to this stat.

Code 2, 3, 4

373 **AVERAGE** *TIME* **SPENT** *AT SUBJECT HOSPITAL* **BY** *SUBJECT AMBULANCE*

This is an important stat to know. It involves all past organizational responses of the subject ambulance (not necessarily both crew members) during the same tour, within a particular time frame. You can compare the at-hospital time of the call which is under investigation to this stat.

Code 2, 3, 4

374 **AVERAGE** *TIME* **SPENT** *AT SUBJECT HOSPITAL* **BY** *SUBJECT CREW*

This is an important stat to know. It involves all past organizational responses by the subject crew when they worked together within a particular time frame. You can compare the at-hospital time of the call which is under investigation to this stat. This number will be different than the preceding report.

Code 1, 2, 3, 4

375 **AVERAGE ORGANIZATIONAL *TIME* SPENT *AT SUBJECT HOSPITAL* BY *COMPLAINT TYPE***

This is an important stat to know. You can compare the at-hospital time of the call which is under investigation to this stat.

Code 2, 3, 4

376 **ALL *HOSPITAL* COMPARISON OF ORGANIZATIONAL AVERAGE *TIME* SPENT *AT HOSPITAL***

The average time organizational units spend at individual hospitals for a specific time frame no matter what the call type was.

Code 3, 4

377 *CASES CLOSED* **BY** *COMPLAINT TYPE*

This is a traffic sheet related report. How many cases were closed during a particular period of time broken down by complaint type. This report should include both complaints and self-generated complaints.

Code 3, 4

378 *CASES CLOSED* **BY** *INVESTIGATIVE CLASSIFICATION*

This is a traffic sheet related report. How many cases were closed during a particular period of time broken down by call type? This report should include both complaints and self-generated investigations.

Code 3, 4

379 **HOW LONG DOES IT TAKE FROM THE TIME A *COMPLAINT* IS ASSIGNED TO AN *INVESTIGATOR* UNTIL THE INVESTIGATOR CONTACTS THE COMPLAINANT TO ACKNOWLEDGE RECEIPT OF THE COMPLAINT**

How long after a case being assigned, does it take an individual investigator to make actual contact with the complainant? If this process is handled correctly by the Investigative Unit, it will reap immediate rewards, and it will become a very important positive stat for the IU. This should be calculated by using calendar days. This report only pertains to complaints.

Code 2, 3, 4

380 **AVERAGE NUMBER OF DAYS *COMPLAINTS* REMAIN OPEN BY THE *IU*, BY *INVESTIGATOR* AND BY *COMPLAINT TYPE***

This is a traffic sheet related report. This report should be calculated by using calendar days. This report should only include complaints.
Code 3, 4

381 **AVERAGE NUMBER OF DAYS *SELF-GENERATED INVESTIGATIONS* REMAIN OPEN BY THE *IU*, BY *INVESTIGATOR* AND BY *COMPLAINT TYPE***

This is a traffic sheet related report. This report should be calculated by using calendar days. This report should only include self-generated investigations.
Code 3, 4

382 **AVERAGE NUMBER OF DAYS *CASES* REMAIN OPEN BY THE *IU*, BY *INVESTIGATOR* AND BY *COMPLAINT TYPE***

This is a traffic sheet related report. This report should be calculated by using calendar days. This report should include both complaints and self-generated investigations.
Code 3, 4

383 **AVERAGE NUMBER OF DAYS *COMPLAINTS* REMAIN OPEN BY *INVESTIGATIVE CLASSIFICATION***

This is a traffic sheet related report. This should be calculated by using calendar days. This report should include only complaints.
Code 3, 4

384 **AVERAGE NUMBER OF DAYS *SELF-GENERATED INVESTIGATIONS* REMAIN OPEN BY *INVESTIGATIVE CLASSIFICATION***

This is a traffic sheet related report. This should be calculated by using calendar days. This report should include only self-generated investigations.
Code 3, 4

385 AVERAGE NUMBER OF DAYS *CASES* REMAIN OPEN BY *INVESTIGATIVE CLASSIFICATION*

This is a traffic sheet related report. This should be calculated by using calendar days. This report should include only self-generated investigations.

Code 3, 4

386 NUMBER OF *COMPLAINTS* WHERE THERE WAS AN *OBSERVER* RIDING ON THE SUBJECT *AMBULANCE* OR *VEHICLE*

In this context, an "observer" is an individual (usually, but not exclusively) a non-organizational employee) who has obtained official permission to ride in a particular ambulance or supervisor's vehicle on a particular date and time. This shouldn't happen often, but it could occur. This information could come in handy when brought up by someone from your organization who is involved with the observer program. This report should only include complaints.

Code 2, 3, 4

387 NUMBER OF *SELF-GENERATED INVESTIGATIONS* WHERE THERE WAS AN *OBSERVER* RIDING ON THE SUBJECT *AMBULANCE* OR *VEHICLE*

An "observer" is an individual (usually, but not exclusively) a non-organizational employee) who has obtained official permission to ride in a particular ambulance or supervisor's vehicle on a particular date and time. This shouldn't happen often, but it could occur. This information could come in handy when brought up by someone from your organization who is involved with the observer program. This report should only include self-generated investigations

Code 2, 3, 4

388 NUMBER OF *CASES* WHERE THERE WAS AN *OBSERVER* RIDING ON THE *SUBJECT AMBULANCE* OR *VEHICLE*

An "observer" is an individual (usually, but not exclusively) a non-organizational employee) who has obtained official permission to ride in a particular ambulance or supervisor's vehicle on a particular date and time. This shouldn't happen often, but it could occur. This

information could come in handy when brought up by someone from your organization who is involved with the observer program. This report should include both complaints and self-generated investigations
Code 2, 3, 4

389 NUMBER OF *INVESTIGATIONS* WHERE THERE WAS AN *OBSERVER* RIDING ON THE *SUBJECT AMBULANCE* OR *VEHICLE*

This is an interesting stat. It could come into play when someone in the organizations asks about observers when re-configuring the observer program. This report includes only self-generated investigations.
Code 2, 3, 4

390 NUMBER OF *CASES* WHERE THERE WAS AN *OBSERVER* RIDING ON THE *SUBJECT AMBULANCE* OR *VEHICLE*

This is an interesting stat. It could come into play when someone in the organizations asks about observers when re-configuring the observer program. This report includes both complaints and This is an interesting stat. It could come into play when someone in the organizations asks about observers when re-configuring the observer program. This report includes only self-generated investigations.
Code 2, 3, 4

391 NUMBER OF *COMPLAINTS* WHERE THE *OBSERVER* WAS THE *SUBJECT* OF THE COMPLAINT

This should be a lower number than the above report would be, but it could happen.
This report should only include complaints.
Code 2, 3, 4

392 NUMBER OF *INVESTIGATIONS* WHERE THE *OBSERVER* WAS THE *SUBJECT* OF THE INVESTIGATION

This report should also yield a low number. This report should include only self-generated investigations.
Code 2, 3, 4

393 **NUMBER OF *CASES* WHERE THE *OBSERVER* WAS THE *SUBJECT* OF THE INVESTIGATION**
This report should also yield a low number. This report should include both complaints and self-generated investigations.
Code 2, 3, 4

394 **PERCENTAGE OF *CASES* WHERE THE *OBSERVER* WAS THE *SUBJECT* OF THE INVESTIGATION VERSUS NOT BEING THE SUBJECT**
This is an interesting stat to have. This report should include both complaints and self-generated complaints.
Code 2, 3, 4

395 **PERCENTAGE OF *CASES* THAT INVOLVE AN *OBSERVER* VERSUS THOSE THAT DON'T**
The percentage of cases that involve an observer (in any capacity) versus those cases that do not. This report should include both complaints and self-generated investigations.
Code 2, 3, 4

396 **NUMBER OF *"HOAX 9-1-1 CALLS"*- *COMPLAINTS***
This is another area that hopefully doesn't happen often, but it is an important stat. This report only includes complaints.
Code 2, 3, 4

397 **NUMBER OF *"HOAX 9-1-1 CALLS"*- *INVESTIGATIONS***
This is another area that hopefully doesn't happen often. This report includes only self-generated investigations.
Code 2, 3, 4

398 **NUMBER OF *"HOAX 9-1-1 CALLS"* - *CASES***
This is another area that hopefully doesn't happen often. This report includes both complaints and self-generated investigations.
Code 2, 3, 4

399 PERCENTAGE OF *"HOAX 9-1-1 CALLS"* COMPLAINTS TO NON-HOAX *COMPLAINTS*

This should be a very low number. This report only includes complaints.
Code 2, 3, 4

400 PERCENTAGE OF *"HOAX 9-1-1 CALLS"* INVESTIGATINS TO NON-HOAX INVESTIGATIONS

This is an important background report. This report only includes self-generated investigations.
Code 2, 3, 4

401 PERCENTAGE OF *"HOAX 9-1-1 CALLS"* CASES TO NON-HOAX CASES

This is another important background report. This only includes self-generated investigations.
Code 2, 3, 4

402 *INTER-AGENCY TRANSFER* ISSUE - *COMPLAINT* RELATED

This should not happen often. This report should include only complaints.
Code 2, 3, 4

403 *INTER-AGENCY TRANSFER* ISSUE - *SELF-GENERATED INVESTIGATIONS* RELATED

This should not happen often. This report should include only self-generated investigations.
Code 2, 3, 4

404 *INTER-AGENCY TRANSFER* ISSUE - *CASES* RELATED

This should not happen often. This report should include both complaints and self-generated investigations.
Code 2, 3, 4

405 **NUMBER AND *COMPLAINT TYPES* OF *COMPLAINTS* WHERE ORGANIZATIONAL ISSUED *GPS* WAS USED**
This is just an interesting investigative-tool stat to have. This report includes only complaints.
Code 4

406 **NUMBER AND *COMPLAINT TYPES* OF *INVESTIGATIONS* WHERE ORGANIZATIONAL ISSUED *GPS* WAS USED**
This is an important background report. This includes only self-generated investigations.
Code 4

407 **NUMBER AND *COMPLAINT TYPES* OF *CASES* WHERE ORGANIZATIONAL ISSUED GPS WAS USED**
This is an important background report. This includes both complaints and self-generated investigations.
Code 4

408 **PERCENTAGE OF *COMPLAINTS* WHERE ORGANIZATIONAL ISSUED *GPS* WAS USED VERSUS NOT USED**
This is an interesting stat to have. This report includes only complaints.
Code 4

409 **PERCENTAGE OF *INVESTIGATIONS* WHERE ORGANIZATIONAL ISSUED *GPS* WAS USED VERSUS NOT USED**
This is also an interesting stat. This report involves only self-generated investigations.
Code 4

410 **PERCENTAGE OF CASES WHERE ORGANIZATIONAL ISSUED *GPS* USED VERSUS NOT USED**
This is also an interesting stat. This report involves both complaints and self-generated investigations.
Code 4

411 **NUMBER OF *COMPLAINTS* WHERE *CELL PHONE RECORDS* (EMPLOYEE OR ORGANIZATIONAL) WERE OBTAINED AND/OR USED**

This is an important investigative tool. This report includes only complaints.
Code 4

412 **NUMBER OF *INVESTIGATIONS* WHERE *CELL PHONE RECORDS* (EMPLOYEE or ORGANIZATIONAL) WERE OBTAINED AND/OR USED**

This is an important background report. This report includes only self-generated investigations.
Code 4

413 **NUMBER OF *CASES* WHERE *CELL PHONE RECORDS* (EMPLOYEE OR ORGANIZATIONAL) WERE OBTAINED AND/OR USED**

This is an important background report. This report includes both complaints and self-generated investigations.
Code 4

414 **PERCENTAGE OF *COMPLAINTS* WHERE *CELL PHONE RECORDS* (EMPLOYEE OR ORGANIZATIONAL) WERE OBTAINED AND/OR USED**

This is an important investigative tool. This report includes only complaints.
Code 4

415 **PERCENTAGE OF *INVESTIGATIONS* WHERE (EMPLOYEE OR ORGANIZATIONAL) CELL PHONE RECORDS WERE OBTAINED AND/OR USED**

This is an important report. It involves only self-generated investigations.
Code 4

416 **PERCENTAGE OF CASES WHERE (EMPLOYEE OR ORGANIZATIONAL)** *CELL PHONE RECORDS* **WERE OBTAINED AND/OR USED**

This is an important report. It involves both complaints and self-generated investigations.

Code 4

417 **NUMBER OF** *COMPLAINTS* **WHERE** *CELL PHONE GPS* **(TOWER INFORMATION) WAS OBTAINED AND UTILIZED**

The number of complaints where cell phone GPS was obtained and used. This report includes only complaints.

Code 4

418 **NUMBER OF** *INVESTIGATIONS* **WHERE** *CELL PHONE GPS RECORDS* **(TOWER INFORMATION) WAS OBTAINED AND UTILIZED**

The number of investigations where cell phone GPS was obtained and used. This report includes only self-generated investigations.

Code 4

419 **NUMBER OF** *CASES* **WHERE** *CELL PHONE GPS RECORDS* **(TOWER INFORMATION) WAS OBTAINED AND UTILIZED**

The number of cases where cell phone GPS was obtained and used. This report includes both complaints and self-generated investigations.

Code 4

420 **PERCENTAGE OF** *CASES* **WHERE** *CELL PHONE GPS RECORDS* **(TOWER INFORMATION) WAS OBTAINED AND UTILIZED**

The percentage of cases where cell phone GPS was obtained and used. This report includes both complaints and self-generated investigations.

Code 4

421 ***RESPONSE TIME* AND *CALL VOLUME* VERSUS *COMPLAINT VOLUME***

A comparison of three issues which can be useful when an organization is looking into the issue of rising response time and its relationship to complaint volume. This report only includes complaints.
Code 4

422 ***RESPONSE TIME* AND *CALL VOLUME* VERSUS *INVESTIGATIONS VOLUME***

A comparison between three important issues. A comparison of three issues which can be useful when an organization is looking into the issue of rising response time and its relationship to investigations. This report includes only self-generated investigations.
Code 4

423 **RESPONSE TIME AND *CALL VOLUME* VERSUS *CASES VOLUME***

A comparison between three important issues. A comparison of three issues which can be useful when an organization is looking into the issue of rising response time and its relationship to investigations. This report includes both complaints and self-generated investigations.
Code 4

424 ***CALL VOLUME* VERSUS *COMPLAINT VOLUME***

A comparison between two important issues. This report only includes complaints.
Code 4

425 ***CALL VOLUME* VERSUS *INVESTIGATIONS VOLUME***

A comparison between two important issues. This report includes only self-generated investigations.
Code 4

426 ***CALL VOLUME* VERSUS *CASES VOLUME***

A comparison between two important issues. This report includes both complaints and self-generated investigations.
Code 4

427 *RESPONSE TIME* VERSUS *COMPLAINT VOLUME*

This is simply a comparison of two stats. This report includes only complaints.
Code 4

428 *RESPONSE TIME* VERSUS *INVESTIGATIONS VOLUME*

This is also a comparison of two stats. This includes only self-generated investigations.
Code 4

429 *RESPONSE TIME* VERSUS *CASE VOLUME*

This is another comparison of two stats. It includes both complaints and self-generated investigations.
Code 4

430 OTHER - *COMPLAINTS*

This report captures all complaints that are not encapsulated in any of the other complaint related reports. This report includes only complaints.
Code 4

431 OTHER - *INVESTIGATIONS*

This report captures all investigations that are not encapsulated in any of the other investigations related reports. This report includes only self-generated investigations.
Code 4

432 *OTHER - CASES*

This report captures all cases that are not encapsulated in any of the other investigations related reports. This report includes both complaints and self-generated investigations.
Code 4

433 *EMPLOYEE ASSAULTED* (ON DUTY) - *COMPLAINTS*

While this type of incident will probably be investigated by others (law enforcement), if a particular employee gets involved in this type of matter multiple times, it warrants further investigation. Likely it shows an aggressive behavior pattern of the employee that could

suggest the likelihood of future serious multiple complaints. It is likely that the IU will only hear about this type of situation via internal organizational reports. This report should only include complaints.
Code 1, 2, 3, 4

434 ***EMPLOYEE ASSAULTED* (ON DUTY) - *INVESTIGATIONS***
While this type of incident will probably be investigated by others (law enforcement), if a particular employee gets involved in this type of matter multiple times, it warrants further investigation. Likely it shows an aggressive behavior pattern of the employee that could suggest the likelihood of future serious multiple complaints. It is likely that the IU will only hear about this type of situation via internal organizational reports. This report should only include self-generated investigations.
Code 1, 2, 3, 4

435 ***EMPLOYEE ASSAULTED* (ON DUTY) - *CASES***
While this type of incident will probably be investigated by others (law enforcement), if a particular employee gets involved in this type of matter multiple times, it warrants further investigation. Likely it shows an aggressive behavior pattern of the employee that could suggest the likelihood of future serious multiple complaints. It is likely that the IU will only hear about this type of situation via internal organizational reports. This report should only both complaints and self-generated investigations.
Code 1, 2, 3, 4

436 **LAPSE OF EMPLOYEE *MEDICAL CERTIFICATION(S)* – BY *RANK***
This is a report of investigations into allegations that job required medical certifications have expired, and that the subject employees are still working their jobs. This issue is a serious one, and if left alone can "snowball" into involving many employees over time. This includes both complaints and self-generated investigations.
Code 3, 4

437 LAPSE OF CERTIFICATION(S) – SUPERVISORS/ MANAGERIAL

This report pertains to supervisor's who oversee employee certifications, who, either purposely or accidentally, allow employee certifications to expire, thereby permitting employees with expired certifications to continue to work and provide patient care while uncertified. There could be instances where supervisory or managerial personnel might have knowledge of some or all of the lapses of certifications and fail to take appropriate corrective action. If that turns out to be the case, they too should become the subjects of an investigation.
Code 3, 4

438 FALSIFICATION OF *CERTIFICATIONAL* PAPERWORK

This report involves allegations that subject employee(s) falsified official paperwork to obtain a re-certification or a new certification, a requirement of the job. Unfortunately, this happens more than you would think. While researching material for this book, I performed a quick internet search and came up with a number of articles about cheating on certification or re-certifications in ten different states. On first glance, it would appear that the majority of these cases involved firefighters more so than EMTs or Paramedics. I am not suggesting EMTs or Paramedics haven't been involved in this type of activity, because they have. This is one of those areas where notifications may have to be made, and where the matter may have to be turned over to an authorized outside agency for investigation, or it could become a joint investigation between the Investigations Unit and the outside investigative agency. This type of investigation is not as difficult to conduct as you might think, especially if your organization is adamant about preserving its integrity. On occasion these cases can involve multiple personnel that are assigned to training academies, which would lead to a large-scale investigation.

Once you become aware of issues of falsified certification paperwork (usually this goes hand-in-hand with cheating) you'll want to open up a historical investigation. One of the articles I read on this type of activity reported that a number of firefighters were found to have falsified their certification once, while a smaller group were found to

have done this twice. The second group was punished more harshly than the first group.
Code 3, 4

439 LAPSE OF EMPLOYEE NON-MEDICAL CERTIFICATION(S) – BY RANK

This is a report of investigations into allegations that job required non-medical certifications have expired, and that the subject employees are still working their jobs.
The most common example of this is a driver's license.
Code 3, 4

440 PROVIDING PATIENT CARE ABOVE/BELOW AN EMPLOYEE'S LEVEL OF MEDICAL CERTIFICATION

This breach of conduct does happen more than you would think, and usually is an issue of providing patient care above an employee's organizational certification level. An employee for your organization is authorized to provide medical care at a certain medical level based upon organizational records of the employee's level of medical training, as well as appropriate refresher training and continuing medical educational (CME) requirements. What could happen is an employee could obtain a higher level of medical training for a second job (not for your organization). This higher level of certification may even have been obtained from another state. Then one day while working for your organization the employee comes across a medical situation at a 9-1-1 call and uses techniques from the higher level of training. This may be admirable but is likely against policy. This includes both complaints and self-generated investigations.
Code 1, 2, 3, 4

441 ALLEGATIONS OF HAZING - AT TRAINING ACADEMY

Any case that alleges there was hazing occurring at the Organizational Training Academy. This includes both complaints and self-generated investigations.
Code 4

442 **ALLEGATIONS OF** *HAZING* **- AT** *AMBULANCE STATION - CASES*

Any case that alleges there was hazing occurring at an Organizational Ambulance Station. This includes both complaints and self-generated investigations.
Code 4

443 **ALLEGATIONS OF** *HAZING* **- AT FIRE HOUSE**

Any case that alleges there was hazing occurring at an Organizational Fire House. This includes both complaints and self-generated investigations.
Code 4

444 **PERCENTAGE OF** *HAZING* **ALLEGATIONS – BY LOCATION**

The percentage of all hazing allegations at the Training Academy, EMS Stations or at Fire Houses, compared to each other.
Code 4

445 **NUMBER OF TIMES ORGANIZATIONAL** *PREVENTIVE MAINTENANCE* **RECORDS WERE OBTAINED RELATED TO A** *COMPLAINT*

This is an informative report. This report only includes complaints.
Code 3, 4

446 **NUMBER OF TIMES ORGANIZATIONAL** *PREVENTIVE MAINTENANCE* **RECORDS WERE OBTAINED AND USED FOR AN** *INVESTIGATION*

This is an interesting report. This report only includes self-generated investigations.
Code 3, 4

447 **NUMBER OF TIMES ORGANIZATIONAL** *PREVENTIVE MAINTENANCE* **RECORDS WERE OBTAINED AND USED FOR** *CASES*

This can be an important s report. This report only includes complaints and self-generated investigations.
Code 3, 4

448 PERCENTAGE OF *CASES* WHERE ORGANIZATIONAL *PREVENTIVE MAINTENANCE RECORDS* WERE OBTAINED AND USED VERSUS CASES WHERE THEY WEREN'T OBTAINED

This is an interesting report. This report includes both complaints and self-generated investigations.

Code 3, 4

449 NUMBER OF TIMES ORGANIZATIONAL *RADIO REPAIR* RECORDS WERE OBTAINED AND USED FOR A *COMPLAINT*

This is an interesting report. This report only includes complaints.

Code 3, 4

450 NUMBER OF TIMES ORGANIZATIONAL *RADIO REPAIR* RECORDS WERE OBTAINED AND USED FOR AN *INVESTIGATION*

This is an interesting report. It includes only self-generated investigations.

Code 3, 4

451 NUMBER OF TIMES ORANIZATIONAL *RADIO REPAIR RECORDS* WERE OBTAINED AND USED FOR *CASES*

This is an interesting report. It includes both complaints and self-generated investigations.

Code 3, 4

452 PERCENTAGE OF *CASES* WHERE ORGANIZATIONAL *RADIO REPAIR* RECORDS WERE OBTAINED AND USED VERSUS CASES WHERE THEY WEREN'T OBTAINED

This is an interesting report. It includes both complaints and self-generated investigations.

Code 3, 4

453 **NUMBER OF TIMES *A FALSE AMBULANCE CALL REPORT (ACR)* WAS FILED - *COMPLAINT* RELATED**

This is an interesting report. This report only includes complaints.
Code 3, 4

454 **NUMBER OF TIMES A *FALSE AMBULANCE CALL REPORT* (ACR) WAS FILED - *INVESTIGATION* RELATED**

This is an interesting report. This report includes only self-generated investigations.
Code 3, 4

455 **NUMBER OF TIMES A FALSE *AMBULANCE CALL REPORT* (ACR) WAS FILED - *CASES* RELATED**

This is an interesting report. This report includes both complaints and self-generated investigations.
Code 3, 4

456 **PERCENTAGE OF *CASES* WHERE A *FALSE AMBULANCE CALL* REPORT (ACR) WAS FILED VERSUS CASES WHERE ONE WASN'T FILED**

This is an interesting report. It includes both complaints and self-generated investigations.
Code 3, 4

457 ***COMPLAINTS* BY EXTERNAL *IDENTIFICATION NUMBERS***

As important as a complaint related case number is to the IU, external ID numbers are just as important to the sender. This report only includes complaints.
Code 3, 4

458 ***INVESTIGATIONS* BY EXTERNAL *IDENTIFICATION NUMBERS***

As important as an investigation's related case number is to the IU, external ID numbers are just as important to the sender. Senders can include the Police, Fire Marshals or the local State Department of Health. This report includes only self-generated investigations.
Code 3, 4

459 *CASES* **BY EXTERNAL IDENTIFICATION NUMBERS**

As important as an investigation's related case number is to the IU, external ID numbers are just as important to the sender. Senders can include the Police, Fire Marshals or the local State Department of Health. This report includes both complaints and self-generated investigations.

Code 3, 4

460 NUMBER OF *COMPLAINTS* **WHERE** *CELL PHONE VIDEO* **WAS PROVIDED DIRECTLY TO THE INVESTIGATIVE UNIT BY THE** *COMPLAINANT* **OR A** *WITNESS*

This is a managerial investigative tool. This report only includes complaints.

Code 2, 3, 4

461 NUMBER OF *INVESTIGATIONS* **WHERE** *CELL PHONE VIDEO* **WAS PROVIDED DIRECTLY TO THE INVESTIGATIVE UNIT BY THE** *COMPLAINANT* **OR A** *WITNESS*

This is a managerial investigative tool. This report only includes self-generated investigations.

Code 2, 3, 4

462 NUMBER OF *CASES* **WHERE** *CELL PHONE VIDEO* **WAS PROVIDED DIRECTLY TO THE INVESTIGATIVE UNIT BY THE** *COMPLAINANT* **OR A** *WITNESS*

This is a managerial investigative tool. This report includes both complaints and self-generated investigations.

Code 2, 3, 4

463 PERCENTAGE OF *COMPLAINTS* **WHERE** *CELL PHONE VIDEO* **WAS PROVIDED DIRECTLY TO THE INVESTIGATIVE UNIT**

This is a managerial investigative tool. This report only includes complaints.

Code 2, 3, 4

464 **PERCENTAGE OF *INVESTIGATIONS* WHERE *CELL PHONE VIDEO* WAS PROVIDED TO THE INVESTIGATIVE UNIT**

This is a managerial investigative tool. This report includes both complaints and self-generated investigations.

Code 2, 3, 4

465 **PERCENTAGE OF *CASES* WHERE *CELL PHONE VIDEO* WAS PROVIDED TO THE INVESTIGATIVE UNIT**

This is a managerial investigative tool. This report includes both complaints and self-generated investigations.

Code 2, 3, 4

466 **NUMBER OF *COMPLAINTS* THAT WERE SUBSTANTIATED WHERE *CELL PHONE VIDEO* WAS PROVIDED TO THE INVESTIGATIVE UNIT**

This is a managerial investigative tool. This report only includes complaints.

Code 2, 3, 4

467 **PERCENTAGE OF *COMPLAINTS* THAT WERE SUBSTANTIATED WHERE *CELL PHONE VIDEO* WAS PROVIDED TO THE INVESTIGATIVE UNIT VERSUS COMPLAINTS WHERE THERE WAS NO CELL PHONE VIDEO PROVIDED**

This is a managerial investigative tool. This report only includes complaints.

Code 2, 3, 4

468 **NUMBER OF *INVESTIGATIONS* THAT WERE SUBSTANTIATED WHERE *CELL PHONE VIDEO* WAS PROVIDED TO THE INVESTIGATIVE UNIT**

This is a managerial investigative tool. This report only includes self-generated investigations.

Code 2, 3, 4

469 PERCENTAGE OF *INVESTIGATIONS* THAT WERE *SUBSTANTIATED* WHERE *CELL PHONE VIDEO* WAS PROVIDED TO THE INVESTIGATIVE UNIT VERSUS COMPLAINTS WHERE THERE WAS NO CELL PHONE VIDEO PROVIDED

This is a managerial investigative tool. This report only includes complaints.
Code 2, 3, 4

470 NUMBER OF *CASES* THAT WERE *SUBSTANTIATED* WHERE *CELL PHONE VIDEO* WAS PROVIDED TO THE INVESTIGATIVE UNIT

This is a managerial investigative tool. This report includes both complaints and self-generated investigations.
Code 2, 3, 4

471 NUMBER OF *COMPLAINTS* WHERE IT WAS ALLEGED THAT A *CREW MEMBER* PHYSICALLY KNOCKED A *CELL PHONE* OUT OF THE COMPLAINANT'S OR WITNESSES HANDS

This is a managerial investigative tool. This report only includes complaints.
Code 2, 3, 4

472 NUMBER OF *INVESTIGATIONS* WHERE IT WAS ALLEGED THAT A *CREW MEMBER* PHYSICALLY KNOCKED A *CELL PHONE* OUT OF THE COMPLAINANT'S OR WITNESSES HANDS

This is a managerial investigative tool. This report only includes complaints.
Code 2, 3, 4

473 NUMBER OF *CASES* WHERE IT WAS ALLEGED THAT A *CREW MEMBER* PHYSICALLY KNOCKED A *CELL PHONE* OUT OF THE COMPLAINANT'S OR WITNESSES HANDS

This is a managerial investigative tool. This report only includes complaints.
Code 2, 3, 4

474 PERCENTAGE OF *CASES* WHERE IT WAS ALLEGED THAT A *CREW MEMBER* PHYSICALLY KNOCKED A *CELL PHONE* OUT OF THE COMPLAINANTS OR A WITNESS'S HANDS

This is a managerial investigative tool. This report only includes complaints.

Code 2, 3, 4

475 WEARING ORGANIZATIONAL *UNIFORM* OFF DUTY - WITHOUT AUTHORIZATION-*COMPLAINT* RELATED

This is a managerial investigative tool. It includes only complaints.

Code 3, 4

476 WEARING ORGANIZATIONAL *UNIFORM* OFF DUTY - WITHOUT AUTHORIZATION - *INVESTIGATIONS* RELATED

This is a managerial investigative tool. It includes only self-generated investigations.

Code 3, 4

477 WEARING ORGANIZATIONAL *UNIFORM* OFF DUTY - WITHOUT AUTHORIZATION - *CASES* RELATED

This is a managerial investigative tool. It includes both complaints and self-generated investigations.

Code 3, 4

478 *COMPLAINT* RISE PERCENTAGE COMPARED TO THE PERCENTAGE OF *EMPLOYEES WITH MULTIPLE COMPLAINTS*

The comparison of complaint rises to the number of employees that have multiple complaints associated with them is an investigative vital sign that should be closely monitored. You are looking to determine if the pool of employees with multiple complaints is rising, and if it is to what degree? This might be a cause or partial cause for the rise in complaints. This report only includes complaints.

Code 3, 4

479 **NUMBER AND TYPES OF *COMPLAINTS* WHERE ORGANIZATIONAL RELATED *E-Z PASS RECORDS* WERE USED**

This is an interesting report. This report only includes complaints.
Code 3, 4

480 **NUMBER AND TYPES OF *INVESTIGATIONS* WHERE ORGANIZATIONAL RELATED *E-Z PASS RECORDS* WERE USED**

This is an interesting report. This report only includes self-generated investigations.
Code 3, 4

481 **NUMBER AND TYPES OF *CASES* WHERE ORGANIZATIONAL RELATED *E-Z PASS RECORDS* WERE USED**

This is an interesting report. This report includes both complaints and self-generated investigations.
Code 3, 4

482 **PERCENTAGE OF *COMPLAINTS* WHERE ORGANIZATIONAL *E-Z PASS RECORDS* WERE USED VERSUS THOSE COMPLAINTS WHERE THEY WEREN'T**

This is an interesting report. This report only includes complaints.
Code 3, 4

483 **PERCENTAGE OF *INVESTIGATIONS* WHERE ORGANIZATIONAL *E-Z PASS RECORDS* WERE USED VERSUS THOSE INVESTIGATIONS WHERE THEY WEREN'T USED**

This is an interesting report. This report includes only self-generated investigation.
Code 3, 4

484 **PERCENTAGE OF *CASES* WHERE ORGANIZATIONAL *E-Z PASS RECORDS* WERE USED VERSUS THOSE INVESTIGATIONS WHERE THEY WEREN'T USED**

This is an interesting report. This report includes both complaints and self-generated investigation.

Code 3, 4

485 ***PATIENT* PROFILE INFORMATION WHERE A COMPLAINT HAS BEEN FILED**

This report is strictly for developing profiles of all patient information for integrity testing, (a subject I covered in my first book). Prior to developing and using this report, I would run it past your organization's legal division to ensure there could be no problems gathering this information. This report is for complaints only.

Code 3, 4

486 ***MEDICAL RESOURCE* "BUFFING" A CALL - NO *PATIENT CARE* PROVIDED – CASES RELATED**

Any medical resource that that responds to the scene of a call without authorization and did not provide any patient care. This report includes both complaints and self-generated investigations.

Code 3, 4

487 ***MEDICAL RESOURCE* BUFFING A CALL - *PATIENT CARE* PROVIDED CASES RELATED**

Any medical resource that responds to the scene of a call without authorization and provided any patient care. This report includes both complaints and self-generated investigations.

Code 3, 4

488 **ASSIGNED ORGANIZATIONAL *MEDICAL RESOURCE* DID NOT RESPOND ON A CALL - CASES RELATED**

Any organizational medical resource (EMT ambulance, Paramedic ambulance, EMS supervisor or Fire Department unit) that was assigned to a call but did not respond. This report includes both complaints and self-generated investigations.

Code 3, 4

489 COMPLETED *COMPLAINTS, SUBSTANTIATED,* WHERE *WRONGDOING* WAS NOTED

This is both a traffic sheet related report and a managerial related report. It includes only complaints.

Code 3, 4

490 COMPLETED *INVESTIGATIONS, SUBSTANTIATED,* WHERE *WRONGDOING WAS* NOTED

This is both a traffic sheet related report and a managerial related report. It includes only self-generated investigations.

Code 3, 4

491 COMPLETED *CASES, SUBSTANTIATED, WHERE WRONGDOING WAS NOTED*

This is both a traffic sheet related report and a managerial related report. It is a listing of all cases that were substantiated with wrongdoing noted. This includes both complaints and self-generated investigations.

Code 3, 4

492 PERCENTAGE OF COMPLETED CASES, SUBSTANTIATED, WHERE WRONGDOING WAS NOTED

This is both a traffic sheet related report and a managerial related report. It is a listing of all cases that were substantiated with wrongdoing noted. This includes both complaints and self-generated investigations.

Code 3, 4

493 COMPLETED *COMPLAINTS, SUBSTANTIATED,* WHERE *NO WRONGDOING WAS* NOTED

This is both a traffic sheet related report and a managerial related report. It is a listing of all cases that were substantiated with no wrongdoing being noted. This report includes only complaints.

Code 3, 4

494 COMPLETED *INVESTIGATIONS*, SUBSTANTIATED, WITH *NO WRONGDOING* NOTED

This is both a traffic sheet related report and a managerial related report. It is a listing of all investigations that were substantiated with no wrongdoing being noted. This report includes only self-generated investigations.

Code 3, 4

495 COMPLETED *CASES, SUBSTANTIATED, NO WRONGDOING NOTED*

A listing of all cases that were substantiated with no wrongdoing being noted. This includes both complaints and self-generated investigations.

Code 3,

496 PERCENTAGE OF COMPLETED *CASES, SUBSTANTIATED*, NO *WRONGDOING* NOTED

A listing of all cases that were substantiated with no wrongdoing being noted. This includes both complaints and self-generated investigations.

Code 3,

497 COMPLETED COMPLAINTS PARTIALLY SUBSTANTIATED, WRONGDOING NOTED

A listing of all complaints that were partially substantiated with wrongdoing being noted. This includes only complaints.

Code 3,

498 COMPLETED INVESTIGATIONS PARTIALLY SUBSTANTIATED, WRONGDOING NOTED

A listing of all investigations that were partially substantiated with wrongdoing being noted. This includes only self-generated investigations.

Code 3,

499 COMPLETED CASES PARTIALLY *SUBSTANTIATED, WRONGDOING NOTED*

A listing of all cases that were partially substantiated with wrongdoing being noted. This includes both complaints and self-generated investigations.
Code 3, 4

500 PERCENTAGE OF COMPLETED CASES PARTIALLY SUBSTANTIATED, WRONGDOING NOTED

A listing of all cases that were partially substantiated with wrongdoing being noted. This includes both complaints and self-generated investigations.
Code 3, 4

501 PARTIALLY *SUBSTANTIATED COMPLAINTS, NO WRONGDOING NOTED*

A listing of all complaints that were partially substantiated with no wrongdoing noted. This report includes only complaints.
Code 3, 4

502 PARTIALLY *SUBSTANTIATED INVESTIGATIONS, NO WRONGDOING NOTED*

A listing of all investigations that were partially substantiated with no wrongdoing noted. This report includes only self-generated investigations.
Code 3, 4

503 PARTIALLY *SUBSTANTIATED CASES, NO WRONGDOING NOTED*

A listing of all cases that were partially substantiated with no wrongdoing noted. This report includes both complaints and self-generated investigations.
Code 3, 4

504 PERCENTAGE OF CASES PARTIALLY SUBSTANTIATED, NO WRONGDOING NOTED

A listing of all cases that were partially substantiated with no wrongdoing noted. This report includes both complaints and self-generated investigations.
Code 3, 4

505 **UNSUBSTANTIATED COMPLAINTS**
A listing of all complaints that were unsubstantiated with no wrongdoing noted. This report includes only complaints.
Code 3, 4

506 **UNSUBSTANTIATED INVESTIGATIONS**
A listing of all investigations that were unsubstantiated with no wrongdoing noted. This report includes only self-generated investigations.
Code 3, 4

507 *UNSUBSTANTIATED CASES*
A listing of all cases that were unsubstantiated. This includes both complaints and self-generated investigations.
Code 3, 4

508 **PERCENTAGE OF UNSUBSTANTIATED CASES**
A listing of all cases that were unsubstantiated with no wrongdoing noted. This report includes both complaints and self-generated investigations.
Code 3, 4

509 **UNFOUNDED COMPLAINTS**
A listing of all complaints that were partially unfounded with no wrongdoing noted. This report includes only complaints.
Code 3, 4

510 **UNFOUNDED INVESTIGATIONS**
A listing of all investigations that were partially unfounded with no wrongdoing noted. This report includes only self-generated investigations.
Code 3, 4

511 *UNFOUNDED CASES*
A listing of all cases that were unfounded. This includes both complaints and self-generated investigations.
Code 3, 4

512 *DUPLICATE COMPLAINTS*

A listing of all complaints that were closed as being a duplicate of another complaint, investigation or case. This report includes only complaints.

Code 4

513 **DUPLICATE INVESTIGATIONS**

A listing of all investigations that were closed as being a duplicate of another complaint/investigation or case. This includes only self-generated investigations.

Code 4

514 **DUPLICATE CASES**

A listing of all cases that were closed as being a duplicate of another complaint/investigation or case. This includes both complaints and self-generated investigations.

Code 4

515 **ALL *FINAL DISPOSITION* REPORT, NUMBER AND PERCENTAGE**

A breakdown of all referenced cases by their final disposition (Substantiated-A, Substantiated-B, Partially Substantiated-A, Partially Substantiated-B, Unsubstantiated, Unfounded or Duplicate Case). This report includes both complaints and self-generated investigations.

Code 3, 4

516 **THE NUMBER OF ALL *OFF-DUTY ARRESTS***

The number of all employee off duty arrests no matter the charge. This includes both complaints and self-generated investigations.

Code 3, 4

517 **THE NUMBER OF ALL *ON-DUTY ARRESTS***

The number of all employee on duty arrests no matter the charge. This number will certainly be lower than the previous report. This includes both complaints and self-generated investigations.

Code 3, 4

518 **THE NUMBER OF ALL *OFF-DUTY ARRESTS* BY *RANK***
The number of all off duty arrests no matter the charge. This includes both complaints and self-generated investigations.
Code 3, 4

519 **THE NUMBER OF *ON-DUTY ARRESTS* BY *RANK***
The number of all on duty arrests no matter the charge. This includes both complaints and investigations.
Code 3, 4

520 **THE NUMBER OF ALL *OFF-DUTY ARRESTS* BY *AMBULANCE STATION***
The number of all off duty arrests no matter the charge. This includes both complaints and self-generated investigations.
Code 3, 4

521 **THE NUMBER OF ALL *ON-DUTY ARRESTS* BY *AMBULANCE STATION***
The number of all on duty arrests no matter the charge. This includes both complaints and self-generated investigations.
Code 3, 4

522 **THE NUMBER OF ALL ON-DUTY ARRESTS BY AMBULANCE STATION AND BY RANK**
The number of all on duty arrests no matter the charge. This includes both complaints and investigations.
Code 3, 4

523 **THE NUMBER OF ALL OFF-DUTY ARRESTS BY AMBULANCE STATION AND BY RANK**
The number of all on duty arrests no matter the charge. This includes both complaints and investigations.
Code 3, 4

524 **SUBJECT *LOCATION* BASIC INTERNET *CHECKS***
A quick internet check of the subject address, as well as adjoining addresses for background information might provide you with a quick investigative avenue to pursue. There are a certain class of cases that

will require more extensive location checks. The internet location check is meant for the other cases.
Code 1, 2, 3, 4

525 ORGANIZATIONAL OVERTIME ABUSE

Overtime refers to working an extra tour and receiving additional money (over and above the normal salary). You want to make sure that all overtime is used for legitimate purposes.
Code 3, 4

526 COMPLAINANT REPORT

This report breaks down complainants into one of the following four categories:
- Patient
- Witness
- Family member
- Other

This report includes only complaints
Code 2, 3, 4

INVESTIGATIVE TURN-AROUND REPORTS

Investigative Turn-Around-Reports are time specific barometers which document how long it takes the investigative unit as a whole, or each individual investigator to process investigations from beginning to end. If these reports are set up properly, they can document investigative activities as well. By running specific turn-around-reports, you can tell how well the investigative unit is doing. In terms of importance, turn-around stats are to the investigative unit, what response time and call volume stats are to the EMS organization. With that being said, I have learned that when dealing with individual investigators, what you will find is that each individual investigator will close cases or complete investigative tasks at their own individual pace. If such an investigator conducts quality investigations, then in my opinion there is nothing wrong with a slightly longer individual pace.

Much like a performance evaluation, individual investigator turn-around report information should not be shared with other investigators. Individual information should only be shared with the respective investigator. Generally speaking, each individual investigator's turn-around time should remain basically consistent. There will be the occasional case that can't be closed for an extended period of time, and when the case is finally closed, it will cause the referenced investigator's turn-around time, as well as the investigative unit's turn-around time to spike. You have to expect this type of situation to occur periodically. If an individual investigator's turn-around-time continues to spike month after month, the director of the investigative unit must speak with the investigator to determine what the problem is, and then try to correct it.

I recommend that all turn-around-reports be calculated by using calendar days rather than business days.

527 *CASE LOAD* VERSUS *TURN-AROUND-TIME*

Case load number versus turn-around time for the investigative unit as a whole. Add in case load broken down by case class versus turnaround time (unit and investigators). This report should include both complaints and self-generated investigations.
Code 4

528 *TURN-AROUND-TIME* BROKEN DOWN BY *INVESTIGATIVE CLASSIFICATION*

Monthly unit "turn-around time" broken down by "investigative classification". (This will document which "classification of cases" are closed the quickest, and which types take longer to close). This report should include both complaints and self-generated investigations.
Code 4

529 *TURN-AROUND-TIME* BY *COMPLAINT TYPE*

Determining the average turn-around-time for the IU is an important stat to have. This report should include both complaints and self-generated investigations.

The average turn-around-time for each individual investigator is equally important. This report should include both complaints and self-generated investigations.
Code 4

530 *COMPLAINT SOURCE TURN-AROUND-TIME*
This is an important stat to have at your fingertips. Some complaint sources received by the IU will require more special attention than others do. This report only includes complaints.
Code 4

531 *TURN-AROUND-TIME* FOR *REFERRALS* OUT
Investigative turn-around time for referrals. This report should include both complaints and self-generated investigations.
Code 4

532 **AVERAGE NUMBER OF DAYS *CASES* REMAIN OPEN BY *INVESTIGATOR* AND BY *INVESTIGATIVE CLASSIFICATION***
This is a managerial investigative tool. It includes both complaints and self-generated investigations.
Code 4

MAPPING REPORTS
Mapping reports take longer to prepare, but the final result can be impressive, especially when they are not overused. There may be occasions where because of the numbers, individual markings might not be possible, so groupings might have to be utilized instead. I can foresee mapping being utilized in the annual review report (in section 5), as well as in the following situations:

533 **MAPPING OF THE TOTAL *RESPONSE AREA* BROKEN DOWN BY EITHER ALL OR A SELECT GROUP OF *COMPLAINT TYPES***
Code 3, 4

534 **MAPPING THE TOTAL *RESPONSE AREA* BROKEN DOWN BY ONE SPECIFIC *COMPLAINT TYPE***
Code 3, 4

535 **MAPPING OF ONE SPECIFIC *GEOGRAPHIC AREA* BROKEN DOWN BY MULTIPLE *COMPLAINT TYPES***
Code 3, 4

536 **MAPPING OF ONE SPECIFIC *AMBULANCE STATION* BROKEN DOWN BY *TOTAL RESPONSES* FOR INDIVIDUAL RESPONSE RESOURCES THAT ARE ASSIGNED TO THE STATION**
Code 3, 4

537 **MAPPING OF TOTAL AREA *HOSPITALS* BROKEN DOWN BY THE TOTAL NUMBER OF *PATIENTS* THAT WERE TRANSPORTED THERE**
Code 3, 4

538 **MAPPING OF TOTAL AREA *HOSPITALS* BROKEN DOWN BY ONE INDIVIDUAL CATEGORY**
Code 3, 4

539 **MAPPING OF *TOTAL RESPONSE AREA* BROKEN DOWN BY *RESPONSE TIME***
Code 3, 4

540 **MAPPING OF INDIVIDUAL *GEOGRAPHIC AREA* BROKEN DOWN BY *RESPONSE TIME***
Code 3, 4

541 **MAPPING OF *TOTAL RESPONSE AREA* BROKEN DOWN BY *COMPLAINT VOLUME***
Code 3, 4

542 **MAPPING OF INDIVIDUAL *GEOGRAPHIC AREA* BROKEN DOWN BY *COMPLAINT VOLUME***
Code 3, 4

543 **MAPPING OF *TOTAL RESPONSE AREA* BROKEN DOWN BY ONE INDIVIDUAL *COMPLAINT TYPE* SPIKE**
Code 3, 4

SECTION 5

PRESENTATION OF STATS

I always chuckle to myself when I hear that statistics can make an issue look anyway a person wants them to. I do this because I have always looked at my investigative statistics strictly from an "it-is-what-it-is" point of view. In other words, the stats were always just what they were, no matter how good or how bad, how high or how low. They weren't changed, they weren't altered, they weren't rounded up, they weren't rounded down, they weren't discarded, and they weren't dreamed up. They were always reported truthfully, win-lose-or-draw.

I have found that without using charts or graphs as visual aids, it is difficult to comprehensively transmit your statistical information to superiors or outsiders. Using categories and numbers alone to document statistics is boring, and will not keep the reader's attention for long, and will certainly not have the impact that you are looking for. Remember, once the person that you are trying to convey the statistical information to becomes bored, or thinks that you can't answer questions intelligently, you have lost the battle, and maybe the war as well. Some report graphs are shown below.

Some of the information you might need to convey might not be utilized specifically for investigative purposes. Information could involve other organizational issues such as budgetary issues or performance statistics. Most will involve investigative issues such as:

- Totaling all individual investigative activities for any given period-of-time.
- Itemizing investigative activities by number, average or by total investigative time spent on each case.

- Justification of the number of employees assigned to the investigative unit
- A specific incident that was reported in the media.
- A large spike in an individual complaint type that seems out-of-control.
- A specific geographic area spike within an organization's response area.

On the other hand, years could go by where no additional information, other than routinely provided information is requested or required. That is probably good and usually means that things are running smoothly. But just because only routine information is being passed along, that doesn't mean that tomorrow some manager won't start asking for additional information. So, if your database is constructed properly, whatever additional information may be requested, it should be immediately available. But if your database is not set up properly, it could take days or weeks to manually obtain the requested information. If this is the case, you are not going to look professional. On the other hand, if your database is set up correctly, and you can provide the information on the same day it was requested, the investigative unit will be looked upon in a favorable light. When new subjects arise, where there aren't existing database reports, new reports should be created and put into use.

The following is a fictitious listing of all the 435 cases for the year 2016 that a fictitious EMS organization's investigative unit received. (A small ambulance organization might think that this list is large, while a bigger ambulance organization might think that it is small). This listing reflects the case number, date if the incident, complaint types, call location and the geographic area (north, east, south and west):

2016 CASES

1	1/1/2016	Delay		Georgia / Long Streets	East
2	1/1/2016	Delay		12 Barful Drive	North
3	1/1/2001	Discourtesy		100 Langer Circle	West
4	1/1/2016	Discourtesy		Highway 12 Rest Stop	West
5	1/2/2016	Delay	Discourtesy	Main Street Bridge	East
6	1/2/2016	Hospital Select		17 Acre Drive	West

7	1/3/2016	Missing Property		1010 Simpson Street	South
8	1/3/2016	Driving	Name Refusal	12 Cleveland Avenue	North
9	1/4/2016	Shield Refusal		141 Broadway	North
10	1/4/2016	Documentation		N/A	N/A
11	1/4/2016	Misconduct		111 Johnson Avenue	South
12	1/6/2016	Drug		Belvedere Park	South
13	1/6/2016	Delay		17 Central Avenue	East
14	1/6/2016	Billing	Discourtesy	100 Tiger Lane	East
15	1/7/2016	Discourtesy		1000 Business District Drive	West
16	1/7/2016	Driving		End Ave / Main Street	East
17	1/8/2016	Name Refusal		111 15 Avenue	North
18	1/9/2016	Civilian Injury		1212 South Drive	South
19	1/9/2016	Hospital Select		17 Seaver Street	West
20	1/10/2016	Other		75 Jackson Avenue	North
21	1/10/2016	Patient Care	Hosp Selection	1000 Carver Loop	West
22	1/11/2016	Audit		Station 3	North
23	1/11/2016	Driving		Park Drive / Park Lane	East
24	1/11/2016	Discourtesy		177 Riverdale Lane	South
25	1/12/2016	Sexual Abuse		10 Barnum Place	West
26	1/12/2016	Name Refusal		250 Denver Avenue	West
27	1/13/2016	Hospital Select		129 Beaver Place	South
28	1/13/2016	Death in Custody		200 Strathmore Place	North
29	1/13/2016	Drug	Discourtesy	1000 Lemon Drive	North
30	1/14/2016	Physical Abuse		111 Butter Boulevard	South
31	1/14/2016	Driving		Carver Loop / 12 Avenue	West
32	1/14/2016	Documentation		2000 Jackson Avenue	North
33	1/15/2016	Missing Property		459 Intervale Avenue	South
34	1/15/2016	Delay		1210 Tenth Avenue	West
35	1/16/2016	Patient Injury	Shield Refusal	1 Liver Lane	North
36	1/18/2016	Billing	Hospital Select	174 Cleveland Avenue	North
37	1/18/2016	Sexual Abuse		12 Beatrice Place	North
38	1/18/2016	Delay		River Park Lane/ 9 Street	East
39	1/18/2016	Patient Care – Death		452 Denver Avenue	West

40	1/19/2016	Misconduct		17 Sway Street	South
41	1/19/2016	Delay		1400 Broadway	North
42	1/20/2016	Billing		100 Avenue C	East
43	1/20/2016	Name Refusal		124 Park Lane Drive	East
44	1/20/2016	Hosp Selection		91 Nebraska Street	West
45	1/21/2016	Patient Care		199 Fox Street	South
46	1/21/2016	Delay		1 Smith Street	South
47	1/21/2016	Delay/Death	Pt Care	1 21 Avenue	North
48	1/21/2016	Discourtesy		1507 Jackson Avenue	North
49	1/22/2016	Leave Abuse		Station 3	South
50	1/22/2016	Documentation		111 Trinity Place	South
51	1/23/2016	Patient Care		33 Forester Avenue	East
52	1/23/2016	Patient Care		77 Prospect Avenue	East
53	1/24/2016	Driving		Smith Street / Benjamin Avenue	South
54	1/25/2016	Billing		111 Columbia Circle	West
55	1/26/2016	Delay		11 Kingsley Street	North
56	1/26/2016	Discourtesy		14 Barn Place	North
57	1/26/2016	Physical Abuse	Discourtesy	1132 Boston Avenue	South
58	1/26/2016	Driving		Wheatly Street /Avenue Z	South
59	1/27/2016	Discourtesy		12 Trenton Avenue	West
60	1/27/2016	Documentation		14 Georgia Place	West
61	1/28/2016	Delay		10 Vermont Way	West
62	1/28/2016	Patient Care		124 Park Lane Drive	East
63	1/29/2016	Discourtesy		4 Degraw Avenue	South
64	1/29/2016	Billing		17 Alaska Street	West
65	1/30/2016	Driving		Park Lane / Prospect Avenue	East
66	1/30/2016	Patient Injury		402 Burger Place	East
67	1/31/2016	Physical Abuse		111 Gun Hill Road	South
68	1/31/2016	Discourtesy		129 Capitol Street	West
69	1/31/2016	Delay		371 Zerega Avenue	South
70	2/1/2016	Driving		143 Broadway	North
71	2/1/2016	Discourtesy		33 Scotch Avenue	East
72	2/1/2016	Patient Care	Billing	99 Serious Street	East
73	2/2/2016	Driving		Avenue Z / Track Road	West
74	2/2/2016	Documentation		74 Sterling Street	North
75	2/3/2016	Billing		Main Street Bridge	East

76	2/3/2016	Misconduct		77 Roulette Way	North
77	2/3/2016	Hospital Select		12 Canadian Avenue	West
78	2/5/2016	Missing Property		111 Prospect Place	South
79	2/5/2016	Delay		223 Maine Drive	South
80	2/5/2016	Other		1 Barrell Lane	East
81	2/6/2016	Patient Care		45 Neveldy Loop	East
82	2/6/2016	Delay		200 Strathmore Place	North
83	2/6/2016	Audit		Station 4	East
84	2/7/2016	Driving		North-South Highway / Bell Lane	East
85	2/7/2016	Patient Care		88 Suburbs Way	West
86	2/7/2016	Documentation		N/A	N/A
87	2/8/2016	Other		76 Bering Circle	North
88	2/9/2016	Delay		147 Prospect Avenue	East
89	2/9/2016	Hospital Select		999 Atlanta Way	South
90	2/10/2016	Billing		121 Avenue P	West
91	2/10/2016	Misconduct		149 Capital Street	West
92	2/10/2016	Discourtesy		1253 Triple Place	North
93	2/10/2016	Hospital Select		199 Prospect Place	East
94	2/11/2016	Other		12 Livermore Street	North
95	2/11/2016	Missing Property		936 Sacramento Street	South
96	2/11/2016	Documentation		12 Plaza Street	South
97	2/11/2016	Drug	Discourtesy	182 Trinity Place	South
98	2/12/2016	Missing Property		23 Avenue D	West
99	2/14/2016	Patient Care	Hospital Select	124 Park Lane Drive	East
100	2/14/2016	Delay/Death		112 Atlantic Lane	East
101	2/14/2016	Hospital Select	Discourtesy	900 Avenue M	West
102	2/14/2016	Leave Abuse		N/A	N/A
103	2/15/2016	Audit		Station 4	South
104	2/15/2016	Discourtesy		54 Eagle Avenue	North
105	2/16/2016	Shield Refusal		237 Prospect Place	East
106	2/16/2016	Hospital Select		11 Everly Way	East
107	2/16/2016	Driving		88 Avenue Q	West
108	2/17/2016	Documentation		12 Clark Street	North
109	2/17/2016	Other		34-36 Steinway Avenue	West
110	2/18/2016	Delay	Discourtesy	11N Nevada Avenue	South
111	2/18/2016	Discourtesy		8 Sycamore Drive	North

112	2/19/2016	Other		880 Zerega Avenue	East
113	2/19/2016	Audit		Station 6	West
114	2/20/2016	Patient Care	Hospital Select	22 Maspeth Avenue	South
115	2/10/2016	Missing Property		776 Idaho Avenue	South
116	2/21/2016	Driving		9 McCoy Way	East
117	2/21/2016	Patient Care		345 Washington Street	South
118	2/21/2016	Missing Property		12 Starch Street	West
119	2/22/2016	Discourtesy		100 Maple Street	North
120	2/22/2016	Documentation		97 Avenue B	West
121	2/23/2016	Other		120 Jerome Street	East
122	2/24/2016	Discourtesy		12 East 149 Street	East
123	2/25/2016	Drug		109 Lying Lane	West
124	2/25/2016	Hospital Select		44 Flowerbed Street	West
125	2/26/2016	Other		124 Forest Street	North
126	2/26/2016	Discourtesy		33 Mercer Avenue	South
127	2/27/2016	Delay	Discourtesy	32 Dyer Avenue	East
128	2/27/2016	Billing		17 Central Avenue	East
129	2/28/2016	Discourtesy		67 Birch Lane	North
130	2/28/2016	Delay		109 Pleasant Avenue	West
131	2/28/2016	Missing Property		444 Toledo Way	South
132	3/1/2016	Discourtesy	Hospital Select	1212 Broadway	North
133	3/1/2016	Patient Care		18 Rainbow Avenue	South
134	3/2/2016	Discourtesy		100 Central Avenue	South
135	3/4/2016	Hospital Select		80 Circle Drive	West
136	3/7/2016	Delay		Broad Street / North Avenue	East
137	3/7/2016	Delay		Tree Lane / Broadway	North
138	3/9/2016	Discourtesy		125 Billings Street	North
139	3/12/2016	Missing Property		1000 South First Street	West
140	3/15/2016	Discourtesy		18 Rainbow Avenue	South
141	3/18/2016	Audit		Station 1	West
142	3/21/2016	Delay		Main Street Bridge	East
143	3/21/2016	Delay		Broadway / Tree Lane	North
144	3/21/2016	Billing	Discourtesy	River Edge Lane / 12 Street	East
145	3/23/2016	Hospital Select		Lennon Street / 18 Avenue	West
146	3/25/2016	Delay-Death		18 Sands Lane	South

147	3/25/2016	Delay		Broadway / Spruce Avenue	North
148	3/25/2016	Patient Care		12 Bruce Street	North
149	3/25/2016	Delay		Broadway / Ocean Drive	West
150	3/30/2016	Missing Property		18 Jewel Avenue	East
151	3/30/2016	Delay		18 Rainbow Avenue	South
152	4/1/2016	Audit		Station 3	South
153	4/1/2016	Discourtesy		32 Avenue Y	West
154	4/1/2016	Hospital Select		17 Avenue P	West
155	4/3/2016	Name Refusal		23 East Drive	East
156	4/4/2016	Missing Property		12 Holiday Place	North
157	4/6/2016	Patient Care		12 Street / Bridge Street	East
158	4/7/2016	Patient Care		88 Cloudless Way	South
159	4/8/2016	Discourtesy		124 Park Lane Drive	East
160	4/9/2016	Delay		77 Bancock Street	North
161	4/11/2016	Delay-Death	Discourtesy	77 Sunrise Lane	South
162	4/13/2016	Drug		67 Suspenders Way	West
163	4/14/2016	Misconduct		99 Avenue U	West
164	4/16/2016	Documentation		2 Beck Avenue	North
165	4/19/2016	Delay		18 Covered Wagon Place	South
166	4/21/2016	Patient Care		17 Jilly Avenue	East
167	4/24/2016	Hospital Select	Discourtesy	34 Everton Place	South
168	4/24/2016	Discourtesy		Jewel Street / North Avenue	East
169	4/27/2016	Other		22 Beckham Street	North
170	4/28/2016	Billing		17 Seaver Street	West
171	4/28/2016	Patient Care		39 Circle Drive North	South
172	4/29/2016	Billing		1010 Simpson Street	South
173	4/29/2016	Discourtesy		222 Ave C	West
174	4/30/2016	Patient Care		54 Port Rogers Place	East
175	4/30/2016	Documentation		74 Sunrise Loop	East
176	5/1/2016	Delay		68 Page Avenue	South
177	5/2/2016	Death-in-custody		1 Lake Front Drive	North
178	5/4/2016	Audit		Station 2	East
179	5/7/2016	Patient Care		97 Foster Place	South
180	5/8/2016	Discourtesy		2 Avenue C	West
181	5/9/2016	Sexual Abuse		99 Flounder Place	West
182	5/10/2016	Hospital Select		999 Avenue Y	West
183	5/14/2016	Physical Abuse		74 Riverdale Avenue	South

184	5/15/2016	Delay		12 Jessup Place	East
185	5/16/2016	Discourtesy		200 Strathmore Place	North
186	5/17/2016	Patient Injury		Barnum Street / Twitch Place	East
187	5/19/2016	Patient Care		98 Gleason Way	South
188	5/21/2016	Documentation		142 Broadway	South
189	5/22/2016	Civilian Injury		Bancock Street / Holiday Place	North
190	5/23/2016	Patient Care		75 Avenue F	West
191	5/25/2015	Delay		43 Foster Place	South
192	5/25/2016	Documentation		1000 Simpson Street	South
193	5/25/2016	Discourtesy		17 Tractor Place	North
194	5/27/2016	Drug		Station 3	East
195	5/28/2016	Audit		Station 5	North
196	5/30/2016	Discourtesy		43 Bellows Loop	North
197	5/31/2016	Delay		12 Church Lane	East
198	5/31/2016	Driving		Broadway / Spruce Avenue	North
199	6/1/2016	Discourtesy		75 Atlantic Lane	East
200	6/2/2016	Audit		Station 2	West
201	6/3/2016	Patient Care		82 Ebitts Street	South
202	6/5/2016	Documentation		1010 Simpson Street	South
203	6/5/2016	Discourtesy		Strathmore / Broadway	North
204	6/6/2016	Hospital Select		17 Westchester Avenue	South
205	6/7/2016	Patient Injury		37 Jessup Place	East
206	6/8/2016	Driving		Jilly Avenue / North Avenue	East
207	6/9/2016	Patient Care		18 Spruce Lane	East
208	6/11/2016	Physical Abuse	Discourtesy	73 Barnes Place	South
209	6/13/2016	Delay		88 Intervale Avenue	South
210	6/15/2016	Civilian Injury		55 Pacific Street	East
211	6/16/2016	Discourtesy		99 Arc Avenue	North
212	6/17/2016	Hospital Select		28 Avenue Z	West
213	6/19/2016	Hospital Select		99 Avenue H	West
214	6/20/2016	Hospital Select		73 Bailey Avenue	South
215	6/20/2006	Audit		Station 1	North
216	6/22/2016	Documentation		Station 2	East
217	6/22/2016	Driving		Port Rogers / Bridge	East
218	6/23/2016	Other		80-82 Avenue P	West
219	6/24/2016	Delay		44 Eagle Street	South

220	6/24/2016	Physical Abuse	77 Avenue Q	South
221	6/25/2016	Discourtesy	55 Barclay Place	North
222	6/26/2016	Hospital Select	17 Linda Lane	North
223	6/26/2016	Documentation	N/A	N/A
224	6/27/2016	Hospital Select	100 Langer Circle	West
225	6/27/2016	Billing	2000 Jackson Avenue	North
226	6/27/2016	Driving	I/F/O Station 2	East
227	6/28/2016	Documentation	33 Long Bridge Road	East
228	6/28/2016	Billing	4 Degraw Avenue	South
229	6/29/2016	Billing	936 Sacramento Street	South
230	6/29/2016	Hospital Select	44 Sampson Street	South
231	6/30/2016	Driving	Avenue Z / 12 Street	West
232	6/30/2016	Discourtesy	39 Bard Avenue	North
233	6/30/2016	Documentation	94 Binnum Loop	East
234	7/2/2016	Discourtesy	12 Front Lake Drive	North
235	7/4/2016	Delay	5 Cleveland Street	South
236	7/4/2016	Delay	77 Maryland Place	South
237	7/4/2016	Physical Abuse	86 Avenue R	West
238	7/4/2016	Hospital Select	12 Avenue Z	West
239	7/6/2016	Discourtesy	12 Steamship Lane	East
240	7/8/2016	Audit	Station 3	East
241	7/9/2016	Billing	1 21 Avenue	North
242	7/10/2016	Driving	78 Carlyle Street	East
243	7/11/2016	Patient Injury	66 Vermont Place	South
244	7/12/2016	Delay	762 Veronica Loop	South
245	7/14/2016	Documentation	93 Delaware Place	South
246	7/14/2016	Driving	817 Avenue R	West
247	7/15/2016	Hospital Select	237 Lakeland Drive	South
248	7/15/2016	Civilian Injury	49 Pension Drive	East
249	7/16/2016	Other	530 Long Bridge Road	East
250	7/17/2016	Patient Care	99 Drapper Loop	North
251	7/17/2016	Misconduct	Station 1	North
252	7/18/2016	Delay-Death	83 Georgia Street	South
253	7/19/2016	Driving	Avenue Z / 12 Street	West
254	7/20/2016	Discourtesy	78 Avenue T	West
255	7/20/2016	Billing	52 Eagle Avenue	North
256	7/21/2016	Shield Refusal	3 Bank Place	East

257	7/23/2016	Billing		12 Toll Lane	East
258	7/23/2016	Misconduct		Station 1	North
259	7/24/2016	Other		Avenue Z / Circle Lane	West
260	7/25/2016	Missing Property		33 Pensacola Street	South
261	7/26/2016	Documentation		11 Avenue A	West
262	7/26/2016	Misconduct		71 Avenue X	West
263	7/26/2016	Name Refusal		12 Arlene Drive	North
264	7/27/2016	Physical Abuse		124 Park Lane Drive	East
265	7/27/2016	Delay		76 Pruden Place	South
266	7/28/2016	Patient Injury		82 Avenue Y	West
267	7/28/2016	Documentation		N/A	N/A
268	7/29/2016	Discourtesy		17-19 Olive Street	East
269	7/29/2016	Hospital Select		82 Tampa Street	South
270	7/31/2016	Driving	Discourtesy	Vermont Place / Degraw Avenue	South
271	7/31/2016	Documentation		12 Roberta Lane	North
272	8/2/2016	Delay		23 Balloon Place	East
273	8/2/2016	Hospital Select		32 Austin Street	South
274	8/3/2016	Audit		Station 5	North
275	8/3/2016	Driving		Avenue A / Smith Street	West
276	8/4/2016	Documentation		12 Bryant Lake	North
277	8/5/2016	Delay		42 Dennis Place	South
278	8/5/2016	Civilian Injury		97 Tuscon Place	South
279	8/6/2016	Misconduct		674 Dyer Place	North
280	8/6/2016	Other		17 Ocean Drive	East
281	8/7/2016	Physical Abuse		78 Wisconsin Street	South
282	8/7/2016	Discourtesy		8 Delaware Drive	South
283	8/9/2016	Delay		9 Avenue C	West
284	8/9/2016	Driving		Wisconsin Street / Boston Way	South
285	8/11/2016	Documentation		44 Reno Street	South
286	8/11/2016	Hospital Select		992 Bangor Place	South
287	8/11/2016	Documentation		74 Destination Avenue	East
288	8/12/2016	Patient Care		21 Prince Street	North
289	8/12/2016	Discourtesy		70 Dove Court	East
290	8/13/2016	Delay-Death		21 Idaho Circle	South
291	8/13/2016	Patient Care		93 Deer Place	East
292	8/14/2018	Driving		82 Avenue J	West

293	8/14/2016	Misconduct	3 Fort Worth Place	South
294	8/15/2016	Hospital Select	99 Avenue U	West
295	8/15/2016	Documentation	4 Smile Place	East
296	8/17/2016	Patient Care	8 Sox Court	North
297	8/17/2016	Delay	24 Columbus Street	South
298	8/17/2016	Physical Abuse	92 Avenue I	West
299	8/18/2016	Driving	Peach Street / Dennis Place	South
300	8/18/2016	Driving	Lemon Drive/ 21 Street	South
301	8/19/2016	Hospital Select	82 Avenue Z	West
302	8/19/2016	Documentation	200 Strathmore Place	North
303	8/20/2016	Audit	Station 3	South
304	8/20/2016	Missing Property	91 Avenue B	West
305	8/21/2016	Misconduct	9 Avenue R	West
306	8/22/2016	Delay	12 Beacon Lane	East
307	8/22/2016	Billing	112 Atlantic Lane	East
308	8/23/2016	Driving	Pension Drive / Bridge Street	East
309	8/23/2016	Missing Property	17 Avenue T	West
310	8/25/2016	Driving	Long Street / Boone Street Circle	South
311	8/25/2016	Billing	34 Bush Street	East
312	8/26/2016	Hospital Select	6 Plane Road	North
313	8/27/2016	Billing	17 Stillwell Avenue	East
314	8/28/2016	Audit	Station 4	West
315	8/28/2016	Name Refusal	77 Avenue D	West
316	8/29/2016	Billing	77 Lenovo Avenue	North
317	8/30/2016	Delay	Jackson Avenue / Holiday Place	North
318	8/31/2016	Misconduct	33 Varsity Place	East
319	9/3/2016	Documentation	N/A	N/A
320	9/5/2016	Audit	Station 1	South
321	9/8/2016	Discourtesy	17 Basket Place	North
322	9/9/2016	Driving	Atlantic Lane / Dove Court	East
323	9/9/2016	Other	43 Stilwell Avenue	East
324	9/12/2016	Driving	Avenue Z / Question Avenue	West
325	9/14/2016	Hospital Select	39 Michigan Street	South
326	9/15/2016	Missing Property	48 Lexington Street	South
327	9/17/2016	Hospital Select	72 Avenue Y	West

328	9/19/2016	Patient Injury	44 Churchill Road	South
329	9/21/2016	Discourtesy	11 Killips Place	East
330	9/23/2016	Hospital Select	54 Oak Street	South
331	9/23/2016	Documentation	Michigan Place / Oregon Way	South
332	9/25/2016	Other	67 Seattle Street	South
333	9/27/2016	Patient Care	68 Avenue U	West
334	9/28/2016	Billing	147 Prospect Avenue	East
335	9/30/2016	Billing	23 East Drive	East
336	9/30/2016	Documentation	74 Avenue S	West
337	10/1/2016	Driving	Tampa Lane / Worth Avenue	South
338	10/2/2016	Patient Care	43 Glass Place	North
339	10/2/2016	Civilian Injury	98 Avenue T	West
340	10/3/2016	Audit	Station 5	West
341	10/4/2016	Hospital Select	82 Bethleham Loop	South
342	10/5/2016	Discourtesy	88 Post Road	North
343	10/6/2016	Driving	23 Horse Street	East
344	10/7/2016	Driving	Peach Lane / Montreal Way	South
345	10/8/2016	Patient Care	17 Bismark Lane	South
346	10/9/2016	Other	92 Victory Street	East
347	10/9/2016	Missing Property	51 Avenue J	West
348	10/11/2016	Documentation	82 Avenue Y	West
349	10/12/2016	Other	12 King Street	North
350	10/12/2016	Hospital Select	43 Bishop Place	South
351	10/14/2016	Discourtesy	12 Verizon Lane	North
352	10/15/2016	Documentation	127 Marathon Way	East
353	10/15/2016	Documentation	83 Sullivan Street	North
354	10/16/2016	Patient Care	25 Dallas Street	South
355	10/17/2017	Driving	Port Reading Avenue / Wood Avenue	South
356	10/18/2016	Leave Abuse	N/A	N/A
357	10/19/2016	Name Refusal	73 Arlene Avenue	North
358	10/19/2016	Other	83 Sprocket Avenue	North
359	10/21/2016	Hospital Select	93 Avenue U	West
360	10/21/2016	Audit	Station 4	West
361	10/22/2016	Documentation	Orange Street / Revolver Lane	South
362	10/22/2016	Missing Property	72 Columbia Street	South

363	10/23/2016	Hospital Select	1 Oklahoma Street	South
364	10/25/2016	Documentation	98 Queen Avenue	East
365	10/25/2016	Billing	75 Atlantic Lane	East
366	10/26/2016	Driving	75 Avenue W	West
367	10/27/2016	Patient Care	54 Artica Way	East
368	10/28/2016	Hospital Select	98 Avenue L	West
369	10/30/2016	Billing	99 Flounder Place	West
370	10/31/2016	Discourtesy	12 Rook Avenue	North
371	11/2/2016	Patient Care	12 Tributary Street	East
372	11/2/2016	Hospital Select	56 Coconut Street	South
373	11/3/2016	Audit	Station 5	South
374	11/3/2016	Discourtesy	25 Tempest Street	South
375	11/4/2016	Driving	34 Avenue X	West
376	11/5/2016	Other	43 Prospect Street North	North
377	11/5/2016	Discourtesy	11 Squirrel Street	North
378	11/7/2016	Hospital Select	34 Denver Oaks	South
379	11/10/2016	Hospital Select	28 Avenue T	West
380	11/11/2016	Driving	Avenue C / Ross Avenue	West
381	11/13/2016	Missing Property	25 Ritz Avenue	South
382	11/14/2016	Driving	Carlyle Street / Binnum Loop	East
383	11/16/2016	Patient Care	124 Park Lane Drive	East
384	11/17/2016	Missing Property	87 Avenue J	West
385	11/18/2016	Hospital Select	867 Mason Street	South
386	11/19/2016	Delay	84 Frost Street	East
387	11/20/2016	Other	83 Jessup Place	North
388	11/23/2016	Billing	1 21 Avenue	North
389	11/24/2016	Delay	81 Silver Cup Way	East
390	11/24/2016	Delay	17 Pappas Lane	North
391	11/28/2016	Billing	09 Avenue H	West
392	11/29/2016	Billing	91 Montgomery Lane	South
393	11/30/2016	Missing Property	12 Clock Street	East
394	12/1/2016	Documentation	97 Chesterfield Place	East
395	12/1/2016	Hospital Select	83 Grave Watch Street	North
396	12/2/2016	Missing Property	45 Avenue Q	West
397	12/3/2016	Misconduct	11 Avenue Y	West
398	12/5/2016	Audit	Station 3	West
399	12/6/2016	Discourtesy	45 Congress Avenue	North

400	12/8/2016	Patient Care	92 Empire Boulevard	North
401	12/8/2016	Misconduct	74 Squad Street	East
402	12/9/2016	Hospital Select	83 Billingsway Street	South
403	12/10/2016	Delay	12 Dubbs Lane	South
404	12/10/2016	Discourtesy	92 Feiler Place	North
405	12/11/2016	Missing Property	29 Justin Way	North
406	12/12/2016	Patient Care	200 Strathmore Place	North
407	12/14/2016	Other	29 Oxford Walk	East
408	12/15/2016	Patient Care	18 Dream Lane	South
409	12/15/2016	Missing Property	29 Avenue U	West
410	12/15/2016	Missing Property	33 Virginia Street	South
411	12/15/2016	Other	92 Oklahoma Way	South
412	12/16/2016	Misconduct	29-31 Stassburg Street	South
413	12/16/2016	Driving	Baltimore Lane / Montana Street	South
414	12/17/2016	Hosp Selection	87 Avenue T	West
415	12/17/2016	Patient Care	75 Avenue W	West
416	12/18/2016	Shield Refusal	42 Shill Street	East
417	12/18/2016	Missing Property	93 Broadway	North
418	12/19/2016	Documentation	Long Street / Short Avenue	North
419	12/20/2016	Physical Abuse	97 Avenue J	West
420	12/20/2016	Discourtesy	89 Forest Road	North
421	12/20/2016	Driving	Alabama Street / Oregon Road	South
422	12/22/2016	Physical Abuse	88 Avenue U	West
423	12/22/2016	Missing Property	35 Avenue Y	West
424	12/22/2016	Name Refusal	124 Park Lane Drive	East
425	12/24/2016	Missing Property	Pitt Street / Basket Lane	South
426	12/25/2016	Delay	Livermore Drive / Tropical Lane	South
427	12/25/2016	Delay	12 Avenue G	West
428	12/25/2016	Billing	Avenue Z / Question Avenue	West
429	12/26/2016	Driving	Shore Boulevard / Spruce Street	South
430	12/27/2016	Billing	43 Stilwell Avenue	East
431	12/27/2016	Hospital Select	81 Riverdale Street	West
432	12/28/2016	Discourtesy	83 Blessings Street	North
433	12/30/2016	Billing	39 Rover Road	North

| 434 | 12/31/2016 | Discourtesy | 92 Foster Street | East |
| 435 | 12/31/2016 | Billing | 11 Killips Place | East |

2016 COMPLAINT TYPES BY GEOGRAPHIC AREAS

TYPE	NORTH	SOUTH	EAST	WEST	N/A
Audit	4	3	5	7	0
Billing	7	15	4	7	0
Civilian Injury	1	2	2	1	0
Death in Custody	2	0	0	0	0
Delay	10	14	18	6	0
Delay/Death	1	1	4	0	0
Discourtesy	27	14	14	20	0
Documentation	9	9	9	5	5
Driving	3	13	13	12	0
Drug	1	1	2	2	0
Hospital Selection	5	5	20	23	0
Leave Abuse	0	0	1	0	2
Misconduct	4	2	4	5	0
Missing Property	3	2	12	10	0
Name Refusal	4	3	0	2	0
Other	8	9	2	3	0
Patient Care	8	14	12	5	0
Patient Care/Death	0	0	0	1	0
Patient Injury	1	3	2	1	0
Physical Abuse	0	1	7	4	0
Sexual Abuse	1	0	0	2	0
Shield Refusal	1	1	2	2	0

Remember, there were 435 cases received, but because any case can have more than one complaint type associated with it, individual complaint type numbers don't equal the number of cases. They almost never do. In this case, twenty-two cases had multiple complaint types.

The following diagram roughly depicts a sample organization's response area:

RESPONSE AREA MAP

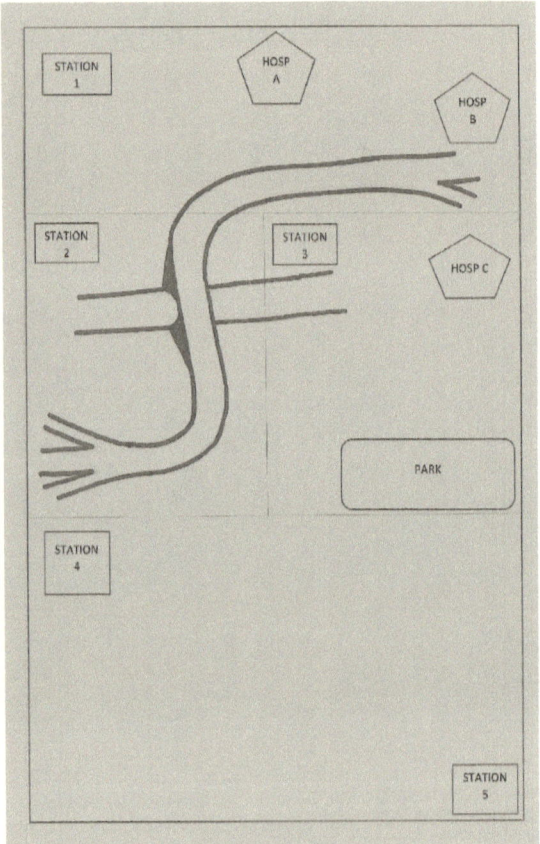

The following information pertains to the above map, some of which is quite evident, and some is not:

- There are five ambulance stations within the organization (1, 2, 3, 4, 5)
- The five ambulance stations provide the only source of medical coverage
- Each Ambulance Station is staffed with five ambulances (4 staffed by EMTs and one staffed by Paramedics) and one supervisory

response vehicle. The fully staffed organizational response force consists of 20 EMT ambulances, 5 Paramedic ambulances and 5 response Supervisors.

- Four Ambulance Stations (1, 2, 3, 4) are located close to, or have easy highway access to area hospitals (Hospitals A, B, C)
- One Ambulance Stations (# 5) is located a good distance away from all of the hospitals. Therefore, it takes those ambulances who are administratively assigned there longer to transport patients to a hospital and longer to return to their response area upon completion of the call than it does for ambulances from other Stations.
- Although Ambulance Station 5 has the lowest number of responses, it generally has the highest number of complaints. Scuttlebutt suggests that this is probably due to their having too much spare time on their hands.
- The north, east and west geographic sectors are both commercial and residential.
- The south sector is completely residential made up of streets, avenues, circles, cul-de-sacs, and dead ends. There is no quick way to drive in, around, or out of the south sector.
- All of the hospitals are located relatively close together.

The following compares which geographic areas have the highest individual complaint types:

- Delay.   South Sector
- Delay with a Death.   South Sector
- Driving.   East Sector and South Sector
- Hospital Selection.   South Sector and West Sector
- Missing Property.   South Sector and West Sector
- Patient Care.   East Sector and South Sector
- Physical Abuse.   South Sector
- Death in Custody.   North Sector

As you can see that the South Sector has the most of the serious complaint types

The following is a listing of the cases which were received for the sample organization for March 2016. It has the same categories as the complete case report above does, plus it displays the dates each a case was opened and closed:

MARCH 2016 CASES RECEIVED

CASE #	D/O/I	TYPE	LOCATION	GEO AREA	OPENED	CLOSED
132-16	3/1/2016	Discourtesy	1212 Broadway	North	3/3/2016	3/15/2016
133-16	3/1/2016	Pt Care	18 Rainbow Avenue	South	3/1/2016	3/30/2016
134-16	3/2/2016	Discourtesy	100 Central Avenue	South	3/3/2016	3/16/2016
135-16	3/4/2016	Hosp Select	80 Circle Drive	West	3/7/2016	3/11/2016
136-16	3/7/2016	Delay	Broad Street / North Avenue	East	3/7/2016	3/10/2016
137-16	3/7/2016	Delay	Tree Lane / Broadway	North	3/8/2016	3/11/2016
138-16	3/9/2016	Discourtesy	125 Billings Street	North	3/12/2016	3/29/2016
139-16	3/12/2016	Missing Property	1000 South First Street	West	3/13/2016	3/13/2016
140-16	3/15/2016	Discourtesy	18 Rainbow Avenue	South	3/15/2016	3/31/2016
141-16	3/18/2016	Audit	Station A	West	3/20/2016	3/30/2016
142-16	3/21/2016	Delay	Main Street Bridge	East	3/21/2016	3/23/2016
143-16	3/21/2016	Delay	Broadway / Tree Lane	North	3/21/2016	3/25/2016
144-16	3/21/2016	Delay/ Discourtesy	River Edge Lane / 12 Street	East	3/22/2016	3/31/2016
145-16	3/23/2016	Hosp Selection	Lennon Street / 18 Avenue	West	3/23/2016	open
146-16	3/25/2016	Delay/ Death	18 Sands Lane	South	3/25/2016	open
147-16	3/25/2016	Delay	Broadway / Spruce Avenue	North	3/25/2016	3/31/2016
148-16	3/25/2016	Pt Care	12 Bruce Street	North	3/25/2016	open
149-16	3/25/2016	Delay	Broadway / Ocean Drive	West	3/25/2016	3/29/2016

| 150-16 | 3/30/2016 | Missing Property | 18 Jewel Avenue | East | 3/30/2016 | 3/30/2016 |
| 151-16 | 3/30/2016 | Delay | 18 Rainbow Avenue | South | 3/30/2016 | open |

After a review of the March 2016 cases, you can make the following determinations:

- Of the 20 cases that were received, 16 were closed during the same month
- 4 of the cases remained open at the end of the month
- 15 cases (75%) were priority cases (delay, patient care, hospital selectin and missing property)
- It took an average of 6.8 days to close the *priority* cases
- It took an average of 12 days to close the *non-priority* cases
- 3 different cases pertained to the same address
- On three different dates (3/7, 3/21, 3/25) there was more than one delay complaint received. The investigations revealed that it was snowing on all three days.
- For the individual delayed response complaints, there were no employee interviews conducted, with the exception of case 151-16. The interview was necessary because it was the third complaint concerning the address 18 Rainbow Avenue received during the same month. If it had not been for the multiple complaints, is likely that interviews wouldn't have been required.
- The geographical breakdown of the complaints/investigations into one of the four geographic grids (north, east, south and west) are as follows: North 6, East 4, South 5, West 5. The breakdown shows that they were more-or-less equally spread out throughout the imaginary organization's response area.

The following is a chart of "cases" received by month in 2016

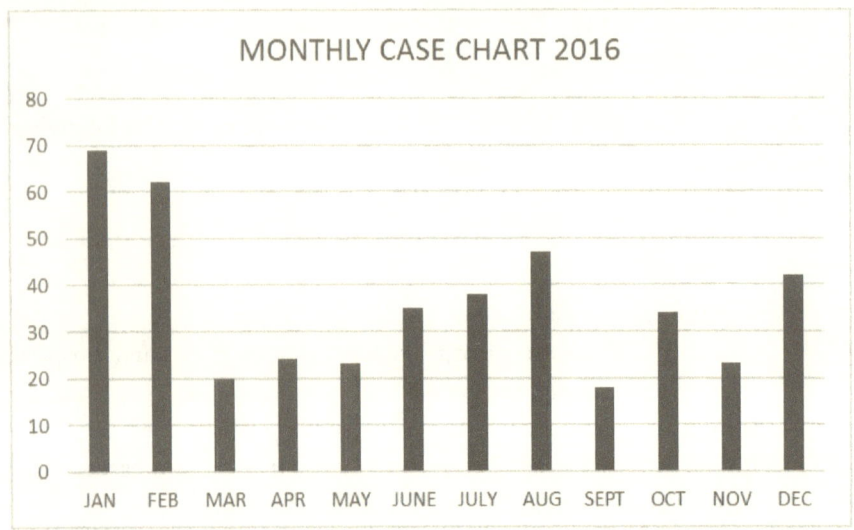

This above chart documents all "cases" (both complaints and self-generated investigations) which were received during each month of 2016. It documents that complaint volume is highest in the winter and the summer.

The following is a chart of "complaints" that were received by month in 2016

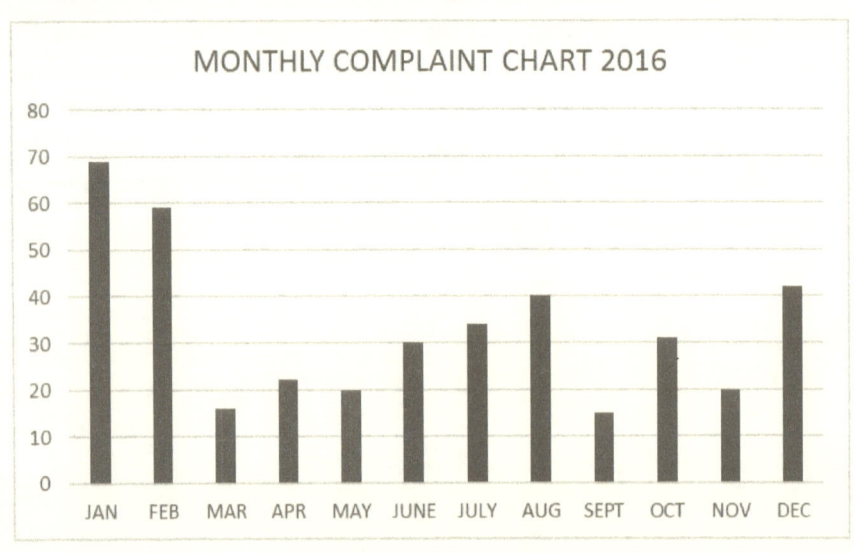

The above chart only includes "complaint" information (it does not include self-generated investigations), and therefore slightly differs from the Monthly Case Chart listed above it.

The following chart contrasts the number of cases per month to the number of investigators assigned to the IU

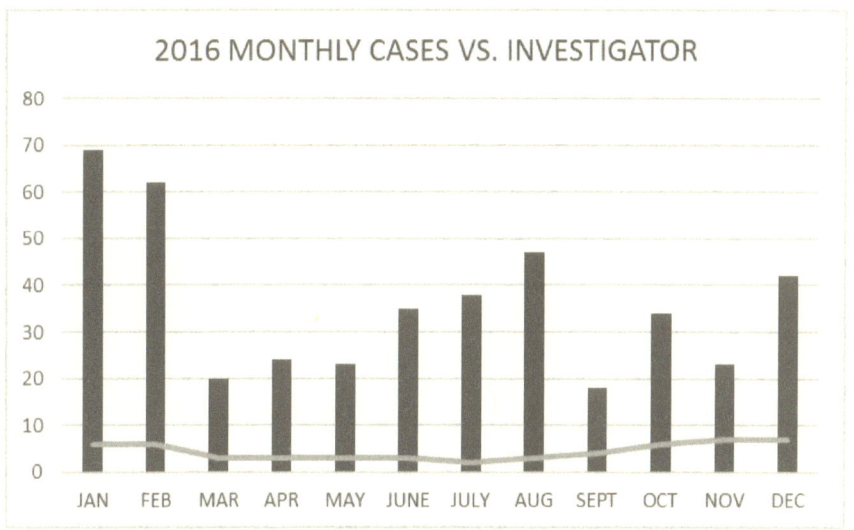

The chart above has always been one of my favorite charts. It compares montly case volume (complaints and self-generated investigations), to the monthly average number of investigators (horizontal line) that were assigned to the Investigative Unit. To me it clearly documents high productivity by the Invetigative Unit.

The following is a chart that documents annual case totals

The above chart is a listing of annual case totals from 1996-2016. It provides a historical perspective towards investigations as it involves twenty years worth of information. You will notice that with the exception of one year (2012), the annual totals are generally consistant, but have been steadily rising. The reason that the 2012 total was so high was there was a special internal project underway requiring additional research and and investigative office work sd well as field work by the Investigative Unit.

The following is a breakdown of "cases" in 2016 by Geographic Area

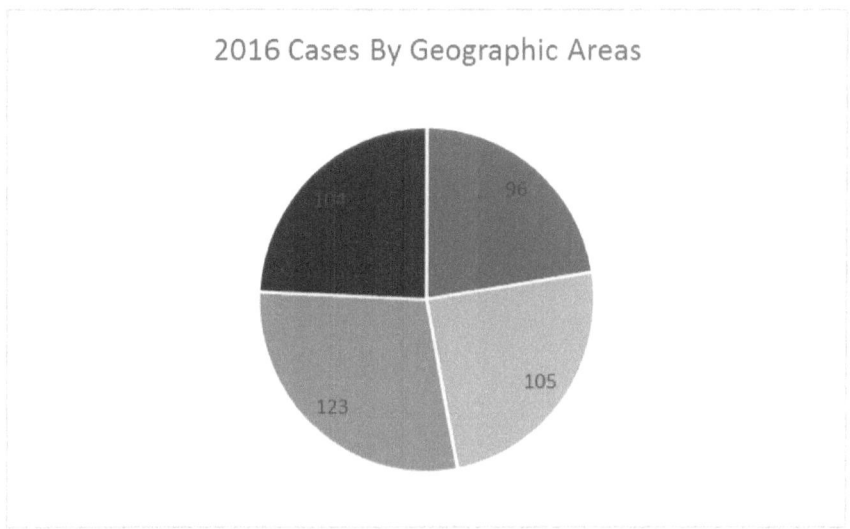

2016 Cases By Geographic Areas

North Sector 96, East Sector 105, South Sector 123, West Sector 104

It documents that the South Sector produced the most cases. (Seven cases did not fit into any geographic area, thus the discrepancy in the numbers).

SECTION 6

ANNUAL RECAP REPORT

Probably the most important historical document for the Investigative Unit (IU) to prepare would be a year-in-review report strictly concerning IU activities. It is important that it be prepared in January of the following year and cover all pertinent material from the previous calendar year. (If you let the preparation drag on for months, it will appear to others that you are not taking the report seriously, and if you don't take it seriously, why should anybody else?).

Nobody is going to "toot" the investigative unit's horn regarding the amount and quality of investigations that they conduct, so it is up to the IU itself to prepare an objective report. It is important that this report be accurate, well thought out, and be professionally printed and bound, because it could potentially wind up anywhere. Obviously, it will wind up on the desk of many of the organizations top echelon of managers. It could potentially wind up in the hands of politicians, the media, and who knows where else. New organizational managerial employees might also receive a copy. The bottom line is that the Annual Recap Report must be p-e-r-f-e-c-t. Unlike the charts listed in section five above, the charts/graphs which are used in the Annual Recap Report must be printed in color to grab the reader's attention.

The first section of the report should be a historical look back at the Investigative Unit over time, not just the previous year. It should include information about the types of cases the IU can and cannot investigate. This section should also include information about how and when the IU was created, who created it, why it was created, and how over time the IU has expanded, including workload, the number of investigators and office space. There should also be a listing of all past and present investigators and directors. I believe that it is important to have all investigators recognized. Once this section has been completed for the first time, it can easily be repeated every subsequent year requiring only minimal updates that encompass the most recent statistics.

The second section of the annual report should be an informative narrative of the year in review. It might even include a brief recap of one or two noteworthy cases.

The third section of the annual report should include important charts, graphs and mapping that document the subject year in review, with statistical comparisons to previous years. Some charts should go all the way back to the year that the IU was created. Other charts should include selected individual complaint types, investigative turn-around-time, average time it takes to close a case broken down by investigative classification, the number of assigned investigators, and various investigative activities. It should also include total unit time spent on individual investigative activities.

Section four of the report should be a brief narrative section about:

- Any initiatives that are either planned or being considered for the new year
- Follow up on any initiatives that were listed in the previous year's report
- The use of any new investigative or equipment or technique which was applied during the year

If you have prepared this report correctly, readers should come away thinking some, or all of the following:

- Wow, the Investigative Unit does a lot more work than I realized.
- The Investigative Unit does all that work with so few investigators?
- I didn't realize that there are so many different types of cases that the Investigative Unit investigates.
- The Investigative Unit maintained their case turn-around-time average even though complaint volume rose so dramatically.
- We can't take away any of the Investigative Unit's staff, their work is too important to the organization.
- Why can't other investigative type units be as productive as the Investigative Unit is?

SECTION 7

FINAL THOUGHTS

The EMS investigations field is important and rewarding. It involves far more than just investigating a case. You never know when the next complaint is going to be received, or how serious it might be, and what any short-term and long-term ramifications might occur. Closed cases can be revived at any time, and even if they were originally received, managed, investigated and closed out correctly, they can literally blow up due to an unforeseen triggering event. Any investigation can become a media incident or can wind up in a court of law. Any mistake made by an investigator can irrevocably ruin their reputation, or the reputation of the investigative unit or even the organization. There is a lot at stake being an EMS investigator. Both the lives of patients, and the livelihood and reputations of investigators can be on-the-line. Because the workforce operates in a relatively unsupervised environment, EMS Administrators must use every tool available to ensure that all their personnel are providing optimal patient care and are operating within your organization's policy and procedure guidelines. At the end of the day EMS investigators should be proud of the work that they do. I know that I was, and still am.